Fostering Imagination in Higher Education

Imagination and creative teaching approaches are increasingly important across all higher education disciplines, not just the arts. Investigating the role of imagination in teaching and learning in non-arts disciplines, this book argues that a lack of clarity about what imagination looks like in higher education impedes teachers in fostering their students' creativity.

Fostering Imagination in Higher Education tells four ethnographic stories from physics, history, finance and pharmaceutical science courses, analytically observing the strategies educators use to encourage their students' imagination, and detailing how students experience learning when it is focussed on engaging their imagination. The highly original study is framed by Ricoeur's work on different forms of imagination (reproductive and productive or generative). It links imaginative thinking to cognitive science and philosophy, in particular the work of Clark, Dennett and Polanyi, and to the mediating role of disciplinary concepts and social-cultural practices.

The author's discussion of models, graphs, strategies and artefacts as tools for taking learners' thinking forward has much to offer understandings of pedagogy in higher education. Students in these case studies learned to create themselves as knowledge producers and professionals. It positioned them to actively experience the constructed nature of the knowledge and processes they were learning to use – and the continuing potential of knowledge to be remade in the future. This is what makes imaginative thinking elemental to the goals of higher education.

Joy Whitton is an academic developer at Monash University in Australia. Her research interests include imagination, cognition and their interplay with tools/ artefacts and practices, and professional learning.

Routledge Research in Higher Education

Learning Community Experience in Higher Education
High-impact practice for student retention
Susan Mary Paige, Amitra Wall, Joe Marren, Amy Rockwell and Brian Dubenion

Academics Engaging with Student Writing
Working at the higher education textface
Jackie Tuck

Professional Education at Historically Black Colleges and Universities
Past trends and outcomes
Edited by Tiffany Fontaine Boykin, Adriel A. Hilton and Robert T. Palmer

Articulating Asia in Japanese Higher Education
Policy, partnership and mobility
Jeremy Breaden

Global Mobility and Higher Learning
Anatoly V. Oleksiyenko

Universities and the Occult Rituals of the Corporate World
Higher education and metaphorical parallels with myth and magic
Felicity Wood

Developing Transformative Spaces in Higher Education
Learning to transgress
Sue Jackson

Fostering Imagination in Higher Education
Disciplinary and Professional Practices
Joy Whitton

For more information about this series, please visit: www.routledge.com/Routledge-Research-in-Higher-Education/book-series/RRHE

Fostering Imagination in Higher Education
Disciplinary and Professional Practices

Joy Whitton

LONDON AND NEW YORK

First published 2018
by Routledge
2 Park Square, Milton Park, Abingdon, Oxon OX14 4RN

and by Routledge
711 Third Avenue, New York, NY 10017

Routledge is an imprint of the Taylor & Francis Group, an informa business

© 2018 Joy Whitton

The right of Joy Whitton to be identified as author of this work has been asserted by her in accordance with sections 77 and 78 of the Copyright, Designs and Patents Act 1988.

All rights reserved. No part of this book may be reprinted or reproduced or utilised in any form or by any electronic, mechanical, or other means, now known or hereafter invented, including photocopying and recording, or in any information storage or retrieval system, without permission in writing from the publishers.

Trademark notice: Product or corporate names may be trademarks or registered trademarks, and are used only for identification and explanation without intent to infringe.

British Library Cataloguing-in-Publication Data
A catalogue record for this book is available from the British Library

Library of Congress Cataloging-in-Publication Data
A catalog record for this book has been requested

ISBN: 978-1-138-08938-9 (hbk)
ISBN: 978-1-315-10923-7 (ebk)

Typeset in Bembo
by Apex CoVantage, LLC

This book is dedicated to my dad, who always urged me to make things clear. And to Peter, who has lived with this research for as long as I have.

Parts of chapters 2 and 5 were originally published in a chapter entitled 'Using Ricoeur to interpret acts of imagination in a university physics class', p. 83–84, in *Re-imagining the Creative University for the 21st Century*, edited by A.C. Besley and Michael A. Peters, 2013. Reproduced by permission of Springer.

Contents

List of figures	xii
List of tables	xiii
List of exemplars	xiv

1 Introduction

1

Creativity? Imagination? Same difference? – terminology 3
About the research 9
Interpretation and analysis 11
How to read this book 11

2 Theoretical framework on imagination

19

Introduction 19
Ricoeur's theory of imagination 19
Productive imagination and agency 21
Metaphor: paradigmatic of imagination 22
Semantic innovation 22
Agency 24
Productive imagination as forecasting or anticipatory imagination 27
'Models for': epistemological imagination in models 27
Fossilised metaphors and lack of criticality in using models 29
Narrative imagination 32
    Narrative agency in author and reader 33
Imagination: developing possibilities 34
Imagination and action: the heuristic power of narratives as models for action 34
Emotions and their role in imagination and in ethical thinking 35
Imagination used to 'map out' practical action 37
The liminal space of imagination 38
Probable imaginary constructions 39
Grounding imagination: its relationship to reality 41
Vygotsky, imagination, creativity and reason 41

viii   *Contents*

**3   Theoretical linking of imagination with cognition
     and learning theory**   46

Introduction 46
Tool mediation – how cognition is shaped socio-culturally 47
The role of language and other people 49
*Problematising perception: Wartofsky putting artefacts/representations
    back into the activity of perception and learning 51*
*Learning re-imagined: Vygotsky's mediational triangle, Clark's extended
    mind model of cognition and Polanyi's 'tacit knowing' 53*
Extended mind theory 54
Interdependence between cognition, action and culture 56
The perceiver as predictor 58
Predictive processing and imagination 61
    1 The perceiver as imaginer 62
    2 The perceiver as generator of models 62
    3 The cognizer as synthesiser 63
*Relevance of predictive processing to imagination in complex learning
    of higher education 63*
Conclusion: imagination and finding and creating new knowledge 65

4   Defining and practising creativity   69

Creativity as original product 70
Creativity as a process 73
Creativity and problem solving, problem formulation or problem finding 75
Creative and critical thinking 77
    Expertise: bringing into play creativity and critical forms
       of thinking 78
Individual or social origins of imagination and creativity? 79
Can creativity be enhanced or encouraged, and if so, how? 81
    Taking an intentional approach to the development of creativity 81
    Creativity training programs 82
    Encouraging the acquisition/mastery of domain-specific
       knowledge and skills 83
    Stimulating and rewarding curiosity and exploration 83
    Building motivation 84
    Encouraging confidence 84
    Risk-taking 84
    Imagination and higher education teachers' views 85
    Creative imagination and disciplinary learning in higher education 88
    Instruction in imaginative processes: action research reflective
       studies by higher education teachers 90
    Imagination expressed through narrative in educational
       and professional contexts 93

Contents   ix

5 Honours quantum physics ethnography

99

Introduction 99
The setting 99
Dialectical cycling through mathematical reasoning processes 101
Modelling the use of analogy to put an image to an emerging meaning:
an instance of 'reproductive' and 'productive' imagination 102
'Dancing around' a problem mathematically, pictorially, linguistically 103
Learning by projecting the imagination into disciplinary conceptual tools 105
Learning to be resourceful 106
Scientific models – examples of productive imagination – involve
the making of assumptions 108
Teaching for imagination involves teaching openness to future revision or
the reconsideration of explanatory possibilities 109
Abstraction: abstracting from collecting tennis balls in a bucket or photons
in a telescope! 110
Using historical examples to problematise concepts and knowledge
and encourage questioning assumptions 112
Modelling internal standards of knowledge attempts and using error as
an impetus to learning 113
Feelings about knowledge 115
Lifelong learning: the eternal return of the same 116
Productive imagination and creatively linking-up diverse things 117
Teaching for imaginative learning is teaching how to learn new things
(not just existing things) 119
Embodied cognition: forming analogical relationships between
body and concept 120
Conclusion 122

6 First year medieval history ethnography

126

Introduction 126
How to read forensically 128
Interrogation of primary sources: the five 'W' framework 130
Example of 'lecture' that models the historical treatment of a
primary source 132
Introduction to history and gaining confidence: 'No one comes out of
the womb reading Latin' 135
The development of historical skills in assessments 138
The synthesis exercise and – what is an essay anyway? 138
The essay as a creative pedagogy 142
Prompting engagement in historical thinking and avoiding
ahistoricism 144
Emotions and imagination 145
Conclusion 147

x *Contents*

7 Finance ethnography   ʼ 150

Introduction 150
Background and context for the case study 152
Setting expectations of learning 153
The role of creative collaboration 154
Ground rules that release creativity 154
Learning agency through risking error 155
Imagination as mental flexibility and shifting perspectives 156
*Imagination in ethics: how surprise ('affect') can trigger reflection in
    simulation pedagogy 157*
*Loans and deposits module: reproductive imaginary structures and
    productive imagination in strategy formation 160*
   Introducing the simulation game rules of the loans and
        deposits module 161
   Forming strategies: a productive form of imagination that
        builds on reproductive forms of imagination – an analysis
        of student bank reports 163
*Evidence of imagination and formation of strategy in student
    assignments 164*
   Danger, surprise (again) and learning opportunity: managing
        the balance sheet 170
   Contingency strategies and forecasting imaginatively 172
Feedback on learning provided naturalistically and in real time 174
Re-imagining banking: questioning assumptions? . . . or not 174
Student reflection on forecasting and trading strategy 175
Conclusion 177

8 Pharmaceutical science ethnography   181

Introduction 181
Establishing the learning environment 185
Shared critical reflection 187
Underlying structure of the pedagogy 188
Igniting the fire 188
Identifying key features of scientific inquiry and critiquing key concepts 189
Tool-making used to dynamically configure meaning 191
Tooling *active cognition by iterative diagram-making, reflection
    and social learning 202*
Conclusion: imaginative synthesis in diagrammatic narrative 207

9 Conclusion 210

Introduction 210
1 Questioning assumptions, asking 'What if?' questions and openness to knowledge being reconstructed 211
Emotions 214
2 Making new meaningful connections, discerning patterns 215
3 Mastery of skills and knowledge, methodologies, processes: developing expertise 216
4 Repositioning learners as knowledge producers 217
5 Repositioning the student and teacher relationship: educational style 218
Reflection on the usefulness of Ricoeur's theory 219
Implications for practice 221
Questions and ideas for teaching approaches that foster imagination 222
Future directions of research 224

Index 227

Figures

2.1	Representing Ricoeur's two axes of received philosophical theories of imagination: degree of critical consciousness and productive/reproductive imagination	21
3.1	Theoretical linkages in this chapter	47
3.2	Vygotsky's mediational triangle, in which the subject and object are not only directly connected but 'indirectly' connected through the medium constituted by culturally based signs or artefacts	48
4.1	Csikszentmihalyi's systems perspective	79
5.1	The structure of a human activity system	107
5.2	Diagram of a two pinhole experiment with a breakout diagram representing the interference incoherent, partially incoherent and coherent waves indicated but not illustrated in the top diagram	119
7.1	Starlab: a purpose-built, high tech, teaching simulation facility	152
7.2	Student HSBC Loans and Deposits Report	169
7.3	Student HSBC Loans and Deposits Report	171
8.1	Educator instructions for the first part of the assignment	192
8.2	Engeström's (1990a) first generation activity theory model, which incorporates as its top level, Vygotsky's mediational triangle	202
9.1	Features of teaching that foster imagination in disciplines of higher education	222

Tables

1.1	SOLO taxonomy	7
1.2	The Cognitive Process Dimension with suggested verbs	7
1.3	The statistics on enrolments in participating units including numbers of consenting student participants in each 'unit'/ ethnographic site and numbers of weeks of observation	10
4.1	First and second generation creativity concepts	86
7.1	Student assignment table	167

Exemplars

8.1 Student diagram of the scientific method 194
8.2 Student diagram of the scientific method 196
8.3 The third part of the assignment task required mapping
the Showcase presentations by one faculty scientist onto the
student's diagram of the scientific inquiry process 199

1 Introduction

Here is a list of some pressing contemporary world issues: poverty, global warming, sustainable energy use, democratic participatory processes, antibiotic misuse, sustainable farming, armed conflict, city design and waste water engineering, learning and teaching in the age of the digital economy. Modern societies seek to educate their citizens to contribute to the solutions. This book focuses on what is meant by imagination and its role in university education that is outward looking, problem solving, and engaged with the world. I argue that imagination (and its close cousin, 'creativity') is an essential capacity for cultivating novel solutions. It therefore demands greater attention in higher education, but should not be the sole province of the creative arts. Democratisation of the fields for fostering creativity appears to be a fundamental condition for a sustainable future. Underpinning this book is the view that imagination is not only an aesthetic matter, but a way of thinking, and can be directed towards adapting to the local environment or adapting that environment. Its view of learning reflects a concern with in-person changes, which modify how we interpret our surroundings and, in turn, change them by our actions. It encompasses how we learn practices and ways of thinking that are new, not only how we acquire existing knowledge. This is important in university education, for imaginative learning allows students to learn the practices that lead to new knowledge.

There is an interesting paradox in today's world. Industry commentators say that for a successful future, we need people who think creatively and implement new ideas for innovation in products, situations and contexts. In an innovation-driven world, creativity 'might have been a luxury for the few, but by now a necessity for all' (Csikszentmihalyi, 2006, p. xviii). It implies that today's university graduates need more than technical skills and knowledge. Among other things they will require personal attributes that enable them to 'persevere in the face of complexity and unresolvability' (McWilliam & Haukka, 2008, p. 660). And yet there is evidence that our education systems are working against these shifts and systematically suppress creative thinking (Robinson, 1999, 2011; Harris, 2014; Noddings, 2013; Amabile, 2010; Stevens, 2003). According to the landmark Robinson Report (1999) in the UK, *All our future: creativity, culture and education*, the prevailing model of university education is knowledge acquisition and retention, which is inadequate if, as a modern society, we are to

2 *Introduction*

successfully meet future challenges by applying knowledge in innovative ways and constructing new ideas. In addition, societies are currently facing disruption in employment patterns, skill sets and recruitment patterns in a range of different industries. All of this means the future of employment is uncertain. We do not know in advance how artificial intelligence will affect certain current job domains, what skills will be retained and where lie the boundaries where human elements will be augmented by artificial intelligence. Also unknown are how national and international developments will affect future markets including employment markets (Mowbray & Halse, 2010). But many commentators argue that skills associated with creativity – the generation and evaluation of new ideas – will be among them (Cropley, 1992, 2009; Cropley & Cropley, 1998; Hajkowicz et al., 2016, p. 13).

The ubiquity of creativity and critical thinking in university graduate attributes in all disciplines and professional areas suggests their importance is recognised by institutions of higher education. And yet there is no evidence that higher education providers develop creativity through a set of coherent, systematic, course-wide strategies (McWilliam & Dawson, 2007, p. 4; Biggs & Tang, 2007). In the absence of undergraduate course-wide development, it falls to interested teachers to develop it in individual subjects/units they are responsible for. In a post-graduate context, the picture is not dissimilar. In an Australian 2007 Group of Eight[1] survey of PhD graduates 5 to 7 years out, covering employment outcomes, job attributes and quality of research training, completed by the University of Queensland Social Research Centre (Western et al., 2007), graduates rated their doctoral training in creativity and innovation as 3.74 but placed the importance of these capacities in their employment higher, as 4.06 (on a five-point scale where 1 was 'Not at all' and 5 was 'To a great extent') (Western, et al., 2007, p. 18).

The reasons for the lack of educational focus on creativity in non-arts-based disciplines and professions are unclear. Some have argued that many higher education researchers are highly trained in ways that have neglected to develop their own imagination and creative faculties (Trowler, 2013, p. 6). Imagination, the aspect of creativity central to the original research on which this book is based, can be regarded with suspicion by higher education educators because of its connotations of fantasy or 'fancy', subjectivity and daydreaming. Saul, for example, attributes the marginalisation of imagination to the influence of the Romantic period, which ennobled pure artists as rather unstable people (2001, pp. 128–129), but the view has been traced back much further, at least as far as Plato (Bleazby, 2013, p. 79; Egan, 1997, Chapter 1). In the history of Western thought, meaning has been identified with logical thinking, whereas human imaginative thought has been identified with fantasy, the irrational and the instinctual (Policastro & Gardner, 1999) – complete with its associations of danger – a point which has been documented by historians and philosophers (for example Dening, 2000, p. 45; Kearney, 1988; Warnock, 1976). A preference for the first goes without saying. For whatever reason, imagination is often construed as having a binary oppositional relationship to facts, evidence and rigour; there is a reality principle at stake. Asking higher educators to foster imaginative capacity may be interpreted by some as trivial or demonstrating a lack of comprehension of the verifiable or evidentiary base to knowledge, to hard-won acquisition of disciplinary skills and disciplined methods of inquiry (see Chapter 4 on this commonly made distinction) or the sheer hard work and persistence involved in discovery. Most academics focus on the knowledge base but neglect teaching how it might be put to work creatively. Creativity's frequent absence in assessment is a case in point, reflecting its ambiguous position in relation to knowledge. Yet students clearly see the institution placing value on those things it assigns marks to; the assessment *is* the curriculum as far as the students are concerned (Ramsden, 1992; Boud, 2010). And if it is not assessed, the question arises: Why should students value it as something they need to develop? And how are they to understand the role of imagination in advancing knowledge?

Yet the advancement of knowledge through creative synthesis between ideas is the pinnacle of academic achievement. In doctoral research in all disciplines it is reflected in standards for evaluating 'original contributions' (Lovitts, 2007). In addition, higher educators are currently grappling with steep rises in student numbers and a more diverse student body at a time when the sector rewards research more than teaching and has diminished resources to spend on teaching quality and the changes required to provide optimal, personalised learning in large cohorts. For whatever reason, a lack of a deliberate, systematic course-wide strategy to develop students' imagination and creativity in disciplines not usually considered creative persists (Cropley, Cropley, Kaufman, & Runco, 2010, p. 301; McWilliam, 2007, p. 4).

Creativity? Imagination? Same difference? – terminology

My research, which forms the core of this book, investigated how university teachers in non arts-based disciplines and professions foster the creativity of their students, with a particular focus on imagination as a fundamental aspect of creativity in higher education. So what is meant by 'creativity' and imagination in higher education? What distinguishes them? This book uses the term 'creativity' as the overarching term. An Organisation for Economic Co-operation and Development (OECD) working paper adopted a Five Dispositions Model of Creativity (Lucas, Claxton & Spencer, 2013, pp. 16–17), which included five dispositions or aspects:

1 Curiosity or inquisitiveness, challenging assumptions.
2 Persistence; grit.
3 Discipline (by which is meant devoting time to developing expertise or mastery in domain relevant skills).
4 Collaboration including the giving and receiving of feedback.
5 Imagination, which refers to making connections, playing with possibilities and using intuition.

4 *Introduction*

Each of these dispositions or aspects reflect key themes in the psychological and educational literature on creativity (for example, Sternberg & Lubart, 1999; Csikszentmihalyi, 1999; Craft, Jeffrey & Liebling, 2001).

Taking these *five* dispositions further, a fruitful metaphor to understand what imagination is, and its role in creativity, is the thumb's function in the hand. If the creativity of the 'hand' can be composed of five main aspects, or 'fingers', imagination can be considered the thumb, the opposable digit with the power to unlock the potential of the others. In fact, this analogy works from a number of viewpoints. It carries with it the importance of wholes – of the importance of the thumb for the facile functioning of a hand. In an analogous way, imagination is crucial to 'grasping' an insightful new connection, some newly perceived relationship or similarity, some new idea or purpose. The connections referred to are not random or pastiches. These new connections made possible by the imagination offer the foresight to see beyond 'what is' to 'what *could be*'. But imagination needs to work in tandem with a seeking curious impulse, with persistence, confidence to take risks, and to be informed by a deep familiarity with, and skill in, one or more fields – the other four elements that make up the full hand of creativity. The hand metaphor also nicely carries connotations of my contention that imagination is opportunistic in its use of available *tools* in the environment – whether language, things, technologies or social networks, the body itself – to structure this grasping. In this way it plays a fundamental role in cognition and learning. The post-Cartesian framework of the embodied and 'extended mind' thesis (Clark, 1997, 2011; Jeffares, 2010) contends that the body, language and the opportunistic use of things in the environment all play a role in cognition itself. As well, a creative disposition implies a proclivity to use these tools, a shift in priorities, not just competence or possession of the skill (Claxton, Edwards & Scale-Constantinou, 2006).

Even though I focus on imagination, too often higher educators and others use the terms 'creativity', 'imagination' and 'innovation' interchangeably. The effect of this is that imagination's specific teachable aspects remain inadequately described, something my research presented in this book seeks to address. But the way the terms are used interchangeably means my research on particular cases of non-arts subjects/units of study also needed to consider what is implied by these overlapping concepts. Different disciplines have a preference for one or other terms too – for instance, 'creativity' is more frequently used in the psychology and educational literature; 'innovation' is more prevalent in the domains of business, engineering, technology and medicine; both 'imagination' and 'creativity' tend to be the terms of choice in the arts, media, science and philosophy. Another nuance is that the term 'innovation' tends to imply the effective *implementation or application* of creativity in industries and in value-added production of goods or services (Flew & Cunningham, 2010; A. Cropley, 2009). Creativity has sometimes been defined as 'the process through which new ideas are produced' while innovation is 'the process through which they are implemented' (Hartley in McWilliam, 2011). Thus, although my focus in this book is on imagination as one aspect of creativity, I do refer to this broader literature, and my empirical research has included what is implied by these overlapping concepts.

Lucas et al. (2013, p. 6) have rightly declared, however, 'If creativity is to be taken more seriously by educators and educational policy-makers then we need to be clearer about what it is'. Likewise, if educators are to effectively develop skills associated with creativity, particularly across multiple levels of a degree, and if learners are better able to understand what it is they should be developing, greater clarity is needed. In this book I use a theory of imagination by philosopher Paul Ricoeur, which links imagination, reason and language, and which argues that 'productive' imagination involves a form of combinatorial thinking which by synthesising disparate things generates new ideas and shifts in perspectives. The general idea of combinatorial thinking is a commonly shared concept, so readers who are familiar with it may be satisfied simply with that, but throughout this book I prefer to refer to Ricoeur because of the unusually deep and detailed delineation of his theory of imagination. Researchers agree that being imaginative implies a playfulness with possibilities of what could be, that arise through the novel forming of connections (Lucas et al., 2013; Greene, 1995; Craft, Jeffrey & Leibling, 2001). Ricoeur, in my view, offers an explanation better than most about how exactly this happens. This is what makes it a valuable theory for higher education, as creating new ideas and fostering the capacity to develop new ideas in the next generation are central to universities' missions of research, teaching and engagement with wider society. More on this in Chapter 2.

Cultivating students' imagination as an aspect of creativity and cultivating higher order thinking and complex reasoning skills are clearly linked. A foundational concept linking them is Vygotsky's thesis that the definition of higher mental processes must be grounded in the notion of mediation by psychological tools or signs. Human beings internalise forms of mediation, he asserts, which is how historical and socio-cultural processes are linked with individuals' mental processes (Vygotsky, 1978; Wertsch, 2007).

Readers of this book may be more familiar with the term 'higher order thinking skills', and for this reason, an appreciation of the relationship between imagination, creativity and higher order thinking skills is helpful to educators concerned to develop these. Two widely used taxonomies of learning outcomes are Biggs and Tang's SOLO (structure of observed learning outcomes) taxonomy (2007) and Anderson and Krathwohl's (2001) revision of Bloom's Taxonomy of Learning Objectives. The term 'imagination' does not figure in either taxonomy, but 'creativity' and 'synthesis' do. Consequently, what teachers do to cultivate students' imagination does not map neatly onto either of these two taxonomies, and some foundational skills for fostering it are distributed across levels of their taxonomic hierarchies.

One aim I have for this book is that the teaching approaches I analyse will flesh out for readers in non arts-based disciplines what teaching for imagination can look like when it is building a discipline base. Some approaches and tasks at first glance don't appear imaginative, and teachers who use them may never have thought of them as encouraging imagination or creativity. Since taxonomies

6 *Introduction*

such as SOLO and Bloom's are frequently used to help design or check that assessments of students' learning capture the desired range of levels of learning of (lower order and higher order) skills, I hope this book may help them identify, or recognize, when imagination and its close cousin, creativity, are being used.

The SOLO taxonomy's 'extended abstract' learning outcomes are the highest in their hierarchically ordered system and refer to those that *go beyond what has been given*, at a high level of abstraction or as applied to new and broader domains. Verbs used to form intended learning outcomes at this 'extended abstract' level in various fields include theorise, generalise, hypothesise, reflect, generate, create, make, compose, invent, design, perform, originate, prove/solve from first principles, make an original case. Activities that would involve these verbs clearly involve performing knowledge or making something, appropriate to the context or discipline. Used in assessment tasks, the outcomes are high level and involve an open-ended process, where the product is not predetermined. The level immediately below, called 'relational', refers to conceptual restructuring which integrates the components of knowledge; it goes beyond knowing *more* and involves constructing newly conceptual relationships between concepts. Examples of the verbs used to form learning outcomes at this SOLO 'relational' level are compare/contrast, explain causes, analyse, relate, apply, integrate, explain, predict, conclude, summarise, argue, review, transfer, make a plan, characterise, differentiate, organise, debate, make a case, translate, solve a problem (Biggs & Tang, 2007, p. 80). These verbs imply that knowledge is combined in some way new for the learner and can be put to work in analysis or actions. Both these levels refer to functioning skills and knowledge, and they involve imagination because they involve combining or synthesising knowledge in order to generate a new idea or perspective or to perform an action, make an argument, problem solve or generate a prediction or a plan or a product. They are therefore a kind of springboard to extended abstract. As Biggs and Tang say, they 'suggest a sequence, starting with foundation of solid knowledge, prising it open, and generating new possibilities, in a SOLO-type progression from relational to extended abstract' (2011, p. 265). Imagination and critical thinking will be germane to the kinds of tasks involved using these skills.

Anderson and Krathwohl's (2001) revision of Bloom's taxonomy distinguishes between two kinds or dimensions of knowledge: what they call knowledge itself and the cognitive process. Imagination and other creative attributes require both. They divide knowledge into four different kinds: factual, conceptual, procedural and metacognitive. Metacognitive knowledge has most to do with imagination because it implies the agency of the learner. Their taxonomy proposes six 'categories' of cognitive processes: remember, understand, apply, analyse, evaluate and create. Lucas, Claxton and Spencer's (2013) five dispositions of creativity require all these cognitive levels while adding an affective dimension – the personal qualities of inquisitiveness (curiosity, wondering, questioning), persistence/grit, and tolerance of uncertainty. Anderson and Krathwohl define 'create' as 'put[ting] elements together to form a coherent or functional whole; reorganise elements into a new pattern or structure', which is frequently described as imagination in philosophical and psychological literature. 'Create', they say, is associated with generating hypotheses to account for an observed phenomena, planning or designing a procedure or a task or producing or constructing or inventing something – all examples of tasks involving lateral or divergent thought processes and putting knowledge to work. However, imagination is involved at many other levels of their hierarchy: in the fourth dimension of 'analysis' it is involved in organising or structuring elements, for example structuring evidence in relation to an historical explanation. It appears it would be involved in the third dimension, 'apply', such as when a medical or psychological professional diagnoses a condition on the basis of examination and interviews. It is also associated with many of the verbs they say are encompassed in learning involving the second dimension, 'understand'. For examples, 'constructing models' that explain historical events, 'inference' (which Dewey argues is imaginative, see Chapter 2, and which incorporates the notion of prediction), and 'interpret', such as changing from one form of expression, for example, mathematical, to another, for example, verbal.

Table 1.1 SOLO taxonomy

SOLO taxonomy	*Verbs associated with two SOLO levels of declarative and functioning knowledge*
Relational	Compare and contrast, explain, analyse, relate, apply, integrate, predict, conclude, summarise, argue, review, transfer, make a plan, characterise, differentiate, organise, debate, make a case, translate, solve a problem
Extended abstract	Theorise, generalise, hypothesise, reflect, generate, create, make, compose, invent, design, perform, originate, prove/solve from first principles, make an original case, reflect upon and improve

Source: From Biggs and Tang, 2011, pp. 123–124.

Table 1.2 The Cognitive Process Dimension with suggested verbs

Anderson and Krathwohl's revised Bloom's taxonomy, the Cognitive Process Dimension	*Verbs associated with the functioning of those cognitive processes*
Remembering	Recognise, identify, locate, recall, retrieve
Understanding	Interpret, clarify, paraphrase, represent, translate; exemplify, illustrate, instantiate; classify, categorise, subsume; summarise, abstract, generalise; infer, conclude, extrapolate, interpolate, predict; compare, contrast, map, match; explain, construct models
Applying	Execute, carry out a procedure, implement
Analysing	Differentiate, discriminate, focus, select, organise, find coherence, integrate, outline, parse, structure, attribute, deconstruct
Evaluating	Coordinate, detect, monitor, test, check, critique, judge
Creating	Generate, hypothesise, plan, design, devise a procedure, produce, construct, invent a product, build (e.g., a habitat)

Source: Adapted from Anderson and Krathwohl's revised Bloom's taxonomy, 2001.

8 *Introduction*

Attaining academic skills may matter little if people with them are disinclined to move that knowledge into action to make a difference. So, what makes that difference? Research in various fields suggests that learning needs to be meaningfully connected to students' understanding if they are to be able to take effective and appropriate action on the basis of it (Mazur in physics, 2009; Anderson in French language, 2010; Dickson, Thompson and O'Toole in chemistry, 2013). A learning experience needs to go beyond absorbing and feeding information back, or manipulation of notation, if it is to make knowledge available and in accordance with what students would like to achieve. The case of Anderson (2010), a university French educator, is both typical and instructive. She observed the attitudes of her French students, and, contrasting them with the pride of final year art school students as they mounted public exhibitions, she found that most of the French students didn't feel much meaningful attachment to the knowledge they handled or to their own 'products' or ideas. She has argued that although the current emphasis on acquiring skills and knowledge in professional fields appears to value the connection between thought and action, it still often amounts to the ability to reproduce acquired knowledge. Her experiments with her own teaching found that 'deep sustainable learning depends on the connection with students' experience' (Slowey & Watson, 2003, p. 180, quoted in Anderson, 2010, p. 206). She further argued that the prevailing 'habits of thought and types of approach developed in secondary schooling and in higher education tend almost exclusively towards a kind of disembodied intelligence and objective manipulation of knowledge for precise and identifiable outcomes' (p. 206). This is not just a matter of students not enjoying the learning provided in their degree; it is that it constitutes shallow learning, which cannot be applied to real-world contexts. Dickson et al. (2013; Dickson, 2015) found that undergraduate chemistry students' manipulation of the symbolic level (that is, the mathematics and chemistry notation) of submicro chemistry did not reliably translate into conceptual understanding. They investigated whether drawing as a pedagogy was effective in connecting students' conceptualisation with their symbolic level of understanding (2013). Other researchers have documented examples of students being able to produce accurate responses when they do not understand why the responses are accurate (Weimer, 2006; Beghetto & Kaufman, 2009). Lacking an understanding of the significance of knowledge restricts students' ability to interpret and meaningfully apply their knowledge, which is necessary for creatively working with it to affect things in the world. Assessment becomes a key to educators who are looking for conceptual understanding: if it is to truly reflect learning, it needs to provide personally meaningful and relevant forms of application or performance of gained knowledge and skills. 'True knowledge lies in our ability to use it' (Polanyi, 1967).

My empirical research responded to these concerns by offering an interpretation of empirical data of undergraduate cases of teaching that support the contention that imagination is teachable in higher education and, along with other aspects of creativity, is fostered in disciplinary-specific ways and in ways relevant to professional preparation. These teaching cases demonstrate models or examples of teaching that encourage learning the kind of synthetic, abstract thinking that the SOLO and Anderson and Krathwohl taxonomies describe as higher order thinking. By deploying imagination in the practice of learning, including in disciplinary practices, they show students being placed in pedagogical situations and doing certain tasks that place them 'in the way' of making meaningful connections.

The core of this book involves the four ethnographic case studies in Chapters 5, 6, 7 and 8. They are based on ethnographic research I conducted from 2012–17, in four subjects or 'units' of study in three campuses of Monash University, a large research intensive university in the city of Melbourne, Australia, that has approximately 70,000 students. Each unit was chosen because it was non-arts based: fourth year quantum physics; first year medieval European history; post-graduate finance; and first year pharmaceutical science. This was important because I sought to elucidate the neglected and misunderstood role of imagination in these disciplines/professions.

I was interested in the following questions:

- What is the role of imagination in learning in higher education, and what learning experiences do educators devise to encourage their students' imagination?
- How do the students experience learning that is focussed on engaging their imaginative capacity?
- This entails some sub-questions: What learning designs, assessment activities and teacher-student interactions encourage the deployment of imaginative capacity? Do disciplinary thinking and methodologies involve the imagination, and if so, how?
- Does Ricoeur's theory of imagination help us understand how teachers' approaches work to encourage imagination as a facet of learning?

About the research

My research design was ethnography (Geertz, 1973), a qualitative research methodology with its roots in anthropology and sociology that involves fieldwork. Studying phenomena in naturally occurring contexts is a key principle of ethnography. I decided to use a written narrative ethnography as writing notes in a classroom (rather than videoing the class, for example) is unobtrusive. As a social science account, its claims to 'objectivity' differ from the dominant positivist notion of an objective account which transcends subjectivity and is independent of anyone's interpretation of it (and also from Popper's notion of objective accounts in science, which are defined by their falsifiability). However, it shares a concern with what is directly observable and with standardisation of procedures of data collection that are stable enough across observers to be practical but are not presumed to be infallible and absolute. Although my analysis sought to be true to the way the educators progressively built concepts and skills in the students, my task was *not* to give an account of the course but to offer

10   *Introduction*

an interpretation of the role of imagination in the teaching and learning in it. Therefore its claims to validity concern the legitimacy of the application of the theoretical frameworks which establish the interpretation of the findings of how the teaching fostered students' imagination (Maxwell, 1992).

The educators were recruited on the basis of the recognised excellence of their teaching and their interest in being involved in a study of creative and imaginative teaching or teaching for creativity. The student participant pool was derived naturally by being enrolled in the unit taught by the selected lecturer. In the case of history, the lecturing professor was supported by a highly experienced head tutor, and the student participants were from one of the tutorial groups, which represented about one tenth of the total cohort.

Three kinds of data were collected to provide deep, cross-referenced perspectives upon which to base my interpretations: notes of my classroom observations of traditional face-to-face and technology-mediated teacher-student and student-student interaction; course documents, such as learning guides, course readers, textbooks, completed student assignments and the text thread from the weekly online student discussion forum (for history only) contained in the university's course management system; and transcriptions from pre- and post-class interviews with the participating educators and the same for the student focus groups conducted before and after the class observation. Data about enrolments, number of participants and length of observation for each site is set out in Table 1.3.

Table 1.3 The statistics on enrolments in participating units including numbers of consenting student participants in each 'unit'/ethnographic site and numbers of weeks of observation

	Physics *Fourth year Quantum Physics 2012*	*History* *First year Medieval European History 2013*	*Finance* *Post-graduate 'Money Market Dealing' 2013*	*Pharmaceutical science* *First year Scientific Inquiry 2017*
Total numbers in class	8	223 in lectures; about 25 in tutorial	36	104
Number of weeks of classroom observation (out of a 12-week semester)	4 weeks	12 weeks	8 weeks	4 weeks
Consent to observation	7	10	31	Lecture: 85 Workshop: 87
Consent to assignments	7	10	31	66
Consent to discussion board viewing	n/a	10	33[2]	81
Consent to focus groups and recordings	6	8	24	33

Interpretation and analysis

The interpretation of the data uses a socio-cultural perspective. The socio-cultural perspective understands learning not as a process of transmission of knowledge from the head of the teacher to the head of the student, but as a relational process. It asks: What is the relationship between knowledge and learning? How do we make meaning out of knowledge? Observation focuses on visible things – What do learners do when they are learning? How do they interact with others? What is the nature of the relationship between educator and student? What do they do with text, other symbolic modalities, drawings? How is the exterior environment manipulated in order to produce the learners' transformation in understanding and capability? What practices are they being inducted into?

A foundation and assumption of my study of formal education settings in higher education in four disciplines is that a teacher in a formal education setting establishes a culture of learning. Ethnography's 'thick' description and analysis (Geertz, 1973) allowed me to observe teaching and learning contexts, materials and disciplinary or professional practices and display the material evidence in my account. In this way, I endeavour to make sense of how teaching for imagination is woven into the texture of personal approaches to teaching and into disciplinary pedagogical practices in a particular research intensive university. The description that follows of Vygotsky's methodology of studying creativity and development, although in some ways aspirational, matches the living and situated attributes of ethnographic methodology that I used to conduct my research.

> He wanted a methodology that could study creativity and development in motion, in the making. In this way, a researcher could determine not just how the mind worked, but how its interconnected systems and its environment developed and influenced one another.
>
> (Moran & John-Steiner, 2003, p. 7)

How to read this book

Readers of this book may like to begin by reading Chapters 5, 6, 7 and 8, the heartwood of the book, and choosing particularly the chapters closest to their own disciplinary background or interests. Chapter 5 is an ethnography of a fourth year quantum physics subject; Chapter 6 is an ethnography of a first year medieval European history unit; Chapter 7 is an ethnography of a post-graduate finance subject; and Chapter 8 is an ethnography of a first year subject in pharmaceutical science called 'scientific inquiry'. These chapters discuss and analyse themes emerging from observation and analysis of data gathered in the four sites. I encourage readers to range beyond their own discipline and/or profession; there is a lot to be learned from other fields if you are willing to translate approaches into your own context.

12 *Introduction*

In this sense, my research and this book are a two-way street; it is unfinished business. I hope that the narratives I offer in my ethnographies enable the writer and reader to 'exchange experiences' (Benjamin, 1969, p. 83) and 'go visiting' the experience of others (Arendt, 1982, p. 43). Narratives offer the reader a bridge, as it were, and invite readers not only to assimilate different perspectives, but to converse with them and to consider how they differ from her or his own. One of the hopes underpinning this research is that it may provide nuanced exemplars within stories of imagination in teaching and learning that illuminate the diverse guises it takes in different fields. Some readers may be prompted to reflect on their own teaching, or to test if these ideas can provide a framework useful to interpret what aspects of imagination they may develop in students through their teaching. If we want to develop students' imaginative capacities, we need to develop a clearer understanding of what it is we are trying to develop (Lucas et al., 2013). Likewise, by providing students with an awareness of their learning as a kind of journey, and explicitly sharing with them what it is we want them to develop, they will be empowered to use their powers of agency and intelligence to achieve it.

Chapters 2 and 3 set the theoretical landscape of the book. In Chapter 2, I introduce Ricoeur's theory of imagination, which links imagination, reason and language and which I use to interpret the substantive ethnographies of each unit/site in Chapters 5, 6, 7 and 8. I make an argument for how and why it is a useful framework for conceptualising how imagination is integral to the creation of knowledge (as well as to learning existing knowledge) and for understanding its specific and teachable attributes that are of particular relevance to higher education. It is useful because if educators and students are clear about what it is they are developing, they can bring their intelligence to bear on developing it using a shared understanding. I discuss Ricoeur's theory of imagination in relation to three forms of what he terms 'productive' imagination: metaphor, models and narrative.

In Chapter 3, I connect imagination to constructivist views of learning and thinking. I discuss key concepts that relate imagination to learning and cognition theories: Lev Vygotsky's notion of tool mediated action; Wartofsky's (1979) linking of models, representations and perception; Michael Polanyi's (1967) notion of tacit knowing; Andy Clark's 'extended mind' thesis (Clark, 1997, 2011) and the theory of 'predictive processing', which presents a unified framework for understanding perception, embodiment, action and imagination as the engine for producing predictive models of perception (Clark, 2016). Collectively, these theories suggest that if we want to study imagination and imaginative thinking, then we should be looking at the way a tool is used to act on and change the object (what is being worked on). Of particular significance is how the theories provide a perspective that allows us to understand how, when teachers teach students the disciplinary methodologies and tools, students learn to make them their own by imaginatively composing their understandings though the use of these tools and practices. This paves the way for analysing the observations in the ethnographic chapters (5, 6, 7 and 8).

In Chapter 4 I distinguish the overlapping, or conflated, uses of the terms 'creativity', 'innovation' and 'imagination', which in higher education and much education curriculum literature, creative industries literature and economics policy are used interchangeably. Nevertheless, the way the terms are used interchangeably means my research also needed to consider what is implied by these overlapping concepts. Thus, this chapter discusses the major themes in the literature on the broad field of creativity. It then tightens its vision and focuses on that aspect of creativity involving imagination. This is because imagination, as the source of new ideas, is important in a higher education context, which is the focus of my research. This chapter then moves to what is already known about the development and enhancement of imagination and also broader dimensions of creativity within higher education, covering higher education teachers' views and approaches for cultivating and supporting the blending of imaginative and disciplinary knowledge. It discusses some key studies for enhancing imagination in other education sectors, presents what is known about how imagination is cultivated and criticises the lack of conceptual clarity about what imagination is, which stymies shared understandings among educators and students and impedes how it may be developed by students.

Using the theoretical lenses discussed in Chapters 2, 3 and 4, I apply them in the ethnographic chapters, 5, 6, 7 and 8, to interpret how the teachers' creative pedagogies mobilise learners into activities that involve projecting their imaginations in four subjects from non-arts disciplines in a research intensive university. These chapters discuss and analyse themes emerging from observation and analysis of data gathered in the four sites.

The case study in Chapter 5 – the honours quantum physics class – raises interesting issues about the relationship between reproductive and productive imagination in Ricoeur's theory of imagination. Pedagogy in this physics class pointed to what appeared to be a contingent and step-wise relationship between reproductive and productive imagination – something which Ricoeur himself does not expand on, although he does speak about memory's role in anticipation or rehearsal and its interaction. In this case study, the role of the imagination in metaphor and narrative that connects disparate things by combining them into new wholes was applied in a pedagogy designed to promote the imagination. Translated into physics, this led me to interpret the observation that the students were led in a cycle of diagrammatic, mathematical and linguistic forms of reasoning. Each of these skilful forms – or tools – independently offered an approach to understanding, but, *cumulatively and in combination*, they did more. Understanding 'danced' *between* them – they synthesised and organised the students' understanding of quantum concepts that in fact cannot be understood directly but have to be constructed indirectly through the mediation of these multiple cognitive tools. The chapter also reveals how students engaged in resourceful learning activities in the student common room as they became embedded in the social relations involved in physics disciplinary practices.

Chapter 6 – the first year medieval European history class – demonstrates how Ricoeur's emphasis on the semantic innovation involved in combining elements,

14   *Introduction*

and constructivist theorists' focus on tool mediated thinking, can illuminate how the creation of knowledge arises. Of particular interest was that the student assignments in the medieval European history course provided opportunities for students to become cultural producers – historians – rather than simply consumers of history. Wielding the tools and techniques of historians involved the students in a constant interplay of imaginative conjecture and critical analysis, allowing new syntheses of ideas to arise that were grounded in evidence – the kind of imaginative activity that is needed to find solutions to contemporary world problems.

Finance is not generally regarded as an imaginative enterprise, but in Chapter 7, an ethnography of a post-graduate finance class, I describe a subject that was run using a high tech, simulation learning approach, in which students in groups took roles in an imaginary bank. The simulation pedagogy motivated students to form various financial strategies based on their disciplinary-tool-enhanced modelling of financial information. I argue that strategic reasoning is an imaginative process in Ricoeur's sense of 'productive imagination' because it includes imagining the consequences of suggested courses of action if they were applied and because strategy involves mentally positing alternative plans, each designed to produce an outcome. The finance ethnography was also notable because Ricoeur's theory enabled an understanding that simulation pedagogy allows students to imaginatively take up at least two positions – banker and learner – and to construct different learnings by moving flexibly between those two mental positions or identities.

In Chapter 8 three main conclusions emerged from research in a first year pharmaceutical science subject on 'scientific inquiry'. First, students making their own diagram or representation of the process of scientific inquiry is used as a mediating tool for processing a developing and critical understanding of scientific inquiry as the basis for organising their own performance of science. Second, the cognitive work performed to gain competence and creativity in science is done by learning to distribute the thinking across the brain-body boundary and beyond, through the symbolic and material artefacts used to think with. Third, by incorporating pedagogies that encourage reflection, the educator fosters how students can begin to imagine ways of thinking and behaving that belong to an emerging identity as a scientist. Ricoeur's understanding of productive imagination in narrative is useful here, as is work on predictive processing. It illuminates the use of productive imagination to form new connections and to incorporate complexity and reconsideration into processes of discovery.

Chapter 8 discusses some conclusions about Ricoeur's theory of imagination and implications for teaching practice.

In the next chapter, we visit the question of what imagination is. I contend that imagination is a key aspect of creativity in higher education because it is integral to proposals for new ideas and therefore underpins new knowledge and professional practices. I argue that Ricoeur's theory of imagination, which is focused on imagination, reason and language, contributes to a coherent theoretical understanding of imagination.

Notes

1 In Australia, the Group of Eight (Go8) universities are a coalition of the research intensive universities. The Go8 includes Australian National University, Sydney University, University of New South Wales, University of Melbourne, University of Western Australia, University of Adelaide, University of Queensland and Monash University.
2 As it happened, the lecturer did not use the course management system, Moodle, for class discussion. Students communicated with the lecturer and 'traded' with him, as the central bank, in between class sessions using email.

References

Amabile, T. M. (2010). *The three threats to creativity*. HBR Blog. Retrieved from http://blogs.hbr.org/2010/11/the-three-threats-to-creativit/

Anderson, K. (2010). The whole learner: The role of imagination in developing disciplinary understanding. *Arts and Humanities in Higher Education, 9*(2), 205–221.

Anderson, L. W., & Krathwohl, D. R. (Eds.). (2001). *A taxonomy for learning, teaching, and assessing: A revision of Bloom's taxonomy of educational objectives*. New York: Longman.

Arendt, H. (1982). *The human condition*. New York: Doubleday Anchor Books.

Beghetto, R. A., & Kaufman, J. C. (2009). Intellectual estuaries: Connecting learning and creativity in programs of advanced academics. *Journal of Advanced Academics, 20*(2), 296–324.

Benjamin, W. (1969). *Illuminations*. London: Pimlico.

Biggs, J., & Tang, C. S.-K. (2007). *Teaching for quality learning at university: What the student does*. Maidenhead: Open University Press.

Biggs, J., & Tang, C. S.-K. (2011). *Teaching for quality learning at university: What the student does*. Maidenhead: Open University Press, Fourth edition.

Bleazby, J. (2013). *Social reconstruction learning: Dualism, Dewey and philosophy in Schools*. New York: Routledge.

Boud, D., & Associates. (2010). *ALTC report: Assessment 2020: Seven propositions for assessment reform in higher education*. Sydney: Australian Learning and Teaching Council.

Clark, A. (1997). *Being there: Putting brain, body and world together*. Cambridge, MA: The Massachusetts Institute of Technology Press.

Clark, A. (2011). *Supersizing the mind*. Oxford: Oxford University Press.

Clark, A. (2016). *Surfing uncertainty: Prediction, action and embodied mind*. New York: Oxford University Press.

Claxton, G., Edwards, L., & Scale-Constantinou, V. (2006). Cultivating creative mentalities: A framework for education. *Thinking Skills and Creativity, 1*, 57–61.

Craft, A., Jeffrey, B., & Leibling, M. (2001). *Creativity in education*. London: Continuum.

Cropley, A. J. (1992). *More ways than one: Fostering creativity*. Norwood, NJ: Ablex.

Cropley, A. J. (2006). In praise of convergent thinking. *Creativity Research Journal, 18*(3), 391–404. doi:10.1207/s15326934crj1803_13

Cropley, A. J. (2009). *Creativity in education & learning: A guide for teachers and educators*. London: Kogan Page.

Cropley, D. H. and Cropley, A. J. (1998) 'Teaching Engineering Students to be Creative - Program and Outcomes' [online]. In P. Howard, G. Swarbrick, & A. Churches (Eds.), *Waves of Change: Proceedings of the 10th Australasian Conference on Engineering Education, 5th Australasian Women in Engineering Forum, 5th National Conference on Teaching Engineering Designers*. Rockhampton, QLD: Central Queensland University, James Goldston Faculty of Engineering and Physical Systems, 21–25. Retrieved from https://

16 Introduction

search-informit-com-au.ezproxy.lib.monash.edu.au/documentSummary;dn=910238685
681832;res=IELENG ISBN: 1875902929. [cited 13 Feb 18].

Cropley, D. H., Cropley, A. J., Kaufman, J. C., & Runco, M. A. (2010). *The dark side of creativity*. New York: Cambridge University Press.

Csikszentmihalyi, M. (1999). Implications of a systems perspective for the study of creativity. In R. Sternberg (Ed.), *Handbook of creativity* (pp. 313–335). Cambridge: Cambridge University Press.

Csikszentmihalyi, M. (2006). Foreword. In N. Jackson, O. Martin, & M. Shaw (Eds.), *Developing creativity in higher education: An imaginative curriculum*. London: Taylor and Francis.

Dening, G. (2000). Writing, praxis and performance. In A. Curthoys & A. McGrath (Eds.), *Writing histories: Imagination and narration*. Clayton, Melbourne: Monash Publications in History, Department of History, Australian National University.

Dickson, H. (2015). *Developing a common visual literacy amongst first year chemistry students using collaborative drawing tasks*. Masters thesis. Retrieved from https://figshare.com/articles/Developing_a_common_visual_literacy_amongst_first_year_chemistry_students_using_collaborative_drawing_tasks/4679761 DOI: 10.4225/03/58acffd8a2f25

Dickson, H., Thompson, C., & O'Toole, P. (2013). *Poster: How do students visualize the submicro world of chemistry*. Paper presented at the Australian Conference on Science and Mathematics Education. Retrieved from https://openjournals.library.sydney.edu.au/index.php/IISME/issue/view/606/showToc

Egan, K. (1997). *The educated mind: How cognitive tools shape our understanding*. Chicago: University of Chicago Press.

Fanning, R., & Gaba, D. (2008). Simulation-based learning as an educational tool. In J. Stonemetz & K. Ruskin (Eds.), *Anesthesia informatics* (pp. 459–479). London: Springer-Verlag.

Flew, T., & Cunningham, S. D. (2010). Creative industries after the first decade of debate. *The Information Society*, *26*(2), 113–123.

Geertz, C. (1973). *The interpretation of cultures*. New York: Basic Books Inc, Publishers.

Gredler, M. E. (2004). Games and simulations and their relationships to learning. In D. Jonassen (Ed.), *Handbook of research on educational communications and technology* (pp. 571–581). Mahwah, NJ: Lawrence Erlbaum Associates.

Greene, M. (1995). *Releasing the imagination: Essays on education, the arts, and social change*. San Francisco: Josey-Bass Publishers.

Hajkowicz, S. A., Andrew, R., Rudd, L., Bratanova, A., Hodgers, L., Mason, C., & Boughen, N. (2016). *Tomorrow's digitally enabled workforce: Megatrends and scenarios for jobs and employment in Australia over the coming twenty years*. Brisbane: Commonwealth Scientific and Industrial Research Organisation (CSIRO).

Harris, A. (2014). *The creative turn: Toward a new aesthetic imaginary*. Rotterdam: Sense Publishers.

Jeffares, B. (2010). The co-evolution of tools and minds: Cognition and material culture in the hominin lineage. *Phenomenolgy and the Cognitive Sciences*, *9*, 503–520. doi:10.1007/s11097-010-9176-9

Kearney, R. (1988). *The wake of imagination*. London: Hutchinson Education.

Lovitts, B. E. (2007). *Making the implicit explicit: Creating performance expectations for the dissertation*. Sterling, Virginia: Stylus.

Lucas, B., Claxton, G., & Spencer, E. (2013). *Progression in student creativity in school: First steps towards new forms of formative assessments*. OECD Education Working Paper No. 86. OECD Publishing. Retrieved from http://dx.doi.org/10.1787/5k4dp59msdwk-en

Maxwell, J. (1992, Fall). Understanding and validity in qualitative research. *Harvard Educational Review*, *62*(3), 279–300.

Mazur, E. (Uploaded on November 12, 2009). *Confessions of a Converted Lecturer*. YouTube. Retrieved from https://www.youtube.com/watch?v=WwslBPj8GgI

McWilliam, E. L. (2007). *Is creativity teachable: Conceptualising the creativity/pedagogy relationship in higher education.* Paper presented at the 30th HERDSA Annual Conference: Enhancing Higher Education, Theory and Scholarship, Adelaide.

McWilliam, E. L. (Ed.). (2011). *Creativity and innovation: An educational perspective.* Melbourne: University of Melbourne.

McWilliam, E. L., & Dawson, S. (2007). *Understanding creativity: A survey of 'creative' academic teachers: A report for the Carrick Institute for Learning and Teaching in Higher Education.* Retrieved from www.altcexchange.edu.au/system/files/handle/fellowships_associatefellow_report_ ericamcwilliam_may07.pdf

McWilliam, E. L., & Haukka, S. (2008). Educating the creative workforce: New directions for twenty-first century schooling. *British Educational Research Journal, 34*(5), 651–666.

Moran, S., & John-Steiner, V. (2003). Creativity in the making: Vygotsky's contemporary contribution to the dialectic of creativity and development. In R. K. Sawyer, V. John-Steiner, S. Moran, R. J. Sternberg, D. H. Feldman, H. Gardner, J. Nakamura, & M. Csikszentmihalyi (Eds.), *Creativity and development* (pp. 61–90). New York: Oxford University Press.

Mowbray, S., & Halse, C. (2010). The purpose of the PhD: Theorising the skills acquired by students. *Higher Education Research & Development, 29*(6), 653–664.

Noddings, N. (2013). Standardised curriculum and loss of creativity. *Theory into Practice, 52*(3), 210–215. doi:10.1080/00405841.2013.804315

Polanyi, M. (1967). *The tacit dimension.* Garden City, NY: Anchor Books.

Policastro, E., & Gardner, H. (1999). From case studies to robust generalisations. In R. J. Sternberg (Ed.), *Handbook of creativity* (pp. 213–225). Cambridge: Cambridge University Press.

Ramsden, P. (1992). *Learning to teach in higher education.* London: Routledge.

Robinson, K. (1999). *All our futures: Creativity, culture and education (the Robinson report).* London: National Advisory Committee on Creative and Cultural Education (NACCCE).

Robinson, K. (2011). *Out of our minds: Learning to be creative.* Oxford: Capstone Publishing Limited.

Saul, J. R. (2001). *On equilibrium.* Ringwood, Victoria: Penguin Books.

Sternberg, R. J., & Lubart, T. I. (1999). The concept of creativity: Prospects and paradigms. In *Handbook of creativity* (pp. 3–15). Cambridge: Cambridge University Press.

Stevens, R. (2003). *National report on trends in school music education provision in Australia.* Double Bay, NSW: Music Council of Australia. Retrieved from http://hdl.handle.net/10536/DRO/DU:30010255

Trowler, P. (2013). Can approaches to research in art and design be beneficially adapted for research into higher education? *Higher Education Research & Development, 32*(1), 56–69. doi:10.1080/07294360.2012.750276

Vygotsky, L. S. (1978). *Mind in society: The development of higher psychological processes.* Cambridge, MA: Harvard University Press.

Warnock, M. (1976). *Imagination.* London: Faber and Faber.

Wartofsky, M. W. (1979). Perception, representation and forms of action: Towards an historical epistemology. In *Models: Representations and scientific understanding* (pp. 188–210). Dordrecht, Holland/Boston, MA/London, UK: D. Reidel Publishing Company.

Weimer, M. E. (2006). Why and how to look. In *Enhancing scholarly work on teaching and learning: Professional literature that makes a difference* (pp. 1–16). San Francisco: Jossey-Bass.

18 *Introduction*

Wertsch, J. V. (2007). Mediation. In H. Daniels, M. Cole, & J. V. Wertsch (Eds.), *The Cambridge companion to Vygotsky* (pp. 178–192). Cambridge: Cambridge University Press.

Western, M., Boreham, P., Kubler, M., Laffan, W., Western, J., Lawson, A., & Clague, D. (2007). *PhD graduates 5 to 7 years out: Employment outcomes, job attributes and the quality of research training: Final report* (Revised ed.). Brisbane, Queensland, Australia: The University of Queensland Social Research Centre (UQSRC).

2 Theoretical framework on imagination

Introduction

As discussed in Chapter 1, there is a will to foster creativity and its close cousin, imagination, which is shared by industry, government and others concerned with the quality of contributions citizens make to the future. However, there is a problem. Attempts to foster imagination are impeded by a number of factors, the main one being that imagination is not well understood or conceptualised by higher educators. My research responds to this problem. If educators are to develop coherent explanations of imaginative teaching and learning that help progress understanding of how it might be encouraged in higher education institutions, conceptual clarity and consistency are needed. My hope is that they can then bring their students into the conversation about it and that students can lend their intelligence to developing it.

In this chapter, I argue that Paul Ricoeur's theory of imagination suggests that imagination is a form of thinking and that it is therefore useful to try to understand how it may be integral to education and learning, how it is related to reality and why it should be cultivated in undergraduate education. I discuss Ricoeur's theory of imagination in relation to three forms of what he terms 'productive' imagination: metaphor, models and narrative. In the following chapter, Chapter 3, I connect this theory to constructivist views of learning and thinking, in particular Lev Vygotsky's notion of tool mediated action, Michael Polanyi's notion of tacit knowing and Andy Clark's 'extended mind' thesis.

Ricoeur's theory of imagination

In three essays, 'Imagination in discourse and in action' (1991), 'The function of fiction in shaping reality' (Valdes, 1991) and 'Metaphorical process as cognition, imagination, and feeling' (1979), and in a book, *The rule of metaphor* (1975/2003), Ricoeur asks whether the term 'imagination' denotes a homogenous phenomenon or whether it is a collection of loosely related experiences. In answer, he distinguishes four major uses of the term 'imagination' in the philosophical literature, which is helpful in thinking about my research aim and the questions of my study.

20   *Theoretical framework on imagination*

Ricoeur draws a distinction between 'reproductive' imagination, which relies on memory and mimesis, and 'productive' imagination, which is generative. He asserts there are two main types of 'reproductive' imagination: the first refers to the way we bring common objects or experiences to the 'mind's eye' in the form of an image (e.g., yesterday's ravioli lunch with a friend at a seaside café). The second refers to material representations whose function is to somehow copy or 'take the place of' the things they represent (e.g., photographs, portraits, drawings, diagrams and maps). He analyses and criticises the focus on the 'image' in Western philosophy of imagination, arguing that at best the image referred to in reproductive imagination is derivative of reality; at worst it is a deviation from reality (Taylor, 2006). Ricoeur claims that philosophers have focused on 'reproductive' imagination and have given short shrift to what he, after Immanuel Kant, calls 'productive' conceptions of imagination (1991c, pp. 169–171). Productive imagination refers to images of non-existent things (not the same as absent things). Again, there are two types of productive imagination: the first type ranges from images, such as dreams to fictions or inventions like novels, fables and mythical creatures, which involve the projection of things that have never existed in reality (p. 170). However, the imaginer is fully aware that such things do not actually exist. The second type of productive imagination is the category of illusions or illusory beliefs, for example a hallucination of water in the desert: non-existent to an external observer but believed in by the subject. The distinction in awareness of the fictiveness of imaginative products is something noted also by Policastro and Gardner's (1999) distinction between fantasy or illusion (which they call the 'subjective expression of needs, conflicts and wishes' [p. 217]) and imagination. They maintain that many scholars conflate the two, generating unwarranted confusion, putting them in agreement with Ricoeur.

These four usages, Ricoeur maintains, are contrary, and he argues that philosophical theories of the imagination, as well as common sense notions and usages of the word, tend to focus on one or other of these usages and, therefore, seem like rival theories, when in fact they are considering different aspects of the imagination. Ricoeur maps received theories and ideas about the imagination in the space formed by two axes, one showing the degree of reproductive or productive imagination implied and the other showing the human subject's critical consciousness of the difference between the imagined and the real (see Figure 2.1). Understandings or positions could be taken up at particular points along the axes and in different quadrants.

Under this scheme, he says that Hume's idea of image as a weak trace of the existing (real) object would be located at the extreme left along the x axis, while Sartre's notions of portrait, dream and fiction would be at the extreme right end of the same axis. Extrapolating on this, a lie I tell about why I came home late last night would be located at the northern end of the y axis, as I am fully aware of its fictional status. In contrast, Macbeth's imagination when he is conceiving Duncan's murder and says, 'My thought, whose murder is yet fantastical/ . . . that function/ Is smothered in surmise, and nothing is,/ But what is not' (*Macbeth*, 1.iii) would be located in the lower quadrants because he finds he believes his

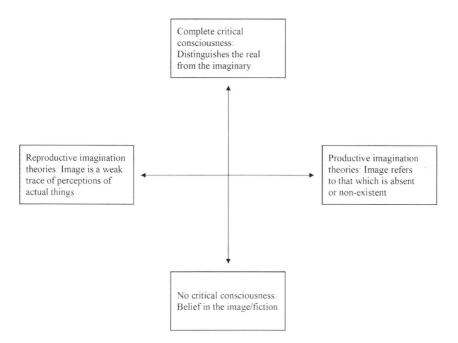

Figure 2.1 Representing Ricoeur's two axes of received philosophical theories of imagination: degree of critical consciousness and productive/reproductive imagination

Source: First published in *Departures in Critical Qualitative Research*, 3(3), 1999. Reproduced with the permission of University of California Press.

own imaginings. However, it would fall to the right of the y axis because the murder has not yet taken place. It is a thing he will 'create'.

Productive imagination and agency

Ricoeur's point is that reproductive forms of imagination tend to be less illuminating in terms of understanding human action, agency and creativity because they merely reproduce the perceived world. His focus is on 'productive' imagination, embodied in inventions like novels and fables – which are not intended to be straightforward descriptions of the world. Hence, they cannot be categorised as correct or incorrect accounts of reality because they imply a consciousness of the fictiveness of the account.

These empiricist (reproductive) notions of imagination (exemplified, he argues, by Hume and Sartre) in which an image is associated with perception go hand in hand with a problematic notion of experience and the subject. They suggest that experience involves a passive subject who is imprinted on by sense impressions from the outside world. This strips the subject of playing any active part in how s/he experiences the world. The phenomenologists and

22 Theoretical framework on imagination

constructivists that Ricoeur is influenced by reject this notion of experience and the subject. They see the subject and the 'external world' as interdependent and interconnected. They describe the subject as having intentions and interests and as actively shaping reality to accord with his or her intentions and interests, from the subject's own particular point of view. The latter presents a more active, creative, autonomous and dynamic notion of the self and experience.

Metaphor: paradigmatic of imagination

Ricoeur's theory offers a new way of putting the problem. Instead of approaching the issue of the imagination through perception, and asking if and how it passes from perception to image, his theory invites us to relate imagination to a use of language. Ricoeur argues that metaphors are paradigmatic of the process of productive imagination, combining hitherto separate things and creating relations of resemblance to one another (1975/2003, p. 271). In doing so, metaphors 'split' their direct reference to everyday objects and *offer up models for understanding reality in new ways*. Ricoeur suggests that metaphor is a rhetorical technique by which discourse unleashes the power that fictions have to 'redescribe' reality, to make meaning or to be 'semantically innovative' and offers a new way of thinking about the imagination. Because it involves analogy and redescription, it is a more productive and creative notion of imagination than the empiricist conceptions discussed earlier because it presupposes will or volition.

Ricoeur argues that metaphors also provide a pictorial or figurative dimension to what is newly discovered or semantically innovative because the imagination *schematises* (in Kant's idiom) an image which is an emerging meaning (1979, p. 149). In support of this idea, he quotes Aristotle, 'Ordinary words convey only what we know already; it is from metaphor that we can best get hold of something fresh' (1975/2003, p. 19). This notion follows Kant's assertion that one of the functions of a schema is to provide images for a concept, but in the sense of depicting relations, rather than having a mental picture *of* something (1979, p. 150). These relations could describe unsaid, unheard similarities or could refer to qualities, logical structures, localisations, situations, attitudes or feelings.

Semantic innovation

Aristotle described metaphors as referring to words (not sentences, or works) in which a label or meaning is *transferred* (or displaced) from one familiar domain onto another unfamiliar one. The effect of this transfer of meaning is to produce a new meaning about the thing described, hence the term 'semantically innovative'. However, Ricoeur differs from Aristotle in ascribing the extension of new meaning to how metaphors operate at *the level of the sentence* as a whole – to be precise, in the deviant use of *predicates* that describe the subject in the sentence.

> We should more accurately speak of metaphorical utterances rather than words used metaphorically.
>
> (1991c, p. 172)

The resemblance is itself a function of the bizarre predicates. It consists in the coming together that suddenly abolishes the logical distance between hithertofore distinct semantic fields in order to produce a semantic shock, which, in its turn, ignites the spark of meaning of the metaphor . . . . This shift has the effect of shifting our attention from the problems of a change of meaning at the simple level of the word, to the problem of the restructuring of semantic fields.

(1991c, p. 173)

This is a lot more than the given association of ideas through resemblance. The following example from T. S. Eliot's *Four quartets* illustrates the shift in outlook, or the 'restructuring of semantic fields', as Ricoeur refers to it (1991c, p. 173), accomplished by metaphoric usage.

Footfalls echo in the memory
Down the passage which we did not take
Towards the door we never opened
Into the rose garden

(Eliot, *Four quartets*,
'Burnt Norton', 1944, lines 11–14)

While the imagery of footsteps and doors in a passageway is simple and given by our senses, when the new way of 'seeing as' strikes us, in a way that is different to that given by our senses, we see the finiteness of life choices taken and the loss of joy in those not taken, and of past and future combined in the present's ruminations. Imagining is the operation performed at the crossroads of this process. For Ricoeur, the language of fresh metaphors creates the conditions that urge us to make a mental leap and combine heterogeneous ideas or domains of experience and, in doing so, tell us something new about their referents. Therefore, metaphors are not merely rhetorical ornaments but have genuine cognitive import (Ricoeur, 1975/2003). They act as filters, suppressing some details and emphasising others, organising our view of the similar. When they do, the amalgamation offers up a model that can generate new connections that lead to scientific hypotheses, or new and coherent ways of apprehending facets of the world, augmenting and reorganising our experiences – what Ricoeur calls 'second-order redescription' (1991c, p. 175; 1975/2003, p. 287) – and, potentially, generating propositions for new actions. Imagination is this ability to make a mental leap and align heterogeneous ideas or totally different domains of experience. In doing so, they can tell us something new about reality. This is why imagination is important to discovery, as well as to solving problems. It also points the way to the importance of 'mindtools', which will be discussed in the next chapter. Some symbolic forms, like metaphors, can supercharge the imagination. Novelty is built into the system!

Ricoeur's view accords with Murphy's argument that imagination 'integrates unlikely elements. It makes surprising connections. And it does this, animated by a drive for coherence, form and meaning' (Murphy, Peters & Marginson, 2010,

24   *Theoretical framework on imagination*

p. 102). It also essentially aligns with the UK National Advisory Committee on Creative and Cultural Education report, *All our futures*, in which imagination is described as 'generative' because it is responsible for making unusual connections. The report is worth quoting here:

> [Imagination is] a mode of thought which is essentially generative, in which we attempt to expand the possibilities of a given situation. . . . Creative insight often occurs when existing ideas are combined or re-interpreted in unexpected ways or when they are applied in areas with which they are not normally associated. Making unusual connections, seeing analogies and relationships between ideas or objects that haven't been related.
>
> (Robinson, 1999, p. 31)

In contrast, in fossilised or hackneyed metaphors, the transference of meaning directs our perception in ways that become invisible to us by constant usage (e.g., 'she drove me mad', 'to grasp a concept'). They no longer affect the senses; the meaning can be mistaken for literal. In fresh metaphors, the meaning produced is innovative and replete with implications which can give rise to new insights in the listener/reader. That is, they mean – *in these and these and these ways, this (stranger) thing is like this other (more familiar) thing*. Rather than simply recognising similarity, in fresh metaphors, the new meaning, as it were, *creates* a resemblance that can be 'seen' and understood, rather than simply finding an antecedently existing similarity and expressing it (see also Black, 1962, p. 83). In other words, the resemblance is in the eye of the beholder, rather than a resemblance inherent in the things themselves, but once apprehended in the new light, the likeness, expressed in an image and irrigated by memory, opens up new insights about the subject. The deviant predication establishes a 'new relationship between heterogeneous ideas in a way that adds something to or throws new light on, the thing talked about' (Egan, 1997, p. 55).

> It is . . . at the moment when a new meaning emerges out of the ruins of the literal predication that *imagination offers its specific mediation* [my emphasis]. . . . Imagination is the apperception, the sudden glimpse, of a new predictive pertinence, namely, a way of constructing pertinence in impertinence. . . . Imagining is above all restructuring semantic fields. It is, to use Wittgenstein's expression in *Philosophical Investigations* 'seeing as . . . '. . . . The work of the imagination is to schematise metaphorical attribution. Like the Kantian schema, it gives an image to an emerging meaning.
>
> (Ricoeur, 1991c, pp. 172–173)

Agency

It can be seen from this that Ricoeur positions the receiver or reader of a metaphor in an active relationship to the metaphor because it is only when the creative imagination of the reader/receiver is activated that meaning is constructed or made. Ricoeur's theory explains a logic of discovery – it is here that the generativity of productive imagination can be seen. However, the value we put on it depends on point of view. This same generativity contains within it the potential illusory power of metaphor that, I would conjecture, lies behind the suspicion that imagination is dangerous – a kind of conjuring trick – and that truth claims that come from our own minds are delusional because they have not sprung from the world itself. This idea underpins the view of imagination as inherently unreliable.

However, what Ricoeur is proposing falls out of this basic dualism. His description proposes that metaphors imply that something is simultaneously *like* and is *not like* something else – analogous to or identified with it, and yet different from it. He takes a kind of Brechtian position, saying that in our use of metaphors we can hover between distantiation/estrangement and familiarisation and that this looking askance at a situation means critical awareness is part of productive imagination (the y axis in Figure 2.1). This is a crucial idea by Ricoeur. And in fact, the discussion of tired metaphors should remind us that although productive imagination can manifest new realities, it needs to be balanced with critical thinking – fresh metaphors can over time become clichéd, taken-for-granted meanings or realities – something that will be discussed later in this chapter. Although it is only marginally relevant to our argument, Ricoeur's essays on ideology and utopia (1991b) show he was well aware of the pitfalls of productive imagination and that he saw a judgement and balance necessary between both standpoints.

The crucial idea of the imagination producing something which is simultaneously like and not like something else is expanded on by Ricoeur as the concept of 'split reference' (1975/2003, p. 271; 1979, p. 153), which means that the meaning of a metaphorical statement arises when the literal interpretation of the statement is blocked and founders. In that moment, the suspension of the ordinary reference involves a kind of stereoscopic vision. In this way, the image offered by the metaphor gives a shape to, or invents, new meaning – a new model for understanding reality. The split structure of metaphor is, according to Ricoeur, the structure of imagination. The power of metaphor is that, in reassigning the label in an unconventional way, it has the capacity to reorganise experience or apprehension in significant ways. We see here how Ricoeur's focus on productive imagination based in a language model offers a notion of the imagination which is potentially powerful as it has the capacity to 'organise' or to restructure experience.

In an essay called 'On interpretation' (1991d), Ricoeur explains further how this works and in doing so highlights the *agency* of the language user. He says that to 'make sense' of a sentence, given the rules of grammar, the reader will try to resolve sense-making difficulties by means of recalling her/his experience of being in the world to which the sentence about the shared author/reader-world refers. So that if we say, for example, 'light is a wave', the sentence, although grammatically perfect, is deviant in the everyday language sense because light has no correlation to a wave in our everyday experience at all. So, when faced with this seeming paradoxical statement, the listener or reader seeks to find a way that it is still *intelligible*. This is where the imagination comes into operation. The listener/reader will bring her/his knowledge and experience of waves to mind in order to find a correlation between the two and figure out what can be meant by the expression. You could say the nonsense causes a kind of cognitive pressure (Ricoeur calls it the emotion 'shock') on the listener/reader to resolve the 'impertinent attribution' and to make (new) sense of the statement. In the process, the everyday references of language have to be 'split', 'suspended' or neutralised – at least momentarily – and new possibilities or insights attributed to the statement in order that the statement can still 'make sense'. In that moment of suspension of ordinary direct reference, new possibilities of meaning or describing the world arise (1979, p. 154). The new way of seeing or understanding that is produced is contained in the proverbial expression to 'see as', which Ricoeur adopts (others refer to it as adopting the 'as if' stance, which is the same concept). He also refers to it as a 'second-order referencing'. When this new way of 'seeing as' strikes us, in a way that is different to that given by our senses, deeper and equally valid forms of understanding occur. Authors use imagination when they configure new sentences and construct new texts. And readers bring their imagination and experience of being in the world in order to interpret text. To quote Ricoeur:

> Poetic language is no less about reality than any other use of language but refers to it by the means of a complex strategy which implies, as an essential component, a suspension and seemingly an abolition of the ordinary reference attached to descriptive language. This suspension, however, is only the negative condition of a second-order reference, of an indirect reference built on the ruins of the direct reference. This reference is called second-order reference only with respect to the primacy of the reference of ordinary language.
>
> (1979, p. 153)

Thus imagination enables us to suspend the force and validity of immediate experience and to consider things as other than they appear. We see in this how theories of the imaginative process can mistakenly construe the body as a simple input device involving sense perception because it involves the pictorial dimension. But if we can read new understandings from pictorial relations conjured by metaphor (language), it is because of the imagination's capacity to assimilate surprising, even seeming-nonsensical, predicates, which implies active mental work. However, we note that this process connects empirical experience (and memory) of being in the world to productive imagination and describes a movement from one to the other. It encapsulates how cultural tools and memories of sense perceptions are actively fused in making meaning, something which is explored in the next chapter. This is highly significant for pedagogy, suggesting it is a method for active forms of student engagement, examples of which are described in the ethnographic chapters of this book. Whether we produce or listen to a metaphor, it provokes us to mental activity – we have to 'grasp the similar', to synthesise contrary meanings, so that, as Ricoeur says, 'Suddenly, . . . we see old age as the dusk of day, time as a beggar, nature as a temple with living pillars' (1991c, p. 173).

Productive imagination as forecasting or anticipatory imagination

Let it not be assumed that these notions of metaphor, imagination and reassignment of meaning in statements are confined to poetic discourse and not to more objective types of discourse which are concerned with pragmatic reality, such as scientific discourse or the human sciences. On the contrary. Ricoeur's conception is very close to Richard Dawkins's (1989) conception of the imagination as mental representations instrumentally used in the service of the intention or purpose of the person, specifically its power to give rise to the free play of possibilities – or to conjecture. Dawkins construes the imagination as a kind of soft technological ability of consciousness to simulate: 'you *imagine* what would happen if you did each of the alternatives open to you – you set up a model in your head, not of everything in the world, but of the restricted sets of entities which you think may be relevant. You may see them vividly in your mind's eye or manipulate stylized abstractions of them' (1989, p. 59). He stresses the use to which imagination is put in the service of instrumental intentions, or to put it another way, for its capacity to allow us to see possibilities in the intermediate or long-term time frames upon which judgement or decision-making can operate. This model, which focuses on providing foresight (powers of prediction and conjecture), stems from Dawkins's adaptive intelligence model of mind, and the fact that it construes imagination as grounded by facts is a view shared by Lipman, in the context of teaching thinking in education.

> To imagine is to envisage a possible world, or the details of such a world, or the journey one may take to reach such a world. To have other worlds in which to dwell – and to make them available to others to dwell in also – is no mean feat. What matters is that those who explore the realms of possibility must retain as much as possible their sense of fact, just as those who explore the perceivable world must keep their imagination about them.
>
> (Lipman, 2003, p. 245)

This dialectic between imagination and the real is an idea which I will consider again later in more detail in the context of Dewey's notion of imagination and will be discussed in Chapter 4 in relation to the interdependence of creativity and critical thinking.

'Models for': epistemological imagination in models

Ricoeur argues that the function of metaphors is equivalent to the function of models in science. Models in science are used to 'redescribe' phenomenon in terms of functions which are more familiar to us and that may give rise to

28 *Theoretical framework on imagination*

hypotheses – or as Dawkins points out, to prediction and conjecture. Models refer to, but do not reproduce, a pre-existing original. They allude to common attributes between the model and the underlying characteristic/s to which it refers. Ricoeur (1975/2003, p. 283) avowedly borrows this idea from the works of authors such as Max Black in *Models and metaphors* (1962) and Mary Hesse's 'The explanatory function of metaphor' in the appendix to *Models and metaphors in science* (1963). Following Black, he describes a hierarchy of three levels or kinds of models. The first is *scale models*. Examples are a model of a ship; an enlargement of something small, like an insect; a slow-motion sketch of a manoeuvre; or a simulation of a social process. All of these are models of something, and they purport to show how something looks, how it works, what laws govern it.

> It is possible to decode the model and, by reading off its properties, arrive at the properties of the original. . . . The model purports to be faithful only in respect to its relevant features. . . . They are the counterparts of the rules of interpretation that specify the way they are to be read.
>
> (Ricoeur, 1975/2003, p. 284)

The second level of Black's model is *analogue models*: 'hydraulic models of economic systems, or the use of electrical circuits in computers, etc.' (1975/2003, p. 284). What is important in this form of model is to illustrate the structure, that is, 'the web of relationships of the original' (p. 284). The pertinent correlative traits that are modelled constitute what, in mathematics, is called 'isomorphism'. 'The model and the original resemble each other in their structures and not through sensible features' (p. 284).

Black's third level in the hierarchy of models, which Ricoeur refers to, are *theoretical models*. An example would be 'Maxwell's representation of an electrical field in terms of the properties of an imaginary incompressible fluid' (p. 284). Identity of structure, or function, also characterises this level, but they are not things, and they cannot be pointed to; instead what defines them is that they introduce a *new language* that describes. The imaginary medium acts as a mnemonic device for grasping mathematical relationships, but, more than that, its primary value is that 'one can operate on an object that is better known, and in this sense more familiar, and on the other hand is full of implications and in this sense rich at the level of hypothesis' (p. 285). Their fruitfulness exists in knowing how we may deploy or use the model. In other words, the theoretical model is an instrument of discovery, a heuristic tool used to give rise to hypotheses that can be trialled or tested.

The fruitfulness of extending the theory of metaphor to a theory of models is that it shows how the models can be deployed.

> Recourse to scientific imagination in this regard does not signal a deflection of reason, distraction by images, but the essentially verbal power of trying out new relationships on a 'described model'. This imagination mingles with reason by virtue of the rules of correlation governing the translation

of statements concerning the secondary domain into statements applicable to the original domain. Once more it is the isomorphism of relationships that grounds the translatability of one idiom into another and, in so doing, provides the rationale for the imagination. But the isomorphism does not hold now between the original domain and something constructed, but between the domain and something 'described'. *Scientific imagination consists in seeing new connections via a detour of this thing that is 'described. . . .'*

(1975/2003, p. 285; my emphasis)

Ricoeur rediscovers and gains support from the work of Mary Hesse, who explained in *Models and metaphors in science* that 'the deductive model of scientific explanation should be modified and supplemented by a view of theoretical explanation as metaphoric redescription of the domain of the *explanandum*' (1975/2003, p. 249). Hesse's thesis is that if the model, like metaphor, introduces a new language, its description is in fact equivalent to an explanation. Mary Hesse terms it 'an instrument of redescription' (p. 283). Hesse says that things are 'seen as' or *identified with* the redescriptive character of the model – recalling Ricoeur's earlier 'second-order' reference to reality. Ricoeur concurs with Hesse that, without models, discovery is reduced to a deductive procedure (p. 285).

Another aspect of models that Ricoeur notes, which is also of interest to us because it is related to the development of theory, and therefore important in higher education, is that theoretical models often consist of a complex network of statements. Max Black calls them archetypes, and they consist of organised, related metaphors that cohere to form major disciplinary concepts. He cites Black talking about Kurt Lewin's description of a network that interrelates words like 'field', 'vector', 'phase-space', 'tension', 'force', 'boundary', 'fluidity', and so forth (1975/2003, p. 288; Black, 1962, p. 241). The network of statements cover an 'area' of experience or facts and are less local than metaphors but have a parallel in poems or novels in which multiple metaphors will cohere to collectively suggest a predominant mood. What this means is that from the simple idea of imagination as seeing 'new connections, a philosophy of imagination must add that of a breakthrough that is both profound and far-reaching, thanks to "radical" and "interconnected" metaphors respectively' (1975/2003, p. 288; Black, pp. 237, 241). In other words, the imagination can give rise to a series or network of metaphoric models that provide a scheme, system or theory through which we can see and connect a horizon of heterogeneous referents.

Fossilised metaphors and lack of criticality in using models

This is exactly Lakoff and Johnson's point, in their book *Metaphors we live by* (1980): metaphors are a means of structuring our conceptual reality, providing grounds for certain inferences that we make when we act on the world. However, there is an important point of difference of emphasis from Black in their analysis. Black focuses on the power of *new* metaphors to create similarities that

30   *Theoretical framework on imagination*

can generate new and coherent ways of perceiving and understanding our experience. Lakoff and Johnson, on the other hand, point out how hackneyed metaphors or metaphors that are sedimented into our everyday habits of language can pre-structure and fix our thinking and, in the process, blind us from other ways of thinking (1980, p. 145). This can happen when we are so accustomed to them that we take the old, outworn metaphors for literal truth. Michael J. Reddy (1979) provides an extended example of this, including an appendix with dozens of examples of common expressions, which shows the prevalence of what he calls the 'conduit metaphor' of human communication. This conduit metaphor is based on the notion that language is a *container* for messages/ideas and so all the hearer needs to do is to 'unpack' the words and 'take out' the message 'in' it. He points out that this conception has the effect of presupposing the objectivity of language – an objectivity that ignores the contribution of the hearer's or reader's own knowledge, as well as any assumptions built or rooted in language. It has led, he maintains, to erroneous attempts to uncover psychological processes involved in language comprehension, and it influences us to talk about thoughts as if they had the same kind of intersubjective reality as when we talk about tables or lamps. Extending this idea, as anyone familiar with higher education can attest, leads us to the view that, for example, we can 'transfer' ideas to students, 'store' knowledge 'in' data sets or repositories and insert 'content' into courses or student learning management systems and that students will then simply be able to 'go there' and 'get it'. This use of language suggests that knowledge is an external resource to be plundered, rather than understanding it as an active process and an internal resourcefulness, or capacity, to be deepened. Believing these metaphors to be factual may mean, says Reddy, that we neglect fostering the crucial human ability to reconstruct thought patterns on the basis of signs and signals, to train people to rebuild it, to 'regrow' it as the word 'culture' suggests. I would concur and say it may also lead us, pedagogically, to a reliance on didactic methods of teaching ('we've limited time to cover the content in the curriculum') and to undervalue active engagement in learning and the role of linking the imaginative experience of the self of the learner with the material studied.

Reddy's point is that unthinking reliance on metaphors, and languishing in the assumptions they bring with them, leads to rigid thinking. This underscores the point made by Ricoeur that the productive imagination is involved in newly coined or freshly heard metaphors, which configure new meaning and guide new frameworks of thinking. Metaphoric language is not in itself indicative of imagination because tired metaphors that have lost their power to spark the mind to new insights (the forming of new semantic pertinences, in Ricoeur's language) and are allowed to become habitual or fixed assumptions, dull critical consciousness.

Donald Schon (1979) makes a similar point in an essay entitled 'Generative metaphor: A perspective on problem-setting in social policy'. Schon's concern is social policy planning, specifically urban planning, and his argument is that descriptions or stories of society's ills contain, implicitly within them, and often insidiously, 'natural' solutions. He takes two cases: if slums are a cancer, then the metaphor is one of disease and it is clear they have to be cured; or similarly, if described as a 'blight', they naturally have to be removed as unsanitary. If, on the other hand, we see a slum as a community, the clearing of which would entail disrupting that community, what we must do is also clear – it should be protected and restored. In both cases the description contains a tacit frame of reference which contains within itself all the relevant 'facts' because the relevant 'facts' are all contained within the metaphor, and it then generates a 'natural' solution to what is wrong. In so far as metaphoric descriptions lead to a sense of the obvious, they construe explanations and actually *set* problems, the solutions to which may have negative impacts because they are based on skewed assumptions. Thus, these examples show how metaphors can constrain and sometimes negatively control the ways problems present themselves to us. It is a reminder that we need to be able to attend to, and describe, the dissimilarities as well as grasp the similarities between A and B, to be critically aware of how we frame issues and set the problems worth solving.

If creative or fresh metaphors can be a spur to grasping similarities and prompting new thinking, even *provoking* hypotheses, it is equally important that critical thinking be applied to them. Questions need to be asked about how apt is the concordance we want to draw between the two things compared in a metaphor. We might conceive, in this way, how the imaginative grasp of an apt metaphor needs to sit in appropriate tension with critical and ongoing reflection upon its fittingness. It is here that we see the significance of Ricoeur's axis of belief in, or critical consciousness of, the products of imagination (Figure 2.1). Ricoeur's theory of productive imagination is valuable because he distinguishes between critical consciousness and uncritical belief in the imaginative products. This distinction strengthens it as an appropriate theoretic/conceptual framework in which to consider how to facilitate the use of imagination in education and learning. In higher education learning, critical consciousness comes about through a process of reflection and continual critique by processes of peer review. The distinction also raises an interesting question about whether, during teaching, there is a time for imaginative approaches to problem setting and a different time for the process of critical reflection and review. It is also a reminder that, as Anderson (2010, p. 214, as discussed in Chapter 3) found, imaginative intelligence cannot afford to be vague or impressionistic but instead is extraordinarily precise, drawing on a balance of intuition and analytic judgement as well as a deep and detailed knowledge of the resources it is surrounded with. In a higher education context, these resources include the resources of the discipline: its skills and defining concepts.

To sum up, Ricoeur's thesis is that models are to scientific forms of discourse what freshly seen metaphors are to poetic discourse. Metaphors act as filters, suppressing some details and emphasising others, organising our view of the similar. When they do, the amalgamation offers up a model that can generate new connections that lead to scientific hypotheses or new and coherent ways of apprehending facets of the world. The trait common to models and metaphors is their heuristic power: the power to offer up to our consciousness new perspectives

32 *Theoretical framework on imagination*

and meanings. They can guide and enable new interpretations. Ricoeur says the process by which metaphor works is the paradigm of this transfer of meaning that is proper to all displacement of concepts and all creative redescriptions. The redescription does not abolish the earlier understanding or vision of the world, but (like stereoscopic vision) augments it: just as quantum mechanics does not abolish Newtonian mechanics – each has a domain of validity (quantum mechanics describes forces in very small or very large sized spaces; Newtonian describes forces within the small window of human-sized spaces). 'Metaphors, like models, are a strategy by which language divests itself of its function of direct description in order to reach the mythic level where its function of discovery is set free' (Ricoeur, 1975/2003, p. 292).

Narrative imagination

Another linguistic technology that can produce shifts in outlook and may reshape reality is narrative (Ricoeur 1991a, 1983/1984). Ricoeur argues that narrative, like metaphor and models, is a case of semantic innovation. In narrative, the semantic innovation lies in the inventing of another work of recombination and synthesis – plot. It is the synthesis of heterogeneous elements that brings narrative close to metaphor. Just as metaphors are not simply substitutions of nouns for other unexpected nouns, but affect a displacement of an overall meaning, so narrative extracts a configuration from a simple succession of events. By means of emplotment, goals, causes and chance are brought together from a viewpoint that makes them able to be followed in the sense we mean when we say we follow a story by making the appropriate connections. It shapes them into a meaningful, organic whole. The productive imagination '"grasps together" and integrates into one whole and complete story multiple and scattered events, thereby schematizing the intelligible signification attached to the narrative taken as a whole' (1983/1984, vol. 1, p. x). Plot mediates between individual episodes and the story taken as a whole because of the contribution of each episode to the development of the plot. In addition, the plot is more than a successive accumulation of events; it organises them into an intelligible whole. This is a key idea. By imposing a congruence on the organisation of events, it seems to achieve a two-directional dynamic: to understand *the point* of the story, or for its themes to be intelligible, the reader needs to *combine* its presentation of circumstances, characters, episodes and changes of fortune that make up the denouement. 'To understand the story is to understand how and why the successive episodes led to this conclusion, which, far from being foreseeable, must finally be acceptable, as congruent with the episodes brought together by the story' (1983/1984, p. 67).

A great illustration of this from literature is Toni Morrison's *Beloved* (1987), in which Seth, a former slave, murders her two children who are being retaken by slavers. Through the delineation of circumstances and events that led up to the act, it becomes possible to conceive of what, at face value, is a repellent act as one underpinned by love, freedom, refusal and pain. The example also illustrates the way narrative can distinguish between complex notions, such as motivation from

Theoretical framework on imagination 33

cause. Because of its projective function, Ricoeur calls narrative 'that extraordinary laboratory of the probable constituted by the paradigms of emplotment' (1983/1984, p. 184). That is, for the imaginer, it serves the function spoken by Dawkins, of a redescription of reality, providing foresight and allowing us to see possibilities in the intermediate or long-term time frames upon which judgement or decision-making can operate. Without imagining and conjecture, the criticality has nothing upon which to work.

Narrative agency in author and reader

Ricoeur also argues that the way the productive imagination configures narrative is not solely the imaginative work of the productive creator but is the joint work of the reader or receiver of the work – a situation he describes in quite a beautiful visual metaphor as an 'arc of operations'. Drawing on work by linguists, anthropologists and ethnographers, he argues that human actions in society are articulated by signs, rules and norms, which are deciphered by other actors in a social interplay of cultural meaning-making. Actions are meaningful to the extent to which they are set within shared conventions, beliefs and institutional values that make up a symbolic, nested framework for them. This shared symbolism confers a 'readability' on action, which, Ricoeur argues, anchors the way that, at the textual level, we derive meaning from narrative configuration.

The literary domain is not, therefore, a world unto itself – a fantasy world. In Ricoeur's view, this would be to negate fiction's subversive power – a power that can be turned towards the social and moral order of societies and is, for this reason, frequently punished and suppressed (think Solzhenitsyn, *The gulag archipelago* or Rushdie, *The satanic verses*). Ricoeur believes there is an interaction between the levels of signification in social life and that configured in narrative (what he calls, after Gadamer, a 'fusion of horizons' (Ricoeur, 1983/1984, p. 77). The way we read the meaning of actions from contexts, usually implicitly and often unconsciously, and the way we interpret (Ricoeur calls it 'refigure') textual configurations share something of this human ability to confer and to derive meaning about reality or the world in which we find ourselves. In Ricoeur's words,

> Because we are in the world and are affected by situations, we try to orient ourselves in them by means of understanding; we also have something to say, an experience to bring to language and to share. . . . This is the ontological presupposition of reference.
>
> (1983/1984, p. 78)

This is no less true for a reader than a creator. In Ricoeur's view, reading involves judging, comprehending or 'grasping together' the detail and action of the plot into a unity, where interpretation is able to be used by people to model the experience of being in the world, in a similar sense as discussed in this chapter in relation to scientific models.

Imagination: developing possibilities

It can be seen how far Ricoeur's theory of imagination has taken us from empiricist understandings of imagination as an image or picture simply reproduced from our recall of our perception of a given thing-in-itself, or as a weak trace of it imprinted in the mind. Instead, what is proposed by his scheme of imagination is a kind of analogical tool, a 'soft' piece of technology of the mind, by which new dimensions of the world can be entertained, through a momentary suspension of our belief in an earlier description, and then deployed and manipulated in the world we inhabit, for its workability and trenchancy. Thus, he follows Kant in the general idea of imagination as the general function of *developing practical possibilities*:

> Imagination is indeed just what we all mean by the word: the free play of possibilities in a state of non-involvement with respect to the world of perception or of action. It is in this state of non-involvement that we try out new ideas, new values, new ways of being in the world.
>
> (1991c, p. 174)

Imagination and action: the heuristic power of narratives as models for action

Ricoeur's argument then takes the heuristic power that theoretical models in science have and uses it to understand the heuristic power of narrative for human beings figuring out how to understand, be and act in the world. To the extent that models are not *models of* given things, similar and imitating them, but *models for* redescribing reality, they can illustrate how literary fiction can display situation/context, agency, action, cause, motivation, conflict – and construe it meaningfully in plot. Under this scheme, fictions, like models, have valid claims to say something true about reality and experience. They function in parallel ways to the explanatory work of models, analogies and paradigms in the conceptual domain of science. It is not a dissimilar conception to what the educational theorist Gerard Egan has in mind when he says that literature generates conceptions of reality and gauges human limits and extremes, from which readers interpret their everyday experience (1997, p. 88). And it is this conception that has Ricoeur denounce aestheticians who claim that it is only in the arts that imagination is productive, who renounce all truth claims for the arts and restrict their referential power to the domain of feelings, emotions and passions devoid of any ontological weight. 'Nothing is more harmful for sound recognition of the productive reference of the imagination than this dichotomy between the sciences and the arts' (1983/1984, p. 77).

This puts Ricoeur's conceptual framework at odds with much of the literature on imagination and education, such as Elliott Eisner (1991) and even Maxine Greene (1995), who argue that the arts have a unique power to unleash imagination (for example Greene, p. 27). An exclusive focus on the arts is based on a problematic distinction between reason and imagination, and reason and

Theoretical framework on imagination   35

emotion, which Dewey also criticised (Bleazby, 2013, p. 99). It is also the major reason why this study focussed its research on multiple non creative-arts-based disciplinary and professional sites.

What is being claimed here is that Ricoeur's theory presents the relationship of imagination to reality, not in oppositional terms, as it is often understood in lay terms, but as foundational to how humans think about and shape reality. Humans use linguistic descriptions to *think with*, not only to communicate with, and complex manipulations of language, such as occurs when we use or hear metaphors, narrative and models, shape what is possible cognitively. By making novel connections, redescriptions of reality arise, from which flow insights and innovative ways of thinking about reality.

Emotions and their role in imagination and in ethical thinking

Martha Nussbaum argues that emotions are forms of intense attention and engagement, in which the world is appraised in relation to self (Nussbaum, 2001, p. 106). She contends our emotions shape the landscape of our mental and social lives and are 'suffused with intelligence and discernment' (2001, p. 1). They insert us into the world, as it is frequently through feelings that we are attuned to reality – we notice danger or something beautiful or unusual, take stock of our discomfort in a situation, for example. As essential elements of human intelligence, she argues, they form part and parcel of ethical reasoning and involve seeing a complex reality in a lucid and richly responsive way.

Rather than regarding emotions as blindly determining behaviour and judgement, Nussbaum maintains emotions involve appraisals and value judgements that ascribe importance to people and things. They can orient and guide behaviour because they affect the goals we aim for and the issues we should address, as well as how we weigh the probable effects of our actions on other people or relationships (Nussbaum, 2001; Young & Annisette, 2009; Johnson, 1993). Writers such as Dewey (Bleazby, 2013, p. 97), Nussbaum (2001), Johnson (1993) and Ricoeur (1979) agree that emotions are part of purposeful behaviour in relation to reasoning about our environment because they are part of how and why we act and what we want to achieve. Dewey argues that it is because we have emotions that particular situations, people or things appear salient to us and get our attention while others go unnoticed (Bleazby, 2013, p. 99). In addition, by better understanding others' emotions, we can learn much about what is at stake for them in a situation or the environment. Understanding others' emotions involves imagination because by empathising with others, we 'put ourselves in their shoes' in order to understand how their behaviour makes sense in a particular context. Thus, for Nussbaum, imagination enables empathy and the ability to imagine the nature of others' emotional attachments that give rise to their behaviour:

> If emotions involve judgements about the salience for our well-being of
> uncontrolled external objects, judgements in which the mind of the judge is

36 *Theoretical framework on imagination*

projected unstably outward into a world of objects, we will need to be able to imagine those attachments, their delight and their terror, their intense and even obsessive focusing on their object, if we are ever to talk well about love or fear or anger.

(Nussbaum, 2001, p. 2)

Biologists too argue that our ability to read each other's emotions confers a survival ability because it informs us about how we should collaborate, whom we should collaborate with and whom we should fear or avoid. This view is similar to Johnson (1993), who argued that how we frame a situation will determine how we reason about it, and how we frame it will include our imaginative capability to understand others' emotions.

Ricoeur too argues that reasoning and 'feeling' are not oppositional.

[Feeling's] function is to abolish the distance between knower and known without cancelling the cognitive structure of thought. . . . . Feeling is not contrary to thought. It is thought made ours.

(1979, p. 156)

Narrative, as we have seen earlier in this chapter, is a culturally derived imaginative structure which allows us to organise and connect disparate events and situations into synthetic unity. Young and Annisette (2009) argue that stories help us look backward over our lives and reflect and try to understand our actions, motives and thoughts. Through them we can also project ourselves into the future and deliberately try on actions, imagining their consequences in what Dewey calls a 'dramatic rehearsal' of alternatives. Nussbaum suggests this is essentially a liberating idea since it implies that by improving our imaginative capability to empathise and understand others, we can potentially improve our ability to live and act better.

These ideas about the value of emotions and their ability *to inform* intelligent, appropriate responses to the world and to others contrast with prevalent notions that distrust emotions because they are construed as *contrary to* rationality.

This literature which emphasises the role of feelings in relation to imagination emerged in all four ethnographic case studies. In finance, the simulated scenario used surprise to focus attention on ethical reasoning and choices and to imagine the repercussions of unethical trading. In physics, the ambiguity of historical figures' feelings about their findings, and notions of beauty and aesthetics, were used to introduce the notion that students may have feelings about the knowledge or theories they were learning. In history, the role of feelings was potentially also important in students' historical interpretations, and the excitement of *being people* (their identity was affected) who conducted research was mentioned by students in focus groups. In pharmaceutical science, students connected knowledge and emotion when they were given the choice about which scientific discovery excited them and then researched and wrote about the stages of its research inquiry.

Imagination used to 'map out' practical action

As we have seen in relation to metaphor, narrative and models as devices for redescribing reality, Ricoeur claims that imagination is integral to knowledge and cognition. He also extends this to practical action. He reasons that the first condition for an application of the semantic theory of imagination, beyond the sphere of discourse to education or to other professional domains, is that semantic innovation has to have 'referential' power: that is, it has to have practical impact on human action.

> The first way that human beings attempt to understand and to master the "manifold" of the practical field is to give themselves a fictive description of it. Whether an ancient tragedy, a modern drama or novel, a fable or legend, the narrative structure provides fiction with the techniques of abbreviation, articulation, and condensation by which the effect of iconic augmentation is obtained. . . . This is essentially what Aristotle had in mind in the *Poetics* when he tied the "mimetic" function of poetry – that is in the context of his treatise, of tragedy – to the "mythical" structure of fable constructed by the poet. This is a great paradox: tragedy "imitates" action only because it "recreates" it on the level of a well-composed fiction.
>
> (1991c, p. 176)

Ricoeur's proposition is that narrative has referential force – that is, impact on the world – through a similar process to that which John Austin discovered in his famous paper on locutionary and illocutionary speech acts (1975/2003). Austin looked at discourse as an event. The locutionary is what is said in the statement of a discourse; the illocutionary force of a statement is what is accomplished by the act of saying it. (For example, for the bride and groom saying 'I do' at a wedding, they enter into a legally binding contract and alter their legal status.) By analogy, or by extension, Ricoeur argues that narratives have an illocutionary force, or reference effect, by schematising or mapping human action, projecting possibilities of action into the future. 'Imagination . . . has a projective function that is part of the very dynamism of acting' (1991c, p. 177). In this imaginary space, we can foresee consequences without the danger of having to learn everything directly from experience (which is also Dawkins's point).

> And it is indeed through the anticipatory imagination of acting that I 'try out' different possible courses of action and that I 'play', in the precise sense of the word, with possible practices. It is precisely at this point that pragmatic 'play' intersects with narrative 'play' mentioned earlier. The function of the project, turned towards the future, and that of narrative, turned towards the past, here exchange their schemata and their grids, as the project borrows the narrative's structuring power and the narrative receives the project's capacity for anticipating.
>
> (Ricoeur, 1991c, p. 177)

38 *Theoretical framework on imagination*

Ricoeur appears to say here that the work of the imagination is to schematise means and ends, by drawing on memory and using it to project possibilities. Through this dynamic, non-linear thinking we anticipate what will happen, we try out different courses of action and we play with possible practical actions by balancing such considerations as our motivations, desires, constraints, logical reasons, expectations and consequences. Narrative's power is useful in a practical sense because its structure enables us to organise, order, abbreviate, articulate and condense particular experiences and actions; it enables us to play with all the possible combinations of a few basic actions and consider their implications and meanings; it enables us to make sense of, and redescribe, experiences, to weigh goals, beliefs, likely outcomes and different courses of action with an understanding of what each may mean, in our effort to try to foresee outcomes. It is in this sense that Ricoeur contrasts ordinary descriptive language – what he calls 'our first order interest of manipulation and control' – with this second-order redescription, or productive reference, created through imagination. However, I would challenge this distinction. It is not the disembodied ego who weighs goals and different courses of action, but embodied people with needs, aspirations and desires in relation to the world and others. Some of these needs are to understand the world they live in. The same Cartesian dualism responsible for ideas that frame reason as oppositional to imagination is also responsible for a tacit assumption that imagination assumes a disembodied ego (Johnson, 1993). Theories, models and concepts are used every day in science, technology and economics to manipulate outcomes and to invent machines and software to enable practical problems to be solved. New tools are invented that are based on a variety of theories, drawing from multiple disciplines, to be safer, to go faster, to be more energy efficient or to save time. First order interests and second-order references are not always distinct because of our embodiment and our social nature.

The liminal space of imagination

There is a seeming paradox here in the relationship drawn between imagination and the developing of practical possibilities of action, but it tells us something important about imagination. The slight state of non-involvement or detachment from action, this hiatus or momentary suspension of belief that is part and parcel of play, seems to be essential for the imaginative process, even while its final purpose may be to produce effective action in the world. When discussing metaphor, Ricoeur describes this stage as 'the stage in the production of genres where the generic kinship has not reached the level of conceptual peace and rest but remains caught in the war between distance and proximity, between remoteness and nearness' (1979, pp. 148–149). Northrop Frye argues similarly, in an ethics context, when he says,

> In the imagination our own beliefs are also only possibilities, but we can also see the possibilities in the beliefs of others. . . . [W]hat produces the tolerance is the power of detachment in the imagination, where things are removed just out of reach of belief and action.
>
> (1963, p. 32, quoted in Egan, 1997, p. 16)

In Ricoeur's terms, the imaginary process happens in that momentary hiatus when provisional rational fictions are momentarily entertained upon which evaluative thinking can be performed. Imaginary possibilities are 'thrown up' to test relationships or compare characteristics or processes of the model. This suggests imagination may thrive in liminal spaces, or prolonged moments, where possibilities are considered before criticality closes them off. For teachers who seek a way to normalise the conditions for imaginative thinking to flower, this has important implications for teaching and learning. For example, it may mean that teachers follow the hunches of students, even if they know from experience that an idea or procedure is going nowhere. This may be challenging to do while keeping a large cohort of students engaged.

Fleshing out what happens in this space of the momentary retreat from action while playing with ways of organising experience, Ricoeur argues that imagination is not restricted to the reorganisation of understanding: it is also involved in the very process of motivation for action and for having projects – which is important for my argument because it suggests that innovation is dependent upon imagination. However, he locates the activity of imagination as working in and through language. For instance, when we say, imputing power to ourselves, 'I would do this or that, if I wanted to', or, when we use the conditional tense, 'I could' and 'I could have' (1991c, p. 177), which is the grammatical expression of imaginative intentions, the conditional tense offers a neutral uncommitted space in which to play with possibilities, possibilities which could include different motivations, different reasons for doing the thing, or things that could have been otherwise, under different conditions. It allows the space in which I can compare and evaluate my motives, such as my desires, ethical obligations, social customs and personal values, and what I want to achieve in relation to others. The progression starts from the simple schematization of my projects, continues through the way in which I figure out what it is that I want, my desires and motives, and ends with the imaginative variations of 'I can'. I try out my power to act, using my imagination, and 'measure the scope of "I can"' (p. 178). I can figure out what is likely to happen but then have to decide whether I like it that way or not.

The key point here for my research on higher education is that this liminal space opened by imagination is marked by a suspension of judgement. This suspension allows the opening of a process of inquiry and is the start of a dialectical creative process of imaginative and critical thinking. What is important is that 'imagination protects us from the temptation of premature conclusions; the temptation of certainty and the fixed truth' (Saul, 2001, p. 116).

Probable imaginary constructions

There is a further expression of productive imagination that has a bearing on our actions, Ricoeur argues in *Time and narrative*, and is of particular pertinence in studies in education. It is an extension of the practical imaginary, described prior, but in the context of history, when an historian is weighing up the causes of events, Ricoeur calls it the idea of 'objective possibilities' or 'probable imaginary

40 Theoretical framework on imagination

constructions'. To illustrate he quotes from Weber's observations of Bismarck's decision to declare war on Austria-Hungary in 1866:

> As Weber observes, "And yet, despite all this, the problem: what might have happened if, for example, Bismarck had not decided to make war is by no means an 'idle' one" (p.164). We need to understand this question. It consists in asking what "causal significance is properly to be attributed to this individual decision in the context of the totality of infinitely numerous 'factors', all of which had to be in such and such an arrangement and in no other if this result were to emerge, and what role it is therefore to be assigned in an historical explanation" (p. 164, his emphases). It is the phrase "all of which . . . and no other" that marks the entrance on stage of the imagination. Reasoning, from this point on, moves in the arena of unreal past conditionals. But history shifts into the sphere of the unreal only in order to better discern there what is necessary. The question becomes "what consequences were to be anticipated had another decision been taken?" (p. 165). This then involves an exploration of the probable or necessary interconnections. If the historian in his thinking can affirm that, by the modification or omission of an individual event in a complex of historical conditions, there would have followed a different series of events "in certain historically important respects" (p. 166, his emphasis), then the historian can make a judgment of causal imputation that decides the historical significance of the event.
>
> (1983/1984, vol. 1, pp. 183–184)

The probable, imaginary construction (similar to emplotment, which is itself a probable imaginary construction) is similar to an explanation. This is an important consideration in education where role plays, for example in history, have the potential to allow students to consider and weigh situations, motives and decisions that caused historical events. If students have to think through how an historical event could have worked out differently, or what would have prevented it, it sets them to think about key contributing causes and contingent conditions and values, such as how people are affected or how actions might change relationships or institutions. Thus, Ricoeur's work provides a hinge on which to understand the impact of imagination on learning important concepts, as well as to critically weigh the values and choices that underpin them.

The ability to shape ourselves and our projects is essential for freewill or autonomy, which many philosophers maintain defines our humanity. This is why Ricoeur's theory of the imagination has traction and is pertinent in a study in education. Our imagination is our human power to project new possibilities of being in and inhabiting the world. Projecting or foreseeing the consequences of our actions impacts on whether our manipulation and operation of the conditions in which we find ourselves is likely to be effective.

Grounding imagination: its relationship to reality

In this important sense, the productive imagination is not something irrational, Ricoeur says. Ricoeur's notion of the productive imagination and any transformative fictions – like metaphors, models, narrative, poems – suggests that they must have elements of reproductive imagination, must draw from existing reality sufficiently so that its productive distance is not too great (Taylor, 2006). Ricoeur offers the example of Impressionism, which he says is productive but also figurative, still reproductive in part (Taylor, 2006, p. 98).

Ricoeur's ideas share similarities with John Dewey's conception of the imagination as connected to the act of thinking and of reason. Since imagination involves making inferences from what is given to what is possible, it can be seen as a form of reasoning. As Dewey explained, 'suggestion is the very heart of inference, it involves going from something present to something absent' (1910, p. 75). Dewey argued that imagination enables us to create ideas that go beyond what is given in concrete experience but are also 'effective' (Bleazby, 2012, p. 99). This makes sense: ideas that ignore the facts of the problematic situation are unlikely to be effective at meaningfully transforming that situation or solving problems (Bleazby, 2012; Dewey, 2004, p. 52; Policastro & Gardner, 1999, p. 217; Cropley, 2006). Dewey specifically used the term 'imagination' to refer to the process of inferring what consequences would follow if the possible solutions suggested to us by our imagination were actualised. This is why Ricoeur's conception of imagination touches on hallucinations and illusions that are *without* critical consciousness (the y axis in Figure 2.1, this chapter). The salience of this is well made by Lundsteen: 'The ability at will to make creative thinking coordinate with more logical thinking may make the difference between lunacy and creativity' (1968, p. 133, cited by Nickerson, 1999, p. 398).

Vygotsky, imagination, creativity and reason

This coordination or confluence of imagination with reasoning is also a theme in Vygotsky's theory of the development of imagination from childhood, through adolescence and into adulthood. Vygotsky (Ayman-Nolley, 1992; Vygotsky, 1986), in language similar to Ricoeur, defined a creative activity as one which makes something new, and distinguished between *reproductive construction*, which is to build an existing reality (as is Ricoeur's 'reproductive' imagination), and *combinatory reconstruction* (standing in relation to Ricoeur's 'productive' imagination), which combines and changes from existing reality to new entities. The latter requires imagination which Vygotsky saw as the basis of creativity.

> A true understanding of reality is not possible without a certain element of imagination; without a departure from reality, from immediate concrete unity of impression which this reality represents in elements of acts of our consciousness.
>
> (quoted in Ayman-Nolley, 1992, p. 78,
> from Vygotsky, 1932/1987, p. 45)

42 Theoretical framework on imagination

Vygotsky believed that imagination and thinking in concepts come together and influence each other in adolescence when the fantasy of the adolescent becomes volitional and increasingly creative (Ayman-Nolley, 1992, p. 80). Imagination under the influence of thinking in concepts is changed at this point and moves from reconstructing already given concrete concepts to creating new concrete concepts. Reciprocally, thinking in concepts and the development of reasoning sharpen imagination. Imagination is involved in the development of abstract thinking as a process removed from concrete reality

This understanding of the role of imagination in the development of abstract thinking appears also in Vygotsky's view that imaginative games contain implicit rules governing what possibilities for action are ruled in and what are ruled out (1978, pp. 95–96). If, as a child, I play the role of mother, there are rules of behaviour I follow that are embedded in situations and that guide my behaviour even though they are not set in advance. Vygotsky argued that the development of childhood play traced a path starting with an imaginary situation with implicit rules and evolves, later, into games with overt rules, such as chess. It displays the interactive nature of the relationship between development of abstract thinking and imagination.

He also argued that, for example, when a child plays 'horsey' and uses some kind of stick to ride on, the horse-in-the-stick object substitution is used as a *pivot* to detach the meaning of a stick from the stick-in-itself. This involves subordinating her/his perception to a new desire as a source of pleasure (1978, pp. 98–99). The source of this pleasure is the play with signs. The significance of this is the increasing ability of children to direct their own behaviour, a mastery made possible by rules and by signs. Vygotsky proposed a developmental theory of creativity in which creative imagination originates in children's pretend play and develops into a higher mental function that can be consciously regulated through inner speech (Smolucha, 2009, p. 70). In fact, he did more than make a general claim that creativity develops from pretend play; he specified that it develops from object substitutions during play (p. 71). The importance of these ideas in the context of education is expanded on in the next chapter in relation to learning 'tools' or 'mindtools'.

Johnson extends the idea of critical consciousness (and interaction between imagination and reason) to include moral imagination and moral critique (1993). He argues that imagination draws on memory, making criticality possible in the first place, for it provides us alternative points of view and concepts from which to evaluate a particular moral position. Memory in this sense is as Weimer depicts (1977, p. 279), an active ongoing modulation of information rather than a retrieval of stored items. Imagination makes it possible to model, or mentally simulate, possible consequences of a proposed course of action, such as how people are likely to be affected, how relationships may be changed and what possibilities will be opened up, or closed off, concerning how we may grow through action.

Ricoeur's theory of imagination based in language, as opposed to empirical perception-based theories, offers ways to think about the operation of imagination across disciplines in higher education. Despite involving a liminal, detached period or space, productive imagination does not transcend reality or divert us from knowledge or facts. On the contrary, his theory describes how imagination can be used to operate on reality in ways that, crucially, are innovative and are based on creative new 'redescriptions', or understandings of reality, and that may lead to discovery and to considerations of new action. Within contemporary higher education, it may help us to conceive of how imaginative processes of learning can offer ways for students to understand and hold in mind competing theories; to test their possibilities of meaning, compare and contrast them according to domains of validity, think critically about them, have feelings about them and give serious thought to the values underpinning their performance of professional roles; to apply their own metaphors or to role play positions that command different perspectives on knowledge or on action. For these reasons, Ricoeur's theory of imagination, including the concepts of metaphorical process, semantic innovation, narrative configuration and probable imaginary constructions, offers a starting point, and a model for, a consideration of common approaches in different disciplines, as well as space for the different discipline-specific ways they manifest themselves.

In the next chapter, we consider the connection between imagination and certain conceptions of what learning is, including the influence of theories of mind.

References

Anderson, K. (2010). The whole learner: The role of imagination in developing disciplinary understanding. *Arts and Humanities in Higher Education, 9*(2), 205–221.

Austin, J. L. (2003). Performative utterances. In J. O. E. Urmson & G. J. E. Warnock (Eds.), *Philosophical papers* (originally published 1979) (Third ed.). Oxford: Oxford Scholarship Online. doi:10.1093/019283021X.001.0001

Ayman-Nolley, S. (1992). Vygotsky's perspective on the development of imagination and creativity. *Creativity Research Journal, 5*(1), 77–85. doi: 10.1080/10400419209534424

Ayman-Nolley, S. (1999). A Piagetian perspective on the dialectic process of creativity. *Creativity Research Journal, 12*(4), 267–275. doi:10.1207/s15326934crj1204_4

Black, M. (1962). *Models and metaphors.* Ithaca, NY: Cornell University Press.

Bleazby, J. (2012). Dewey's notion of imagination in philosophy for children. *Education and Culture, 28*(2), 95–111. doi:10.1353/eac.2012.0013

Bleazby, J. (2013). *Social reconstruction learning: Dualism, Dewey and philosophy in schools.* New York: Routledge.

Cropley, A. J. (2006). In praise of convergent thinking. *Creativity Research Journal, 18*(3), 391–404. doi:10.1207/s15326934crj1803_13

Dawkins, R. (1989). *The selfish gene* (Second ed.). Oxford: Oxford University Press.

Dewey, J. (1910/1997). *How we think: A restatement of the relation of reflective thinking to the educative process.* Mideola, NY: Dover Publications.

Dewey, J. (2004). *Democracy and education.* Mineola, NY: Dover Publications.

Egan, K. (1997). *The educated mind: How cognitive tools shape our understanding.* Chicago: University of Chicago Press.

Eisner, E. W. (1991). *The enlightened eye: Qualitative inquiry and the enhancement of educational practice.* New York: Macmillan.

44 *Theoretical framework on imagination*

Eliot, T. S. (1944). *Four quartets*. London: Faber and Faber.

Frye, N. (1963). *The educated imagination*. Toronto, ON: Canadian Broadcasting Corporation.

Greene, M. (1995). *Releasing the imagination: Essays on education, the arts, and social change*. San Francisco: Josey-Bass Publishers.

Hesse, M. (1963). *Models and analogies in science*. London: Sheed and Ward.

Johnson, M. (1993). Moral imagination. In *Moral imagination: Implications of cognitive science for ethics*. Chicago: University of Chicago Press.

Lakoff, G., & Johnson, M. (1980). *Metaphors we live by*. Chicago: University of Chicago Press.

Lipman, M. (2003). *Thinking in education*. New York: Cambridge University Press.

Morrison, T. (1987). *Beloved*. London: Vintage.

Murphy, P., Peters, A. M., & Marginson, S. (2010). *Imagination: Three models of imagination in the age of the knowledge economy*. New York: Peter Lang.

Nickerson, R. (1999). Enhancing creativity. In R. J. Sternberg (Ed.), *Handbook of creativity* (pp. 392–430). Cambridge: Cambridge University Press.

Nussbaum, M. (2001). *Upheavals of thought: The intelligence of emotions*. New York: Cambridge University Press.

Policastro, E., & Gardner, H. (1999). From case studies to robust generalisations. In R. J. Sternberg (Ed.), *Handbook of creativity* (pp. 213–225). Cambridge: Cambridge University Press.

Reddy, M. (1979). The conduit metaphor. In A. Ortony (Ed.), *Metaphor and thought* (pp. 284–324). Cambridge: Cambridge University Press.

Ricoeur, P. (1975/2003). *The rule of metaphor: The creation of meaning in language* (R. Czerny, K. McLaughlin, & J. Costello, Trans.). London: Routledge.

Ricoeur, P. (1979). The metaphorical process as cognition, imagination and feeling. In S. Sacks (Ed.), *On metaphor* (pp. 141–153). Chicago: University of Chicago Press.

Ricoeur, P. (1983/1984). *Time and narrative* (K. McLaughlin & D. Pellauer, Trans. Vol. 1). Chicago: University of Chicago Press.

Ricoeur, P. (1991a). The function of fiction in shaping reality: Reflection and Imagination. In M. J. Valdes (Ed.), *A Ricoeur reader* (pp. 117–136). Hertfordshire: Harvester Wheatsheaf.

Ricoeur, P. (1991b). Ideology and utopia (T. K. Blamey & J. B. Thompson, Trans.). In J. M. Eadie (Ed.), *From text to action: Essays in hermeneutics* (Vol. 2, pp. 308–324). Evanston, IL: Northwestern University Press.

Ricoeur, P. (1991c). Imagination in discourse and in action (K. Blamey & J. B. Thompson, Trans.). In J. M. Eadie (Ed.), *From text to action: Essays in hermeneutics* (Vol. 2, pp. 168–187). Evanston, IL: Northwestern University Press.

Ricoeur, P. (1991d). On interpretation. In *From text to action* (pp. 1–20). London: Continuum.

Robinson, K. (1999). *All our futures: Creativity, culture and education (the Robinson report)*. London: National Advisory Committee on Creative and Cultural Education (NACCCE).

Saul, J. R. (2001). *On equilibrium*. Ringwood, Victoria: Penguin Books.

Schon, D. (1979). Generative metaphor: A perspective on problem-setting in social policy. In A. Ortony (Ed.), *Metaphor and thought*. Cambridge: Cambridge University Press.

Smolucha, F. (1992). The relevance of Vygotsky's theory of creative imagination for contemporary research on play. *Creativity Research Journal*, *5*(1), 69–76.

Taylor, G. H. (2006, Spring-Fall). Ricoeur's philosophy of imagination. *Journal of French Philosophy*, *16*(1 & 2), 93–104.

Valdes, M. J. (Ed.). (1991). *A Ricoeur reader*. Hertfordshire: Harvester Wheatsheaf.

Vygotsky, L. S. (1978). *Mind in society: The development of higher psychological processes*. Cambridge, MA: Harvard University Press.

Vygotsky, L. S. (1986). *Imagination and creativity in the adolescent*. Unpublished English translation by F. Smolucha, University of Chicago. (Original work published 1931).

Weimer, W. B. (1977). A conceptual framework for cognitive psychology: Motor theories of the mind. In R. Shaw & J. Bransford (Eds.), *Perceiving, acting and knowing*. Hillsdale, NJ: Lawrence Erlbaum Associates, Publishers.

Young, J. J., & Annisette, M. (2009). Cultivating imagination: Ethics, education and literature. *Critical Perspectives on Accounting, 20*, 93–109.

3 Theoretical linking of imagination with cognition and learning theory

Introduction

In this chapter, I argue that the insights derived from linking Ricoeur's notion of imagination to theories of learning and cognition can lead to a clearer understanding of the role of imagination in disciplinary work and the creation of knowledge. For imagination is a higher order thinking skill which participates in the learning of the practices that may lead to new knowledge. These insights suggest ways of teaching that cultivate it, particularly in higher education.

I discuss key concepts that relate imagination to learning and cognition theories: Lev Vygotsky's notion of tool mediated action (1978); Wartofsky's linking of models, representations and perception (1979) and Michael Polanyi's (1967) notion of tacit knowing; Andy Clark's 'extended mind' thesis (Clark, 1997, 2011) and the theory of 'predictive processing', which presents an integrated framework for understanding perception, action, embodiment and the nature of human experience and imagination as the engine by which generative models produce predictive perceptions (Clark, 2016b). The progression of the argument is broadly represented in Figure 3.1. In one respect, I will have traced a full circle, because Ricoeur's theory of imagination broke away from the notion of imagination proposed by Hume, Kant and others which conceived of imagination as primarily images based on perception or sense data. In contrast, Ricoeur focused on the relationship between imagination and particular forms of language use. However, by resurrecting the role that (cultural) signs, artefacts and tools play in perception, Vygotsky, Wartofsky, Polanyi and 'predictive processing' theory show the co-emergence of imagination in relation to perception and to cultural and social practices of reason and thinking. Hence they are re-united in my argument. They are also both underpinned by the view that imagination is wrongly served by considering it purely as an aesthetic matter rather than as a way of thinking which can be directed towards adapting to the local environment or adapting that environment. It encompasses how we learn practices and ways of thinking that are new, not only how we acquire existing knowledge. This is important in university education, for imaginative learning allows students to learn the practices that lead to new knowledge.

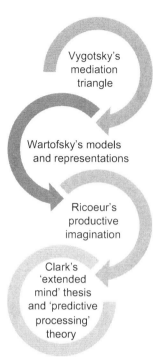

Figure 3.1 Theoretical linkages in this chapter

Tool mediation – how cognition is shaped socio-culturally

Two of Vygotsky's concepts are crucial in understanding the relationship between learning and imagination. The first is the notion of mediation by tools, or signs, particularly language, in the emergence of the higher mental processes of human thinking. This notion provided the foundation for his major themes of historical and socio-cultural processes and their relationship to the individual's mental processes (Wertsch, 2007). Vygotsky included under the heading of signs 'language; various systems for counting; mnemonic techniques; algebraic symbol systems; works of art; writing; schemes, diagrams, maps, and mechanical drawings; all sorts of conventional signs' (Vygotsky, 1981, quoted in Wertsch, 2007, p. 178)

Foremost among these tools is the role of speech in the development of cognition and the organisation of practical activity. In studies of children he and his colleagues found that speech not only accompanied practical action, but played an active role as a resource used to helping carry it out. Vygotsky takes as an example a four-and-a-half-year-old girl who was asked to get candy

48 *Linking of imagination with cognition*

from a tall cupboard, with a stool and a stick as possible tools. His description is as follows:

> (Stands on a stool, quietly looking, feeling along the shelf with the stick.) 'On the stool.' (Glances at the experimenter. Puts stick in other hand.) 'Is that really the candy?' (Hesitates.) 'I can get it from that other stool, stand and get it.' (Takes stick, knocks at the candy.) 'It will move now.' (Knocks candy.) 'It moved, I couldn't get it with the stool, but the, but the stick worked.'
> (Vygotsky, 1978, p. 25)

Her private speech (self-talk) is used by the child to help her solve the practical problem (she is small; the sweets are positioned high; there happen to be a stool and a stick in the local environment; her goal is to get the sweets). Vygotsky represents the problem relationship in what he calls a mediational triangle (see Figure 3.2) in which the subject's encounter with an object is mediated by some (cultural, historical) tool or artefact which is used to control activity in relation to the object.

As the example of the little girl shows, speech – language – is used by the girl to direct her attention to particularities in the field of operation in which her pragmatic action is directed. It is a cognitive *resource*, a tool she uses to organise her thoughts and to coordinate them in relation to the presence of other, pragmatic kinds of tools in the environment in order to solve the problem. Although practical intelligence and speech can operate independently of each other, the dialectical unity of these two systems, Vygotsky asserts, is the essence of complex human behaviour. Signs and other forms of symbolising activity perform what is essentially an organising function for actions. The dialectical relationship between language (or other signs) and practical activity is the key point here. Given this understanding, Vygotsky's research methods suggested that if we want to study thinking, then we should be looking at the way a tool is used to act on and change the object (what is being worked on).

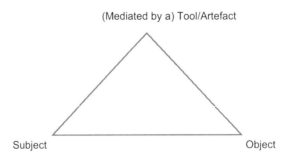

Figure 3.2 Vygotsky's mediational triangle, in which the subject and object are not only directly connected but 'indirectly' connected through the medium constituted by culturally based signs or artefacts

The role of language and other people

Other developmental psychological notions underpinning problem solving relate to learning from others. Smolucha's (1992b) research builds on Vygotsky's thesis that children's social interactions with more capable play partners (parents, older siblings, other children) bring the child into the 'zone of proximal development' (ZPD). For example, children may be talked through learning to tie their shoelaces, a zone in which they are able to learn new concepts and skills supported by experienced others. Children can then carry on a private conversation aloud about tying the shoelaces, which facilitates their ability to complete the task. Like Vygotsky, Smolucha argues this forms evidence that children's private speech fulfils a cognitive role by guiding skill development and action and regulating behaviour. In this sense Smolucha's and Vygotsky's idea of knowledge construction emphasises that a cognitive process is by its nature a social process as well, involving historical–cultural tools, as well as emotions and motivation with respect to what is to be learned. Smolucha applies these mechanisms to argue that the higher mental functions, such as creative imagination, thinking and critical reasoning, are similarly derived from internalised social interactions and object substitution (1992a; 1992b). Specifically she applies them to the use of visual analogies in art and metaphorical thinking (1985). The transformation of processes that is implied by this work was articulated well by Geertz.

> This means that rather than culture acting only to supplement, develop or extend organically based capacities logically and genetically prior to it, it would seem to be an ingredient in those capacities themselves.
>
> (Geertz, 1973, p. 68)

These principles underpinned the focus for observations in my case studies. The physics ethnographic case is a case in point, in which students learned quantum physics concepts by dynamically synthesising diagrammatic, mathematical and linguistic symbolic systems practised by their disciplinary culture in their attempt to grasp the physical conception of a quantum state suggested by these three forms. It suggests that sign-based tools are not only used to organise pragmatic action, but transform thinking and computation itself.

Developing the idea of the role of speech in complex thinking, Vygotsky argues that speech introduces a 'timefield', allowing us to direct our attention in a dynamic way and not be restricted simply to the synchronous visual field. He argues that language aids our ability to redirect our attention away from the momentary sensori-motor operations of perception. The slowing down of perception restructures it in a dynamic way, allowing us to view changes in the immediate situation from the point of view of past activities, as well as in order to act in the present from the viewpoint of the future (1978, p. 36). As we grow and develop and speech moves from outer to inner, the epistemic value of this to self-organisation of thinking expands. Pelaprat and

Cole (2011) make a similar point – that thought occurs over time and that the ability is heavily influenced by language. This is significant for my argument because it creates conditions for thinking which include past, present and future intentions and symbolic representations of purposeful action – planning, in other words.

A related point made by Vygotsky is that there is some cognitive activity that is carried out in order to affect conditions for the agent herself, not to directly change the world or the environment. The simple example Vygotsky uses is of tying a knot in a handkerchief (putting your keys in the fridge is a similar one), which reminds and alerts the agent into constructing a process of remembering by forcing an external object to remind her of something. A temporary link – the knot – is formed owing to the artificial combination of stimuli that triggers the human organism's memory. This demonstrates Vygotsky's key notion of the dialectical nature of learning, as learners recognise demands in tasks and approach those tasks by coupling external signs or symbols as resources for cognitive activity. A well-adapted learner will affect a balance between internal and external computation. It is also suggestive for my research in that analysing key points in processes of thinking may uncover linked psychological functions, including memory's role in thinking. This recalls the relationship between Ricoeur's notion of reproductive imagination, which draws on sense impressions and experience, and productive imagination, which it uses these to generate models and potentialities.

Expanding this idea, Kirsh and Maglio (1994) propose a class of actions which they call 'epistemic action' – 'physical actions that make mental computation easier, faster or reliable' (1994, pp. 513–514). An example is when a player moves chess pieces around the board, rather than merely imagining moving them – physically moving the pieces makes it easier to detect repercussive moves. Or making a shopping list before going to the market. Scrabble players perform epistemic actions when they group the tiles of common combinations of letters in the Scrabble rack in order to cue memory and recall words. Epistemic action involves offloading structure onto the world so that the world pre-empts the need to internally represent the situation. Kirsh and Maglio's research on players who play Tetris – a real-time, interactive video game – unveils how subjects control their ordinary actions (which are not sensor actions such as control of gaze or control of attention) in order to change the informational state of play, in ways that augment their planning ability. Expert players perform actions that can appear superfluous or time-wasting, but which arrange things to revise the sensory input and actually improve performance. These actions are more efficient and reduce the cognitive work involved by offloading some part of the cognitive work onto the world, as it were (similar to the knot in the handkerchief), to achieve a better (faster, more accurate, more plentiful) result.

The significance of this idea is that selecting which actions to take to improve perception and enhance computational space challenges the linear model of information processing, thinking and planning because it means that complex thinking, such as planning, cannot proceed without regard to the agent's mechanisms of attention, perception and the reasoning they use.

> For the stimulus, in these epistemic cases, is not reacted to as an indicator of the state of the task environment, it is used as a reminder to do X, a cue that helps one to recall Y, a hint that things are not as once thought, or as a revision of input so that an internal process can complete faster. To make an analogy, just as the function of a sentence may be to warn, threaten, startle, promise, so the function of a perceived state may be to remind, alert, normalize, perturb, and so on. The *point of taking certain actions, therefore, is not for the effect they have on the environment as much as for the effect they have on the agent.*
>
> (Kirsh & Maglio, 1994, p. 546; their italics)

Instead of a simple 'classify stimulus, then select external response' model, it proposes a more dynamic, complex psychological model – classify stimulus, predict and judge expected utility of responses, select external response. More recent work on perception, information processing and learning (coming up in subsequent sections) has taken these notions even further.

Problematising perception: Wartofsky putting artefacts/representations back into the activity of perception and learning

Kirsch and Maglio's research has an antecedent in Wartofsky's theoretical notions of models and representations (1979). Wartofsky's ideas touch on similar notions of imagination and the power of metaphors as models to those we saw earlier in the work of Ricoeur (see Chapter 2). Recall that Ricoeur posed the 'problem' of imagination by hypothesising what happens if imagination is related to a use of language rather than, as it is traditionally viewed in philosophy, to perception and image. Wartofsky argued that the traditional bottom–up view of perception – that our brain analyses incoming signals, finds patterns of ever-increasing complexity and makes sense of what's out there by matching observed patterns against internal representations as a prelude to action – is wrong; we do not perceive and then act.

Perception, Wartofsky contended, is a specific mode of outward activity continuous with other forms of activity in the world. This is because it is not the eye (to take one sensory example) that sees; the whole organism 'sees' in relation to its goals. Perception is not an activity of the perceptual system, or a specific sense modality, for the genesis of perception is practical interaction with the world; perception derives itself from its function in the life of organisms as a whole (in their ecosystems and in relation to their needs and intentions). The perceptual understanding is not super-added to the pre-interpretative perception upon a purely physiological or psychological base of sensory input; it is inherent in it.

Because perception is rooted in modes of action and intention, Wartofsky argued that human perception is mediated, or conditioned, by modes of

52   *Linking of imagination with cognition*

productive and communicative praxis – and by the 'artefacts' by means of which the praxis is carried out – such as tools, like digging sticks, needles, axes and language, and so forth (these he calls 'primary' artefacts) – to enable existence to flourish. The symbolic communication of the production, reproduction and skilful use of these artefacts constitutes a second level that he calls 'secondary' artefacts because they have a reflexive quality as 'representations' or models which show the highly evolved ways that primary artefacts or tools are acted upon. 'Representations', in Wartofsky's view, are a different class of artefact because of their ability to represent an action or process by symbolic means and thus preserve and transmit it though time to future generations. Thus Wartofsky's representations function in similar respects to Ricoeur's notion of 'models' – the cultural purveyors of semantic innovation (and akin to Dawkins's 'memes': cultural concepts and tools which enhance survival and so are passed on). Moreover, Wartofsky argues, by virtue of models representing action and processes symbolically, perception is therefore historically variable, not ahistorical, transcultural or unchanging, as it is taken to be in traditional accounts. The significance of this is that such representations are governed by conventions which change over time. Variation in modes of representation then produce historical changes *in perception and in other forms of practice* – such as social and technological practices. The variation in perceptual modes both determines, and is determined by, historically changing modes of human action. For example, a forest can be perceived as a source of sustenance, a resource to be cut down and exploited for money or a source of danger – with concomitant practices or actions consistent with those different perceptions. Similarly, a field can be viewed as an arena for action but also as an artefact if it's a tilled field. Extending this idea into art, he argues that artists re-educate us perceptually when they present us with a possible world, different from what is culturally dominant at the time (1979, pp. 206–207). Van Gogh, for example, was not hailed as a significant artist until many years after his death, and yet in our day, his influence is pervasive: people fondly 'recognise' the verisimilitude of his irises, his shaken grass fields and his shimmeringly alive night skies or street cafes. What we have learned to see in perception is important because it can reshape our worldview, making it available for our subsequent outward practical activity. Thus he agrees with Vygotsky that perception is mediated by cultural artefacts. Wartofsky uses the term 'imagination' to describe how activities of modelling in the ways that we represent things impact on perception. Art is one way he finds that cultural perception shifts over time in response to imagination, which underpins innovations in representations.

There are also clear similarities here to Ricoeur's use of Black's work on metaphors and networks of metaphors having the power to model aspects of the world as the field for new actions and to cohere into the creation of new meaning schemas. However, we should recall that Ricoeur rejected the notion that models depict or picture an image or resemblance. In contrast, he emphasised a theoretical model's capacity to represent *relations* between things: 'not to have a mental picture of something but to display relations in a depicting mode' and, following Kant, to schematize an emerging meaning. By making possible *a new language* to describe relations, he argued that models provide tools with which to re-present things anew, thereby transforming what thoughts are possible. As Wartofsky maintains that models or representations cannot be reduced to a simple notion of resemblance, and that representations demonstrate historically variant conventions, it would appear that while there is strong similarity in their arguments, Ricoeur is more interested in the power of models to harness language with which to redescribe relations, whereas Wartofsky focuses on the model's impact on perception itself.

Perception for Wartofsky is not a passive imprint of sense impressions, just as it is not for Vygotsky – it is mediated by an active process involving tools or artefacts. Both Vygotsky and Wartofsky break with the notion of perception as an inner mental process (denuded of culture) distinct from active acts of intervention in the world. The language used is a little different: Vygotsky emphases the language of artefacts, symbols and signs, with Wartofsky using artefacts, models and representations.

Learning re-imagined: Vygotsky's mediational triangle, Clark's extended mind model of cognition and Polanyi's 'tacit knowing'

Ricoeur's proposition was that language offers a new way of understanding the phenomenon of imagination. Instead of approaching the problem through perception and asking if, and how, it passed through perception to image, his theory asks us to relate imagination to a certain use of language – certain technologies of language use, such as metaphors, narrative and hypotheses, which are semantically innovative (1991, p. 171). In this section, I want to consider this central idea of Ricoeur's in relation to Vygotsky's and Wartofsky's common notion that subject-object relations are mediated by the cultural tools/artefacts we are 'born into' in the cultures we inhabit. I then relate this idea to Polanyi's notion of tacit knowing in *The tacit dimension* (1967), which attempts to account for intuitive knowledge (Polanyi, 1967). I also relate it to Andy Clark's thesis of the 'extended mind' (1997, 2008, 2010; Menary, 2010a, 2010b; Rowlands, 2010). Finally, in the last part of this chapter, I will show how recent work in cognitive science, synthesised by Clark (2016a, 2016b, 2013) and called 'predictive processing', offers an overarching framework in which new understandings of perception as actively predictive and structured by a multiple-level system of control suggest a role for imagination in cognition. This overarching theoretical framework of imagination and cognition is used in my ethnographic accounts to explain my observations of imaginative pedagogies used in the ethnographies of higher education classes.

The notion of 'tacit knowledge' is well illustrated by the example of how we recognise faces. We are capable of recognising a face, even when, if asked to describe the features of the face, we are unable to specify features correctly. This is a remarkable attribute: many of us can recognise a face after an interval

54 *Linking of imagination with cognition*

of many years without seeing someone, when the facial features have aged and altered. Implicit learning leads to tacit knowledge that people do not know they possess. Polanyi (1967) argues that in the process of interior integration, we are aware of characteristics only in their relation to their bearing on the comprehensive entity which they constitute – the whole face (p. 18). This unconscious way of knowing is captured in his phrase that we 'know more than we can tell'.

Likewise, Polanyi argues that our own body is the only thing in the world that we normally never experience as an object. We experience our body in terms of *the world to which we are attending from* our body. By making this intelligent use of our body, he says, we are made to feel it is our own body, and not a thing outside (p. 16; my italics). Taking the example of using a walking stick, Polanyi argues that blind people are able to attend to the meaning of the world around them by extending their feeling through the hand via probing with the tip of the stick. In this way, with practised use, we can come to make the tool an 'extension of our body', we come to inhabit the tool itself, incorporating it into our body, as it were, or, as he puts it, 'come to dwell in it' (pp. 12–13). This is what he means by 'tacit knowing': when we make a thing function as a proximate term of tacit knowing – that is, a tool – we incorporate it into our body or extend our body to include it (whichever way you think of it). Anyone who has watched a skilled musician or sportsperson has witnessed what he means by inhabiting their tool. Polanyi compares this idea to William Dilthey and Lipps's idea of 'indwelling', or empathy, or interiorization, which they say are the proper (sic) means of knowing in the humanities (p. 16). For the purposes of education, it also suggests the importance of practice in order to make the skilful use of tools fluent and second nature. I am suggesting that Polanyi's acute observation is essentially another example of Vygotsky's notion of subject-object mediation through tools. However, it extends this idea to an embodied way of knowing. It also raises a new idea that some knowledge is tacit, derived from skilled practice (and therefore related to expertise), and the effect of this is that it becomes intuitive and 'automatic'.

Extended mind theory

Both Polanyi and Clark stress the way we recruit parts of our external environment to scaffold (that is, using some kind of external support) our understanding of the world as well as to problem solve.

Clark (1997, 2008) extends this idea of the mind's extension into the world, but instead of 'indwelling' he posits a more radical notion of the opportunistic use of part of the world to perform thinking – the actual cognitive work that we usually think of as being performed by the brain is distributed across interior *and* exterior fields. He proposes an adaptive form of intelligence which is highly selective and sees adaptive success as inhering in interaction between body, world and brain. Thus he shares a rejection of the subject-object dualism of the Cartesian positivists, just as the phenomenologists and the constructivist, Vygotsky. He argues that cognition is highly selective and functional, geared to making things happen and controlling the biological body. This model of cognition is radically different from classical cognitivism, which proposes an internal, picture-perfect, representational model of the world, in which memory retrieves data from a stored symbolic database, where problem solving is solely understood as logical inference, where cognition is centralised and where the environment is positioned as a problem domain and the body an input device. If imagination is a way of thinking which can be directed towards adapting the environment, it recruits the available tools to do so. Thus, Clark's argument lends weight to Ricoeur's and Dawkins's arguments that imagination is poorly served by restricting it to aesthetics, without appreciating its role in reasoning, in the tools of representation and hence in informing problem solving and guiding and shaping action.

Clark (1997, 2010, 2011) argues that our cognitive tools are part and parcel of human cognition – that is, the mind is not bounded by the brain but is 'extended' into the world. Clark builds on Daniel Dennett's argument that our cultural tools endow us with intelligence (Dennett, 1995, pp. 377–378), which is a relative of Richard Dawkins's idea of 'memes' – concepts/tools that succeed in winning the hearts and minds of their tool wielders and so are passed on. Clark claims that the 'effective circuits of human thought and reason are not entirely "in the head", and invites us to consider technologies, social networks, and institutional structures as proper parts of distributed organs for thought' (Clark, 2015).

Clark's extended mind thesis is that cognitive agents 'engineer their environment to sustain as well as amplify their cognitive abilities' (Colombetti & Krueger, 2015, p. 1157). That is, we control our physical surroundings in ways that alter how we interpret and act in and on them. 'Simple external props enable us to think better and hence to create more complex props and practices, which in turn "turbocharge" our thoughts a little more, which leads to the development of even better props' (Clark, 1997, p. 62).

For Clark, these props or resources can include things like shopping lists, mnemonics to prompt recall (such as tying a knot in a handkerchief or leaving your keys in the fridge with your work lunch), getting help from other people, using a computer or arranging the parts of an engine being dismantled in the shape from which they were removed for easier reassembling. They also include language, mathematics and disciplinary concepts. In extended mind theory, the environment is not simply the location of informational inputs and outputs, with the brain doing the cognitive work. He argues that we actively and resourcefully interact with the world, rather than passively receive it. 'The human organ is linked with an external entity, in a two-way interaction, creating a coupled system that can be seen as a cognitive system in its own right' (Clark & Chalmers, 1998, p. 8).

Deepening the application of his thesis, he demonstrates how we use language and discourse as tools to extend our thought capability. For example, he includes oral and written mythic and narrative 'external scaffolds' which have been passed down as knowledge from generation to generation. Theories, too, record processes of thought and argument, which can be passed around, amended and

56 *Linking of imagination with cognition*

completed by others. After Kirsh and Maglio (1994), he calls these methods 'epistemic action', whose primary purpose is to alter the nature of our own cognitive tasks.

Like Clark, Dennett (1995) argues that human minds import mindtools from the cultural environment and that, like cranes, these do the 'heavy-lifting' that improve both the generators' (of ideas) and the testers' (the community who uses them) chances of acting in ways that improve their competitive advantage or efficacy. In both their conceptions, tools (which are given to us in culture, whether they are scissors or language or complex concepts such as 'evolution' or 'ideology') are a two-way sign of intelligence: not only does it require intelligence to recognise and maintain a tool, let alone fabricate one, but tool use *confers* intelligence on those individuals who are lucky enough to be exposed to the tool (Dennett, p. 377). Neural pathways are actually altered through acquiring skill and knowledge as a result of wielding the tool. This is because the tools transform our inner (mental) environment – they literally shape neural pathways of the brain. What Dennett and Clark both mean is that if individuals can wield these conceptual tools, they can give themselves the ability to conceive longer and more complex trains of thought. This advantages the tool wielders, conferring a superior ability to understand and to act on their will and intentions in order to control the outer environment and solve problems. They argue this ability has been increasing exponentially in recent centuries and that cultural tools, especially new technologies, have now surpassed biological characteristics in the evolutionary adaptive stakes. Dennett talks about teams of generators and testers able to leverage their discoveries by communicating using language (p. 377), continually expanding the opportunities for the use of new ideas, multiplying their influence and building on the work of predecessors. Examples of these include discipline communities whose culturally stored external formalisms can be learned and critiqued over generations, resulting in gradual refinement of concepts, new formulations of concepts and eventually new disciplines that cohere around certain concepts and methodologies for applying them.

Interdependence between cognition, action and culture

Because our responses to the world impact on the world, we are both shaped by, and shape, our world. For this reason, Clark's thesis of the extended mind implies that by studying the traces of human agency in culture, we will gain insight into cognition and thinking. The boundary between brain and cultural world is merged in extended mind, and if the thesis is accepted, this would demonstrate to what extent our culturally bound ways of learning, and knowledge itself, become indistinguishable features of our minds. Educators commonly use words such as 'acquire', 'inculcate' and 'instil' to refer to knowledge 'acquisition' of 'content'. Clark's theory of cognition suggests a re-adjustment to dominant conceptions of learning: It implies that learning should emphasise how students situate themselves in relation to external memory systems to deepen their knowledge and how resourceful they are in leveraging these systems to perform

Linking of imagination with cognition 57

tasks – in other words, how they develop a capacity to connect their thinking loops to these external traces. This theory also has implications for teaching that emphasises the value of application: Assessment may need to focus more on how students *perform* their knowledge using various self-selected thinking tools; formative learning tasks should emphasise developing the ways students can gain fluency in using received tools – 'make them their own' – and use them to probe, test and understand the world in order to develop new questions, gain new knowledge or apply practical intelligence to problems with clear and meaningful goals; it might appear to favour authentic settings for problem solving rather than, for example, multiple-choice tests. If accepted, the theory of extended mind would imply that the *experiences* in which students are involved in order to shape their learning would gain greater importance, and it would seem to favour active conceptions of learning over transmission models which emphasise recall of facts stored in memory. I would expect, in my research, to see evidence of this in classes taught by competent teachers who are interested in vitalising imagination.

What I am building here is an argument that imagination harnesses mindtools (derived from historical-cultural practices – including disciplinary practices – in learning environments in the world) and drives the creation of new ideas which underpin creativity and innovation. Vygotsky's research methods are appropriate for these ideas: by focusing on how subjects acted on and changed the object (what is being worked on), his methods revealed the dynamic mediation of cultural symbolising activity in learning processes and in pragmatic action. Clark's extended mind thesis, like Vygotsky's, Dennett's and Wartofsky's theories, describes an interdependence between cognition, culture and action. My study focuses on how disciplinary and professional methodologies, processes and tools are taught in highly evolved higher education settings and are passed on to new generations. Ethnographic work is apt to try to capture the levels at which this works: institutional, emotional, technical, tool based, skill acquisition and modelling, for example.

Minds cannot be separated from bodies with needs and desires to accomplish things in the world. They are shaped by cultural tools to continually enable the remaking of that culture by developing new ideas, technologies and processes. Whether you use the analogy of crane (Dennett), or bootstrap (Clark), or describe the process as a dialectical blend of sign and practical intelligence (Vygotsky), their mutual contributions bleed into one another. The ideas of Vygotsky, Clark, Polanyi and Dennett on cognition appear to me to usefully conflate the Cartesian subject-object dichotomies, distinctions and preferences which guide some creativity theorists' focus on genius individuals, as well as refuting the argument for symbolic systems or domains as the 'ultimate' sites of creativity (see Chapter 4). Vygotsky, Clark, Polanyi and Dennett persuasively blur the distinction between the contents of the mind, culture and the world. If their ideas are accepted, the internal/external, first generation/second generation dichotomist conceptions of creativity (see McWilliam, 2007; see Chapter 4) could be said to collapse.

The perceiver as predictor

Predictive processing (PP) is a paradigm in computational and cognitive neuro-science that has attracted significant attention across fields including psychology, philosophy, artificial intelligence and robotics (see Clark's 2013 *Behavioural and brain sciences* article which attracted widespread responses from the fields of lin-guistics, computer science, ecology and evolutionary biology, economics, music and management). Predictive processing depicts the brain as a world-engaged, action-orientated, dynamic force that is built to make ongoing predictions about the world (Clark, 2016b; Hohwy, 2013). The predictions are issued in a top-down flow of neural activity from multiple levels of acquired knowledge. By top-down, Clark (2013, 2016b) means they use the mind's best guesstimates (or hypotheses) of the world to drive perception and action, which is why they are 'generative models'. The bottom-up incoming sensory signals are used as cor-rective feedback, feeding in deviations and uncertainty (the 'prediction errors'), which may drive model selection at a higher level in the hierarchy. 'The need for generative models emerges when systems must deal with complex structures of hidden causes in domains characterised by noise, ambiguity, and uncertainty' (2016b, p. 94).

This allows it to, in Clark's words, stay one step ahead, getting a grip on the world by 'lock[ing] onto patterns specifying everything from lines and edges, to zebra stripes, to movies, meanings, popcorn, parking lots, and the characteristic plays of offence and defence by your favourite football team' (2016b, p. xv). It is an embodied conception of cognition, which presents the world as offer-ing affordances in the environment that present opportunities for action and intervention. Predictive brains, Clark argues, enable situated agents to operate smoothly in the world, structuring the received barrage of energetic stimula-tion from our human senses of sight, hearing, taste, smell and touch (p. 5). It is worth remembering here that the energetic stimulation, or sensory signals, also includes our less well-recognised *inward* sensory channels: proprioception, or the sense of the relative position of body parts and the forces being deployed (this allows us, for example, to 'know' where to put our foot when we first get out of bed without working out the relativities of foot to floor height every time), and interoception, or the sense of the physiological conditions of the body (e.g., hunger, pain, cold) – channels that are crucial in forming actions and in accounting for feelings and conscious expectations. Predictive processing allows us, as organisms, to operate smoothly, 'surfing the uncertainty' of negotiating the world in order to act on our needs, goals and intentions.

Importantly, for our argument, Clark argues that learning and predictive pro-cessing are supported using the same basic resources. This is because perceiving our body and the world involves learning to predict our evolving sensory states, states that are responding to the body in action in the world. It turns out, he says, that a good way to predict those changing states is to learn what causes them. This idea, he says, has roots in Helmholtz's (1860) depiction of percep-tion as a process of 'probabilistic, knowledge driven inference' (Clark, 2016b,

Linking of imagination with cognition   59

p. 19) because organisms are in the tricky business of inferring worldly causes from their bodily, sensory effects – like a bet on what's out there (p. 19). Hence the connection to imagination – as predictive inference and meaning-making. According to PP theory, the organism's task is thus: How would the world be for my sensory organs to be stimulated the way they currently are? To answer this question, the agent has to learn how to generate a model of the distal causes whose combination would make up the incoming data. As Clark emphasises, this form of prediction in 'predictive processing' is less a task of looking into the future than one that focuses on perception and the guessing of the present (2016a). A striking example of the brain making meaning where none exists is provided by Clark in recordings of sine-wave speech (see www.lifesci.sussex. ac.uk/home/Chris_Darwin/SWS). Initially, these sound incomprehensible, and I could only recognise speech inflexions. But if you listen to the original sentence, and then re-listen to the sine-wave version, you will start to make sense of and 'hear' the words in the sine-wave version. The theory states this is because your brain now has prior knowledge, which it uses to generate educated guesses about what is creating sine-wave speech. The best guess is what you 'perceive'.

In Clark's (2013, 2016a, 2016b) account of predictive processing, humans do not wait passively for sensory stimulation to arrive. Because we have bodies with needs, desires and particular sensory apparatus, we 'sample' the world actively in terms of those needs, non-consciously predicting the sensory flow from the world to our receptors. We also intervene in the world, probing and acting in ways that assist us to estimate and re-estimate our predictions. He argues that this occurs in a Bayesian fashion, generating a statistical model of how our sensory inputs will change and evolve. We gauge our prediction errors through mismatches between our predictions and the sensory inputs, continually re-adjusting our expectations and re-sculpting our predictions (of 'distal world' causes) accordingly. This implies that the predictive models combine the use of top-down probabilistic models with a vision of how and when to use them (p. 25) – context-dependent decision-making, in other words. This 'precision-weighting' (2016b, p. 9), context-sensitive mechanism alters the influence of specific prediction error signals and optimises the relative influence of top-down prediction against incoming (bottom-up) sensory evidence, according to changing estimations of the context-varying reliability of the sensory evidence itself (Feldman & Friston, 2010). This means we are engaged in rolling cycles or loops that harvest the 'information' (energetic stimulation) we need to refine those predictions. It also means that our learning is self-directed, as we accumulate, over time and in a variety of contexts, top-down knowledge of patterns and regularities, which we match with bottom-up receipt of sensory information. The PP model, in other words, illustrates a neurally grounded model which *learns to learn* (Lake, Salakhutdinov & Tenenbaum, 2015). Let us take an example to see how this may work. If I am studying for a psychology exam, and using online multiple-choice questions to test whether I have adequately understood the material, when I make an incorrect guess, I receive immediate feedback that my answer is wrong. The error in my prediction is alerted to me. This allows me to realise

60 *Linking of imagination with cognition*

that the way I have hitherto constructed my knowledge is in error. I can then the adjust my attention to broaden the concepts which I now need to attend to in my lecture notes, in order to reconfigure a new pattern of relationships and to re-form my understanding. It is in this way that my individual cognitive system uses the niche of a cultural signal in the environment (the online MCQ psych test) to help reduce its prediction error and learn something new. Referring to prediction-driven learning in formal learning practices, such as this, Clark says,

> Those training signals are now delivered as part of a complex developmental web that gradually comes to include all the complex regularities embodied in the web of statistical relations among the symbols and other forms of socio-cultural scaffolding in which we are immersed.
>
> (Clark, 2013, p. 195)

It is in this way that historical-cultural disciplinary practices interact with the prediction-driven overarching framework he proposes.

One advantage of top-down cognitive prediction is that it allows timely body action responses that would not be possible with the clunky signal delays that would occur if the brain had to compute causes by crunching incoming data in order to work out, moment by moment, how to act most appropriately – as would happen with a centralised information processing model. In this predictive processing picture, it is important to emphasise the restrictive use of the word 'model'. As discussed earlier, the PP model does not imply a picture-perfect, richly detailed representation, as might be expected if we deem perception as a print impression of reality on an inert wax. Deeply embedded in evolutionary roots as PP theory is, it interprets information processing ways of 'modelling the data' as cognitively expensive and unnecessary in the wild. PP understands itself as frugal (cognitively speaking), selective, created in response to the agent's specific needs and the demands of the world in the context at hand. This is why, Clark argues, the motor control and perception systems should not be regarded as processes separate from each other, because actions can probe and sample the sensory information needed to increase the likelihood of good predictive capability. This means that perception is indirect (Hohwy, 2007, p. 322, quoted in Clark, 2013, p. 199) and that what is inferred about the world – experience-dependent learning, in other words – is partial and selective, not veridical. In this respect, the argument goes, PP models are unlike scientific models, which aspire to accuracy and detailed representation, because PP models are instrumental and geared for functional capability.

Let us return to Vygotsky's example of the little girl to re-interpret it in the light of predictive processing theory.

While Vygotsky presents the problem relationship as a mediational triangle in which the subject's encounter with an object is mediated by some (cultural, historical) artefact which is used to control activity in relation to the object (as shown originally in Figure 3.1), it is equally clear that the child's performance and her resolution of the problem rely on prediction. What her cognitive predictions are based on are probabilistic models, derived from memory (experience) and reasoning at a range of multiple levels: trial and error of standing and falling off objects (including stools) and accumulated physical adeptness; language competence; the consequences of poking, manipulating and hitting with a stick; and the rewarding taste of candy. I am arguing that imagination emerges from the child's need to predict, or project, alternative possibilities of what *could* happen, in order to reach the candy (the action that accomplishes the goal). Her imagination exploits the affordances of time and space in the power of language (the linguistic tool) to help play with a combination of other affordances in the situation – the stool and stick – to do it. In other words, the internal process of prediction is shaped by its coordination with external resources – where 'external' includes language, in which we are immersed by virtue of our socialisation.

But tools, especially linguistic tools, are not stable entities. The use of a tool is not exhausted by the intentions built into its design – even a hammer can be used a hundred ways. When one thinks of the exponential possibilities for creating novel meanings when words are used as metaphors, for example, one can begin to appreciate the super-charged conceptual power of metaphor as a tool. Novelty is built into the system! To illustrate, if I say, 'The road runs down to the beach', the road is static but the metaphorical expression has the effect on a hearer of affecting a cognitive process involving superimposing a dynamic trajectory line onto the imagined spatial scene. This is not simply a matter of language but is also a matter of knowing how to project a trajectory in an imagined space (Hutchins, 2014). This is an example of extended cognition – extended by metaphor as a linguistic mindtool. In complex higher order learning, as in higher education, I am suggesting that knowledge intensive strategies, and metaphors (as a specialised linguistic artefact), can become integrated into the mind's predictive form of top-down processing.

Predictive processing and imagination

In the following section, I present three features of predictive processing theory, as championed by Andy Clark, involving the imagination. The PP theory reveals imagination as an inseparable part of thinking because perception, understanding, reason and imagination are conceived of as co-emergent.

1   PP's claim that imagination is the generative engine of perception (Swanson, 2016).
2   PP's claim that human cognition uses an architecture of both top-down hierarchical levels and a bottom-up prediction error which together generate models of what causes phenomena in the world. This is aligned with Ricoeur's focus on the generativity of *productive* imagination.
3   PP's claim that the cognizing agent combines and orders sense data through the synthesising activity of the productive imagination (Swanson, 2016).

62 *Linking of imagination with cognition*

1 The perceiver as imaginer

Imagination plays a key role in predictive processing theory as it appears to be the engine that enables generative models at all levels (Swanson, 2016). For example, if, on a rainy night, I see a flash of lightning, I predict the sound of thunder that will follow based on my knowledge of the regular pattern that twins these two sensory perceptions in my experience. The regularity that constitutes the model is a top-down signal that 'primes' my perception cortex areas (I listen expectantly for the clap, or will it be a rumble?). In this instance, 'prime' is neural terminology for making neurons more readily excited. Under the PP framework, the top-down influence includes a precision-weighting aspect which can direct my attention and bias my sensory processes so as to reflect estimates of reliability and salience towards certain sounds I expect to hear and the generative model itself (p. 148). If, on the same night, a gunshot is fired (I live in Brunswick, Melbourne, where biker gangs and mafia-like figures occasionally act out feuds), I will very likely dismiss the sound as nothing more than thunder – until several sirens signal the arrival of police. In that case the model will be revised in response to the subsequent sensory signals which indicate a prediction error in causal attribution. Clark cites several psychological studies which present work on memory as intimately bound up with constructive processes of neural prediction and hence imagination. For example, neuroscience work on perception, recall and episodic future thinking appears to align perception, recall and imagination (2016b, pp. 106–107).

The sine-wave speech example prior also seems to me to nicely illustrate the participation of imagination in the act of perception that joins passive and active elements in thinking and imposes unity on the sound material.

Another reason to suggest the role of imagination in perception is the existence of daydreams, dreams and also delusions. Neuro-scientific research suggests that models of behaviour at higher levels of the model hierarchy can be activated without propagating their output signals down to actual muscle movements and to acts in the world – as we see in dream states or daydreams (Clark, 2016b). This same process allows me to imagine flying without moving my arms when I am imagining the scene – the internal images can be insulated from entrainment in motor control and don't require concomitant propagation of the accompanying neural to muscular activation. This process of mental imagery or rehearsal also applies to more complex planning projected over various time scales (2016b; Perlovsky, Deming & Ilin, 2011). As we saw in Chapter 2 in relation to imagination, foresight and critical thinking, alternative actions can be imagined, along with their likely consequences. This narrative prefiguring allows time for reflexive and deliberate forms of reasoning. Thus the system forms the basis for autonomous, unsupervised learning – which is the aim of higher education.

2 The perceiver as generator of models

Clark's argument is that PP involves predicting the non-actual sensory trajectories that *would* ensure were we to perform some desired action. This is what I might call the 'virtual reality' side of imagination that presents an object or

Linking of imagination with cognition 63

action in 'intuition', which is to say, even without those objects or actions being present. The effect is that downwards connections, in both the motor control and sensory systems, carry complex predictions, and the upwards connections carry prediction errors (the sensory information). The system is a generative model, capable of reconstructing the predicted sensory signal at lower levels of the multi-level model – literally the system can generate 'virtual' versions of the sensory data for itself, assembling cues and remembering (reconstructing) past experiences using knowledge about regular, interacting causes in the world and using them to predict future influences.

3   The cognizer as synthesiser

As we saw in Chapter 2, Ricoeur owned that his theory of imagination drew on Kant's argument that productive imagination schematized a *synthetic* operation which was necessary for perception (Ricoeur, 1979, p. 147). Thus, Kant defined synthesis as 'the act of putting various presentations with one another and of comprising their manifoldness in one cognition' (Kant, 1997/1787, sec. B103, quoted in Swanson, 2016, p. 9). Kant attributed synthesis to the workings of imagination and stressed its crucial role in perception and cognition. 'Synthesis . . . is the mere effect produced by the imagination . . . without which we would have no cognition whatsoever' (Kant, 1996/1787, sec. A78, quoted in Swanson, p. 9).

Similarly, in predictive processing theory, central to the idea of generative models is a strategy of analysing by synthesis (Swanson, 2016, p. 9).

> A generative model . . . aims to capture the statistical structure of some set of observed inputs by inferring a causal matrix able to give rise to that very structure. . . . When the combination of such hidden causes (which span many spatial and temporal scales) settles into a coherent whole, the system has self-generated the sensory data using stored knowledge and perceives a meaningful structured scene.
>
> (Clark, 2016b, p. 21)

For predictive processing, imagination underpins the way generative models generate and construct the incoming sensory signals they expect to receive. This means it is in some way required for perception. 'It means that perception – at least, as it occurs in creatures like us – is co-emergent with (something functionally akin) to imagination' (Clark, 2016b, p. 94).

Relevance of predictive processing to imagination in complex learning of higher education

The key idea of predictive processing is that we *learn* about the world by attempting to *generate the incoming sensory data for ourselves*, from the top down, using the amassed recurrent connectivity which produces models (Clark, 2016b, p. 6). If this understanding is correct, neural expectation, or prediction, is driven by imagination. The models that are produced are *self*-produced, not a sense impression in the Humean sense. This is not to say that these models are chimeras untethered to the corrections of worldly data. First, the models are the organism's best predictions of worldly causation based on past experiences. Second, the margin of error between what we predict and the down-up sensory flow of data over time incrementally produces improved models. We are, according to PP, natural imaginers, but what the theory of predictive processing proposes is that imagination is constrained by functionality in the world, however that is defined. The top-down aspect has been used to explain the phenomena of daydreaming and producing illusions, according to predictive processing theorists (Clark, 2016b; Hohwy, 2013). In support of this, it is argued that neural imaging studies show that the same neuronal resources that produce the top-down approximations or models to explain the sensory states produce them 'off line', as it were, as quasi-sensory states (Clark, p. 94). This is significant and reminds us of the characteristic of liminality of the imagination discussed in Chapter 2 – a hiatus or state of momentary suspension of belief, also part and parcel of play, that seems to be essential for the imaginative process. As I argued there, the imaginary process happens in that momentary hiatus when provisional rational fictions are momentarily entertained upon which evaluative thinking can be performed. In that space, imaginary possibilities are 'thrown up' to test relationships or compare characteristics or processes of the model. Recall Vygotsky's example of the little girl contriving to reach the candy. The predictive processing theory suggests a fundamental cognitive role for this imaginative activity and suggests it may be nested in hierarchical levels of models whose explanations cascade upwards and downwards in attempts to minimise the errors of its predictions of its internal states. If PP has traction as a general theory, there are flexible influences over what models are recruited for a particular goal at a particular time. Used in the upper levels of the hierarchy and fused with human artefacts/mindtools, such as language and mathematics, the stage is then set for cognitive effects that allow reflection or re-examination of the models that represent inferred causes for phenomena. With the human ability to attend to them intentionally, and in loops of enhancement, this helps build a picture of the human capacity for ongoing unsupervised learning. As this is the goal of higher education, it is important that teaching approaches recognise, encourage and not impede this cognitive process.

While the role of imagination in PP related to perception builds a picture of environmentally situated probabilistic models that facilitate world-exploiting action, it includes how deductive inferential models, such as scientific models, or narratives, can be assembled in human cognition at these higher levels in the hierarchy. Once externalised in language and cultural institutions, an idea or thought is able to be passed around, revised, improved or combined in new webs of higher order and more abstract representations – in Wartofsky's sense. These representations are far removed from simple sensory models and include conversation, poems, theories such as quantum theory, concepts such as 'evolution', maths equations, art or politics and general principles such as moral and logical principles. Given material form, they are made available to us and to others, as objects to be deliberately attended to. Through the vehicles of spoken words, text, diagrams, music and art, they are then part of a social process in which they become cultural representations, or tools, that are passed on. In cultures of academia, such representations are made available in journals and critiqued for their ability to answer the questions in the field. They are taught in schools and universities. As Clark says, 'Our best models of the world are this able to serve as the basis for cumulative, communally distributed reasoning, rather than just providing the *means* by which individual thoughts occur' (2016b, p. 279).

The upshot of this externalising is that the human built environment, rather than being simply an arena for living, action and play, becomes filled with cultural representations, practices and tools. As a human-designed environment, it 'repeatedly transforms the activity of the prediction-hungry biological brain' (Clark, 2016b, p. 279). Inevitably, this iterative restructuring – and not the sheer processing power of the individual mind – shapes us more powerfully (arguably) than the neural self-structuring that we initiate. Technologies, mathematics, language, disciplinary methodologies, structured discussion and professional or cultural practices such as processes of peer critique are part of the construction niches by which humans build and control the environmental resources that structure our predictions and enhance and amplify our cognitive capacity (Sterelny, 2010).

When testing the application of these ideas in classes of higher education, I seek to understand the processes of imagination and the encouragement of unsupervised learning implied by PP in these contexts. The classrooms I research are undoubtedly designed environments, complex and purpose-built to develop students' capacities helping them identify, and manipulate, complex 'regularities' in symbols and practices and start to learn the practices that enhance that process. In doing so, such classrooms create environments that will enhance – or impede – students' capacity to self-generate ever more refined, simple, apt, efficient, beautiful and/or powerful abstract representations and complex practices, in order to impact their worlds.

Conclusion: imagination and finding and creating new knowledge

How do bodies of existing knowledge and ways of thinking that are themselves open to change pass inside an individual? And how do we innovate – create new knowledge, new practices and new ways of doing things? These questions are important in education, particularly in higher education. The answers educators give will impact on how students are taught the practices that lead to new knowledge and/or how to apply new knowledge in order to invent, or adapt, new professional practices. I have argued that Vygotsky's and Wartofsky's notion of subject-object mediation by tools situates the subject in relation to her historical social environments and resources she uses to learn. Pedagogical approaches that teach professional and disciplinary practices and processes (i.e. actions) of knowledge creation are some of these subject-object mediating tools. I also am suggesting that they equip the mind with soft technologies that augment and improve the subject's predictive models. In this way, predictive processing provides a theory

66 *Linking of imagination with cognition*

describing how imagination co-emerges with action, perception and understanding – an integrative theoretical framework with which to understand cognition in relation to cultural tools, technologies and practices. Predictive processing theory also provides an explanation for unsupervised learning in relation to hierarchical models positions imagination as co-emergent with perception, reason and action. Imagination is a part of the inner economy which exists in relation to our embodied needs, goals and intentions in worldly activity (Clark, 2016b).

In twenty-first-century higher education, student learning happens through experiences afforded in a variety of learning contexts: classroom activities and tasks, work placements, online simulations, overseas study experiences and study habits. The practical pedagogies set in motion by educators in these 'designer' environments encourage cognitively resourceful responses in their students. This could mean working through simulations or problems, drawing on subject notes or library resources, learning in self-devised study groups, seeking help from others and following other practices in order to act on the problem or task. Therefore, institutions and teachers need to provide: appropriate contexts in which students can practise making critical judgements about how to apply their skills and knowledge; contexts to practice collaboratively building new knowledge with peers and professional communities in appropriate ways; as well as interactive spaces that help develop the attitudes and the know-how to keep learning throughout their professional and personal lives. If higher education is to prepare students to function in, excel in and contribute to the fields in which they live and work, the cognitive dimension of imagination and creativity, and the cultural tools used in various disciplinary domains which education imparts, need to be brought together in course learning. I am not arguing that these things are not already brought together – good teachers do this purposely and to great effect in engaging their students in new understanding, in developing fluency in concepts and skills and generating knowledge by combining and applying them creatively. But combining the ideas of Ricoeur, Dennett, Polanyi and Clark provides a theoretical basis for thinking about how imaginative activity incorporates tools in the environment, including the disciplinary environment, to shift perspectives, produce new ideas, and find and solve problems. This is central to the educative role of universities which prepare the next generation for life in society.

Imaginative approaches underpin the ability to navigate novelty, to make new discoveries, to solve problems in highly complex environments or to offer new perspectives that reconfigure problems so they can be solved in better ways. These approaches can also contribute richly to perspectives about values and social justice questions about who benefits from which problem-solving approaches. It is therefore of fundamental importance to higher education.

References

Clark, A. (1997). *Being there: Putting brain, body and world together.* Cambridge, MA: The Massachusetts Institute of Technology Press.

Clark, A. (2008). Magic words: How language augments human computation. In J. Toribo & A. Clark (Eds.), *Artificial intelligence and cognitive science* (pp. 21–39). New York: Garland Publishing, Inc.

Clark, A. (2010). The extended mind. In R. Menary (Ed.), *The extended mind* (pp. 27–42). Cambridge, MA: A Bradford Book, The MIT Press.

Clark, A. (2011). *Supersizing the mind*. Oxford: Oxford University Press.

Clark, A. (2013). Whatever next? Predictive brains, situated agents, and the future of cognitive science. *Behavioural and Brain Sciences, 36*, 181–253. doi:10.1017/S0140525X 12000477

Clark, A. (2015, March 4). *The extended mind: HDC, a history of distributed cognition* [seminar on web]. University of Edinburgh: Arts and Humanities Research Council. Retrieved from www.hdc.ed.ac.uk/seminars/extended-mind

Clark, A. (2016a). Busting out: Predictive brains, embodied minds, and puzzle of the evidentiary veil. *Noûs*, 1–27. doi:10.1111/nous.12140

Clark, A. (2016b). *Surfing uncertainty: Prediction, action and embodied mind*. New York: Oxford University Press.

Clark, A., & Chalmers, D. J. (1998). The extended mind. *Analysis, 58*, 7–19.

Colombetti, G., & Krueger, J. (2015). Scaffoldings of the affective mind. *Philosophical Psychology, 28*(8), 1157–1176.

Dennett, D. C. (1995). *Darwin's dangerous idea: Evolution and the meanings of life*. New York: Simon & Schuster.

Dilthey, W. (1914–36). *Gesammelte Schriften* (Vol. VII., pp. 213–216). Leipzig and Berlin. Translation by H. A. Hodges, *Wilhelm Dilthey*. New York: Oxford University Press, 1944, pp. 121–124.

Edwards, A. (2005). Let's get beyond community and practice: The many meanings of learning by participating. *Curriculum Journal, 16*(1), 49–65.

Feldman, H., & Friston, K. (2010). Attention, uncertainty, and free-energy. *Frontiers in Human Neuroscience, 4*. doi:10.3389/fnhum.2010.00215

Geertz, C. (1973). *The interpretation of cultures*. New York: Basic Books Inc, Publishers.

Helmholtz, H. (1860/1962). *Handbuch der physiologischen optic* (J. P. C. Southall, Ed., English trans., Vol. 3). New York: Dover.

Hohwy, J. (2013). *The predictive mind*. Oxford: Oxford University Press.

Hutchins, E. (2014). The cultural system of human cognition. *Philosophical Psychology, 27*(1), 34–49. doi:10.1080/09515089.2013.830548

Hutto, D. D., & Myin, E. (2017). Imagining. In *Evolving enactivism: Basic minds meet content*. Cambridge, MA: The MIT Press.

Kirsh, D., & Maglio, P. (1994). On distinguishing epistemic from pragmatic action. *Cognitive Science, 18*, 513–549.

Lake, B. M., Salakhutdinov, R., & Tenenbaum, J. B. (2015). Human-level concept learning through probabilistic program induction, *Science, 350*(6266), 1332–1338. doi:10.1126/science.aab3050

McWilliam, E. L. (2007). *Is creativity teachable: Conceptualising the creativity/pedagogy relationship in higher education*. Paper presented at the 30th HERDSA Annual Conference: Enhancing Higher Education, Theory and Scholarship, Adelaide.

McWilliam, E. L., & Dawson, S. (2007). *Understanding creativity: A survey of 'creative' academic teachers: A report for the Carrick Institute for Learning and Teaching in Higher Education*. Retrieved from www.altcexchange.edu.au/system/files/handle/fellowships_associatefellow_report_ericamcwilliam_may07.pdf

Menary, R. (2010a). Cognitive integration and the extended mind. In R. Menary (Ed.), *The extended mind* (pp. 227–244). Cambridge, MA: A Bradford Book, The MIT Press.

Menary, R. (2010b). Dimensions of mind. *Phenomenology and the Cognitive Sciences, 9*, 561–578. doi:10.1007/s11097-010-9186-7

68 *Linking of imagination with cognition*

Pelaprat, E., & Cole, M. (2011). Minding the gap: Imagination, creativity and human cognition. *Integrative Psychological & Behavioral Science, 2011*(4), 397–418. doi:10.1007/s12124-011-9176-5

Perlovsky, L., Deming, R., & Ilin, R. (2011). Emerging areas. In L. Perlovsky, R. Deming, & R. Ilin (Eds.), *Emotional cognitive neural algorithms with engineering applications: Dynamic logic: From vague to crisp* (Vol. 371, pp. 81–174). New York: Springer.

Polanyi, M. (1967). *The tacit dimension*. Garden City, NY: Anchor Books.

Ricoeur, P. (1979). The metaphorical process as cognition, imagination and feeling. In S. Sacks (Ed.), *On metaphor* (pp. 141–153). Chicago: University of Chicago Press.

Ricoeur, P. (1991). Imagination in discourse and in action (K. Blamey & J. B. Thompson, Trans.). In J. M. Eadie (Ed.), *From text to action: Essays in hermeneutics* (Vol. 2, pp. 168–187). Evanston, IL: Northwestern University Press.

Rowlands, M. (2010). *The new science of the mind*. Cambridge, MA: A Bradford Book, The MIT Press.

Smolucha, F. (1992a). A reconstruction of Vygotsky's theory of creativity. *Creativity Research Journal, 5*(1), 49–67. doi:10.1080/10400419209534422

Smolucha, F. (1992b). The relevance of Vygotsky's theory of creative imagination for contemporary research on play. *Creativity Research Journal, 5*(1), 69–76.

Sterelny, K. (2010). Minds: Extended or scaffolded? *Phenomenology and the Cognitive Sciences, 9*(4), 465–481. doi:10.1007/s11097-010-9174-y

Swanson, L. R. (2016). The predictive processing paradigm has roots in Kant. *Frontiers in Systems Neuroscience, 10*(79). Retrieved from http://dx.doi.org/10.3389/fnsys.2016.00079

Vygotsky, L. S. (1978). *Mind in society: The development of higher psychological processes*. Cambridge, MA: Harvard University Press.

Wartofsky, M. W. (1979). Perception, representation and forms of action: Towards an historical epistemology. In *Models: Representations and scientific understanding* (pp. 188–210). Dordrecht, Holland/Boston, MA/London, UK: D. Reidel Publishing Company.

Wertsch, J. V. (2007). Mediation. In H. Daniels, M. Cole, & J. V. Wertsch (Eds.), *The Cambridge companion to Vygotsky* (pp. 178–192). Cambridge: Cambridge University Press.

4 Defining and practising creativity

If, as is argued in Chapter 1, imagination and creativity are important to help meet present and future challenges, what is already known about how each may be learned, and what approaches to cultivating or teaching them are effective? What distinguishes imagination from creativity? Are they naturally occurring capacities? If so, can the natural capacity be impeded and diminished, and if so, how? Can it be developed? What conditions can cultivate it in higher education, and what teaching approaches are effective? And what is the role of creativity and imagination in various disciplinary domains? What does the interchangeability of creativity, imagination and innovation in the literature have on practical pedagogical implications for fostering imagination in higher education learning and teaching?

The literature on how university educators cultivate the imagination of their students and an appreciation of how the imagination applies in their discipline is relatively small. It sits, however, within a vast, multi-disciplinary literature on the overarching concept 'creativity', which has very different discourses in different scholarly fields of study, such as philosophy, psychology, education, media and the arts, as well as in a proliferating popular literature on creativity (for example, Lehrer, 2012; Tharp, 2008; Catmull & Wallace, 2014). It is usually also situated within national and institutional educational policy frameworks which incorporate creativity into their 'visions' and learning outcomes.

As discussed in Chapter 1, this book uses the term 'creativity' as the overarching term which includes five dispositions or aspects: inquisitiveness, persistence, imagination, being collaborative and discipline (Lucas, Claxton & Spencer, 2013, pp. 16–17). Even though my focus is on imagination, higher educators and others use the terms 'creativity', 'imagination' and 'innovation' interchangeably. The effect of this is that imagination's specific teachable aspects remain inadequately described, something my research on which this book is based seeks to address. Equally, however the way the terms are used interchangeably means my research also needed to consider what is implied by these overlapping concepts. Thus, this chapter begins with a discussion of the major themes in the creativity literature. They include findings frequently observed in my research sites – for example, encouragement of personal persistence, attitudes

70   *Defining and practising creativity*

to risk-taking, developing expertise and fluency in particular disciplinary skills and concepts. It is unsurprising that other creative attributes are fostered by educators simultaneously with imagination because imagination is a tributary of creativity – all are necessary contributions. Or to use another analogy, as I suggest in Chapter 1, imagination is one digit (the thumb) in the full hand of creativity. But I distinguish the role of imagination, which implies making new connections that can shift the perspective, from which things are considered, and that forms new grounds from which to question assumptions and generate alternative possibilities.

Therefore the principle of organisation of the first part of this chapter are the broad themes in the creativity literature that lead towards a meaningful understanding of imagination in higher education, which is my focus. This chapter will first outline the following themes from the broad creativity literature:

- Conceptions of originality in relation to creative products and creativity as a process.
- Creative thinking seen as problem solving and problem finding.
- The relationship between creative and critical thinking.
- Imagination and its role in 'expertise', or domain-relevant skills and knowledge.
- The contribution of individuals versus their social context as the sources of creativity – in which I also include domains of knowledge and professional communities.

These themes are compared with some key notions in Ricoeur's theory of imagination, such as reproductive and productive imagination. Limitations of Ricoeur's theory and the necessity to be aware of other elements involved in the wider process of creativity are discussed.

In the subsequent section, the chapter tightens its vision to focus on the literature covering creativity, imagination and higher education. This includes whether creativity, and imagination (as an aspect of creativity), can be enhanced and the constellation of foundational elements that are activated in pedagogies. Ricoeur's theory interweaves this discussion, which tries to clarify what exactly it is that makes certain activities imaginative. Some key studies for enhancing imagination in disciplinary and professional contexts, particularly focusing on narrative ways of knowing and the issue of personal identity, are also discussed.

Creativity as original product

'Creativity' is typically defined in terms of the *results* of an activity. The products of creativity are typically characterised by their novelty or originality. The focus on originality has led to a body of research that seeks to locate the origins of creativity in the study of psychological traits of individuals who have made eminent or 'game-changing' contributions to their field, such as Albert Einstein, Vincent Van Gogh, J. S. Bach and Steve Jobs. Literature which accepts this

Defining and practising creativity   71

notion tends to argue that creativity is a rare endowment possessed by geniuses or talented individuals (Martingdale, 1999).

However, the principle of originality has been criticised by researchers on a number of counts. Some researchers argue that originality, novelty or innovation of products should be understood, not in terms of a complete break with the past, or unalloyed newness, but as building on the foundations of preceding products, conventions and/or received knowledge (Weisberg, 1999; Ricoeur, 1983/1984, p. 69; Csikszentmihalyi, 1996). This has the effect of de-emphasising the contribution of precursors, peers and collaborators and tends to spruik a commodified idea of the value of 'individual' talent (Csikszentmihalyi, 1999, p. 324).

Another qualification on the idea of originality is the idea that the original product must also be socially useful and/or accepted by others as appropriate or expressive of meaning in order to be deemed creative (Sternberg & Lubart, 1999; Csikszentmihalyi, 1996).

In addition, the rare trait view of creativity has been criticised by Csikszentmihalyi (1999) and others, who have found no necessary corollary between creative personal attributes and works hailed as creative achievements. Csikszentmihalyi makes the point, for example, that women in his study who showed as much potential in art school as their male counterparts did not go on to receive outstanding recognition at all. It is therefore necessary, he argues, to incorporate social recognition as integral to definitions of what counts as creative. This led him to propose a 'systems' approach to understand creativity, in which creativity is not a real objective quality, but involves social recognition or acceptance by a field of judges (p. 316) and occurs when a person makes a change in a domain that has *impact* over that domain which is transmitted over time (p. 315).

Taking a different perspective, Nickerson (1999) takes issue with Csikszentmihalyi's position, arguing that we should not mistake the existence of creativity with the recognition of creativity:

> By definition, we are not aware of creativity that goes unnoticed, but we have every reason to believe that it exists. . . . One cannot rule out the possibility that for every creative product that is eventually recognised as such there are others that go unnoticed indefinitely.
>
> (p. 392)

This reservation for uncounted creativity is worthy of consideration in education because the view of creativity as the preserve of major transformations of domains is not shared by all. Educational researchers, in particular, have argued for a universal notion of creativity occurring in all aspects of life ('lifewide') as well as 'lifelong' – from cradle to grave (Craft, 2003). This more pervasive and democratic notion of creativity, which emphasises informal learning as well as formal processes, has been picked up by educators because it occurs in multiple roles, contexts and places throughout life (Jackson, 2011).

The conception of *creativity as product* underscores the value to society of creativity. Robinson has popularised this idea by advocating that our ability as a

72   *Defining and practising creativity*

society to successfully meet future challenges will be dependent on us 'fashioning' 'imaginative activity . . . so as to produce outcomes that are *both original and of value*' (1999, p. 30). This comment suggests that the value of imaginative activity is its potential for commodification – and the employment that goes with it. The rise of this 'creativity as capital' discourse can be traced to the proliferation of the 'knowledge economy' agenda (Walsh, Anders, Hancock & Elvidge, 2013, p. 1261). Original ideas underpin the value-adding of products and outcomes, especially knowledge assets, such as medical techniques or quantum computer information processing or storm water collection design – an idea implied most by the word 'innovation'. Craft (2003) makes the point that globalisation of economic activity has led to increased cross-border competition for markets and a fear of obsolescence. In this sense, the pervasive promotion of creativity itself can be seen as a high-stakes policy response to the world of capitalist economics (Harris, 2014). The logic drawn by political and industry leaders is that continual innovation and resourcefulness have become necessary to economic competitiveness. Economists and politicians assert that the economy demands creativity because an economy that produces innovative assets for consumption (including knowledge) creates quality employment and wealth. This creates a demand for a highly skilled and knowledgeable workforce and can – if distributed equitably – result in improved public amenities and higher standards of living, health and services. 'Innovation' is frequently the term of choice in these contexts and is associated with tangible research outcomes, patents and spin-off companies in the knowledge economy.

These ideas reflect the attention creativity is commanding globally and constitutes what one researcher argues is a historically significant 'creative turn' in which creativity has been unhitched from the creative arts and is being increasingly identified in the twenty-first century with technology, creative and cultural industries and innovation (Harris, 2014, p. 2). This is reflected in the pervasive use of the term 'innovation' – far more prevalent than 'imagination' – in creative industries and economics discourses, where it is used to depict the value of novel products, systems, practices or services. Innovation is also frequently linked with technology as an enabler of collaboration. Skills associated with the expansion of the 'creative class' producing this innovation (Florida, 2002), which are therefore needed for employment, are used to justify its expansion in education (for example, McWilliam, 2007, 2009; McWilliam & Haukka, 2008; Sternberg & Kaufman, 2010, p. 475). The logic goes: If we can no longer trust time-honoured habits of thinking and doing, how should education respond? These commentators have also observed the contradictions in the policy response to the need for creativity, arguing that its development is impeded by the rise of standardised testing in education systems. Conventional standardised testing has been criticised for its lack of attention to creative thinking (Harris, 2014; Sternberg & Kaufman, 2010; Spencer, Lucas & Claxton, 2012). Responding to this environment, the OECD and Creativity, Culture and Education (CCE) funded a UK project to define and formatively assess creativity (Lucas et al., 2013). In Australia, the Australian Research Council funded a project called 'The creative turn: An Australia-wide

Defining and practising creativity 73

study of creativity and innovation in secondary schools' which studied the ways that creativity and innovation are defined and the ways that creativity presents itself in existing school, student and teacher practices (Harris, 2016). These broad issues and justifications relate to my research discussed in this book in that my argument is that imagination precipitates semantic innovation, which can create or disclose (pick your metaphor) different perspectives on the world, which lead to finding new questions, new ways of seeing and solving problems and new forms of action. This kind of 'upstream' capability provided by education is integral to downstream 'innovation'.

Creativity as a process

More recently, arguably in reaction to emphases in research into creativity as a product of original genius, as well as to the debates mentioned earlier, there has been a shift to an alternative consideration of it as a property of *thinking*. This literature places greater stress on aspects involved in the *process* of creativity.

Emphasising the *process* speaks to the aims of education because of the transformative potential of creative thinking to human society and the quality of life of individuals. Education attempts to improve the kind of thinking individuals bring to their consideration of issues or problems so conceptions of creativity, as a process of thinking, are germane to teachers' work. Craft argues for a broadly conceived, everyday form of creativity (which she calls 'little c creativity'). She says that creativity is considered 'an essential life skill, which needs to be fostered by the education system' (1999, p. 137; also Robinson, 2011). Jackson, Oliver, Shaw and Wisdom (2006) described creativity in higher education in terms of the ability to think through complex indeterminate problems, whether they are abstract or concrete.

Conceived as a process of thinking, creativity sometimes connotes *quantity* – as the ability to get lots of ideas – and emphasises divergent and flexible thinking. Brainstorming programs, for example, stem from these conceptions. They are focused on maximising the number of possible ideas, with a further convergent step in the process involving the evaluation of those ideas. Being imaginative can be seen as the divergent aspect, while being evaluative, or disciplined, can be seen as the convergent (Runco, 2010, p. 424, quoted in Lucas et al., 2013, p. 14; Cropley, Cropley, Kaufman and Runco, 2010).

However, the vast majority of thinkers tend to emphasise various qualitative characteristics of creative thinking. Cropley (1992) describes creativity as being daring and innovative (the latter seems like a tautology). The 'daring' idea is linked to risk and is picked up by educators who try techniques to encourage risk-taking approaches to learning in their students. This characteristic is pertinent to my research in higher education. It may have implications for teachers' attitudes towards mistakes or how they award marks in assessments – the idea here being that assessments which have a high loading of marks tend to discourage students experimenting and taking risks because they are disinclined to risk failing a subject for the sake of an untried idea; therefore, teachers need to be aware of this when allocating marks for tasks that aim to encourage imagination and

74   *Defining and practising creativity*

creativity. It is also easy to see how this connects to emotions about learning. But it is not only disinclination for risk-taking that needs to be taken into account. Pedagogies that allow experimentation can be framed in terms of the heroism of students taking risks; there is also potential for humour in these contexts. For example, I personally know of one educator who suggests his students prepare for exams like Clint Eastwood prepares for an encounter with his nemesis – to be ready for the unexpected! The example indicates there is room for educators to re-frame their students' attitudes to taking risks in learning situations to make them less threatening and more personally attractive, challenging and fun.

One definition of creativity as a process of thinking that is raised in the literature is the capacity to bring together previously unrelated ideas in a new juxtaposition, or to *make connections*. This key idea accords with Ricoeur's theory of 'imagination'. This work is exemplified by Koestler, who defines creativity as consisting of

> combining previously unrelated mental structures in such a way that you get more out of the emergent whole than you have put in . . . each new synthesis leads to the emergence of new patterns of relations – more complex cognitive holons[1] on higher levels of the mental hierarchy.
> (Koestler, 1978, p. 131, quoted in Taber, 2012)

The importance of forming new connections is born out in my empirical study of physics and history, and it is central to the usage of both 'reproductive' and 'productive' forms of imagination in metaphor and narrative as argued by Ricoeur, as we have seen in the last chapter. Koestler's notion of creativity connotes thinking as original to the individual who conceives of this connection, irrespective of how many others in the world may have previously entertained the thought (Nickerson, 1999, p. 394). Under his definition, *re*discoveries by individuals would be signs of their personal creativity. My point is that the process-oriented, cognitive understanding of imagination most closely accords with the subject of my research and was confirmed by pedagogy involving playful forming of links that I observed, for example, in the physics class. The sources for making connections and generating ideas – whether analogical thinking, raising new questions, formulating problems to be solved, envisaging new possibilities, making new links or generating new perspectives on old problems – are all aspects of imaginative thinking that are picked up in the literature on fostering imagination in higher education.

It is also worth pointing out that the other noun form of connection, 'connectivity', is the word chosen in the early twenty-first century to carry the notion of innovation at the social, macro scale at the heart of applications of social networking technology. This work gels with social constructivist perspectives that emphasise, as does Vygotsky, that meaning-making is mediated by skilled others (for example, peers, teachers, parents) who bring the learner into a zone of proximal development. This reinforces that the making of connections may be cognitive and may be individual, but they occur in socialised ways in particular environments. In our century, the rich platform of social networking technology has transformed the possibilities of interaction with these others, who most frequently may be peers rather than senior partners or experts. Yet, while it is true that technology can be a driver of collaboration, the same technology can just as easily be used to find precisely what you want to hear/believe and can narrow our exposure to alternative information or ideas because greater choice can mean we are more selective about what we read or view. Social networking technology can also be used to bully and to sell stuff. And 'intelligent' search engine algorithms also constrain the results of searches. My point is that technology is not necessarily a path to innovation; whether technology leads to creativity depends on the purpose for which it is used. The potential for technology to support collaboration and, therefore, innovation will be discussed in a later section on 'Individual or social origins of imagination or creativity?' and it has links to Csikszentmihalyi's work on social 'fields', which act as gatekeepers for creative ideas, which will also be discussed later in this chapter. However, for individuals, organisations *and* societies in the twenty-first century, it is clear that this potential underlines the importance of striving to adapt their practices to the rich resource of many new technologies. The finance class in which I conducted research is a good example. The technology supported simulation pedagogy and enabled students to take roles in a bank. The educator was expanding the teaching across campuses so that teams of students in Malaysia could play with their Australian-based counterparts. In addition, many higher educators use mobile telephones, clickers, Facebook or similar to check on students' understanding in class or to enable teams to work together on projects.

There is also debate and research about how various qualities in the environment can either inhibit/undermine or encourage the creative process. Amabile, for example, discusses the evidence that interruptions, or, conversely, creating familiar routines in the immediate environment, can induce, or inhibit, individual creativity (1983; Collins & Amabile, 1999). More recently, she has taken issue with education systems for narrow curricula, for lacking challenging goals and scope for students to pursue passions and for not providing sufficient time for students to really think or work together with others (2010). Amabile argues that such curricula and pedagogies constrain intrinsic motivation and are therefore detrimental to creativity. In keeping with this, in higher education as well as in school systems, there has been increasing attention to classroom and learning space design and architecture to encourage certain pedagogies.

So far we have discussed the literature on creativity as product and process (including the environment in which it occurs), with the process conception aligned more closely with cognitive characteristics that relate to imagination – my specific interest. The notion of creativity as a process of thinking about problems (even if the problem is a product of some kind) leads us to the next theme in the literature on creativity: problem *solving* and problem *formulation or finding*.

Creativity and problem solving, problem formulation or problem finding

Some researchers define creativity as a special class of problem solving characterised by novelty, unconventionality, persistence and difficulty in problem formulation (or problem finding), such as in research (Newell, Shane & Simon,

76 *Defining and practising creativity*

1962, and Mumford et al., 1994, cited in Nickerson, 1999). Here, problem solving is an identifying characteristic of creativity, regardless of how uncertain or downstream the solution or product of that creativity. Researcher motivation, for example, is associated with problem solving itself rather than its impact or outcome (Walsh et al., 2013, p. 1265).

Amabile (1983) described situations in which creativity in problem solving included a phased step-by-step process or a combination of pathways of steps, something she argues has much to offer education. However, other writers are sceptical about whether research on step-by-step processes of creativity sheds any light at all on real-world problem solving. Creativity, they say, is characterised by the formulation of an issue or a way of solving a situation that no one has noticed hitherto or that has been taken as given. Inventions, for example, are frequently conceived of by people who notice problems with existing products or practices and are motivated to overcome them. Csikszentmihalyi and Getzels (1988) distinguish between 'presented' (given) and 'discovered' problems and contend that problem *finding* is characteristic of creative thought processes. As evidence, they quote comments by Wertheimer: 'Envisaging, putting the productive question, is often a greater achievement than the solution of a set question'; Darwin: 'Looking back, I think it was more difficult to see what the problems were than to solve them'; and Einstein and Infield: 'To raise new questions, new possibilities, to regard old questions from a new angle, requires creative imagination and marks real advance in science' (1988, p. 91). In the same vein, they cite Dewey's observation that the mental operations involved in original thought are preceded by a period of diffuse dissatisfaction, a feeling that somewhere, in the dilemma one is grappling with, is an as-yet unspecified problem needing definition and specification if the dilemma is to be resolved (p. 91). This suggests, they argue, that there is a seeking, searching impulse that motivates imaginative thought, and this phase, at least, does not resemble a consecutive step-by-step process. There are implications of this finding for curriculum. If the curriculum focuses on broad coverage at the expense of depth of understanding, is it more difficult for students to gain enough knowledge to identify and formulate problems for themselves? Dewey warned about the disabling effects of surface learning on complex higher order thinking, such as creativity.

> Pupils who have stored their 'minds' with all kinds of material which they have never put to intellectual uses are sure to be hampered when they try to think. They have no practice in selecting what is appropriate, and no criterion to go by; everything is on the same static level.
>
> (Dewey, 2004 [1916], p. 152)

Superficial learning may be rectified in later years of university, or in postgraduate work, where choice in assignments or topics is often more prevalent, but how do you preserve the imagination and curiosity until then – the questioning in the mind? Similarly, curricula that fail to provide opportunities for student choice in formulating topics for investigation may provide little opportunity

Defining and practising creativity   77

for the exercise of personal creativity. This suggestive work prompted possible observations in my research sites.

Extending this line of thought, Nickerson (1999) draws a parallel between presented problems and hypothesis testing, contrasted with discovered problems and hypothesis or idea generation – which he contends is an important distinction in science (p. 394). He says that scientists are generally agreed on how hypothesis testing is done – involving the public and replicable checking of the hypothesised dependencies and other relationships among variables of interest against the results of observation and controlled experiment. Hypothesis generation is a different question and not well understood. He locates it at the 'creative' end of the spectrum, suggesting by his language ('spectrum') that he conceives them at ends of a continuum. In the debate around the problem-finding/problem-solving continuum, the terms 'imagination' and 'creativity' and the meanings they denote are closely aligned. Ricoeur's notion of 'productive' imagination is useful here. The theoretical model in the sciences, he argues (offering the example of Maxwell's representation of an electrical field as an incompressible fluid), is an imagined construct offering an image containing functional relationships that can be translated into instruments of discovery. That is, models refer to, but do not reproduce, a pre-existing original. They allude to common attributes between the model and the underlying characteristic/s to which it refers. The model is therefore a heuristic tool used to give rise to hypotheses – that can be trialled or tested.

Creative and critical thinking

The relationship between creative and critical thinking has been the subject of much research. In the past, creative and critical thinking have been understood as polar opposites. Creative thinking was characterised as expansive, divergent thinking associated with curiosity, exploration and idea generation. In contrast, critical thinking was characterised as focused, convergent, disciplined, logical and constrained. Nickerson argues, however, that they are interdependent dimensions and that education should promote both kinds of thinking (Nickerson, 1999).

Recently Bosanquet, Winchester-Seeto and Rowe (2012, p. 332) have reported that there has been a move to combine the teaching of creative and critical thinking because, while distinct, they are viewed as inseparable, dialectical forms of thinking. The logic is that creative thinking generates new ideas and possible solutions and that critical thinking assesses their validity or effectiveness, which leads to new and better solutions (Nickerson, 1999). In other words, to be a creative solution, the solution has to match the task constraints or it is novelty without effect. The terms 'creative' thinking and 'imaginative' thinking are indistinguishable in these discussions. Once again, Ricoeur's discussion of metaphors as paradigms of imagination, and scientific models as heuristic instruments for discovery, covers this ground well. Richard Dawkins's illuminating idea of the imagination as a kind of simulator, giving us the ability to run imaginary alternative models in our heads, which can be manipulated to help anticipate outcomes

78 *Defining and practising creativity*

(1989), is another example of the dialectical contribution of these two kinds of thinking. Also in Chapter 2, Lakoff and Johnson's research (1980) and the discussion of tired metaphors reinforce the idea of the interaction of imagination and critical thinking in relation to problem solving. Scientific models have to be grounded in evidence; hypotheses have to be supported by evidence: both must at some stage explain observations and results of experiments or they will be rejected. In other words, imagination needs to mingle with reason. Most important for my research is the point made by these researchers that *neither form of thinking is effective without the other*. As Lundsteen said, capturing its importance in a nutshell, 'The ability at will to make creative thinking coordinate with more logical thinking may make the difference between lunacy and creativity' (1968, p. 133, cited by Nickerson, 1999, p. 398). Ultimately the creative product has to be contextually relevant. Generating alternatives (divergent thinking) eventually gives way to assessments of value, such as aesthetics, originality and usefulness (convergent thinking). Vygotsky's view on the development of the interaction between what he calls reasoning and imagination, especially during adolescence, adds weight to the idea of a necessary interaction between creative and critical thinking as characteristic of adult creativity.

Much has been written about critical thinking in higher education, and the majority of institutions of higher education in Australia, as well as internationally, include creative and critical thinking as 'graduate attributes', which implies that course graduates will acquire those skills and attributes if they fulfil the requirements of their university course (Oliver, 2011, p. 9).

Expertise: bringing into play creativity and critical forms of thinking

The extensive literature on expertise, or mastery of a domain of activity, encompasses both the critical, evaluative skill and imagination of creative individuals. It is easy to see why. Critiquing a proposed strategy, or a practice, requires imagining all the ways it might fail or cause unanticipated consequences and planning appropriate responses. That involves two things: first, knowing the field extremely well – which involves expertise – and second, using imagination to foresee possibilities. It is not likely that one can be effectively critical without imagining a whole set of outcomes. Thus, creative or imaginative thinking and critical, analytical or evaluative thinking can be understood as dialectical, or as two sides of the same coin, and good, expert thinking requires a balance between their contributions (Johnson, 1993; Saul, 2001; Cropley, 2006). One only has to think of disaster management, aeronautical engineering, space travel, medicine, paramedicine and health care to see the importance of blending such skills. This view seems to be supported by a number of studies that report university educators incorporating both divergent and convergent, creative and critical pedagogical techniques in their teaching (for example, Cropley & Cropley, 1998; Cole, Sugioka & Yamagata-Lynch, 1999; Anderson, 2010; Onsman & Paganin, 2006). In these studies, and in the theoretical work of Dawkins and Ricoeur, the term 'imagination' refers to a specific ability to conjure an image with which to consider a possibility – which seems to be required for creativity to become productive. Hence the problem-solving/problem-formulation theme distinguishes imagination as a cognitive aspect of a larger process of 'creativity'.

Individual or social origins of imagination and creativity?

A debate in the literature on creativity is the contribution of individuals to creative fields or periods versus how much the environment or culture determines how creative that culture will be. For example, Renaissance Italy would not have happened without the discovery of Roman ruins, which yielded new knowledge about construction techniques and sculptural models and motivated young people to become artists and architects (Csikszentmihalyi, 1999, p. 320).

Csikszentmihalyi's 'systems model' of creativity provides a perspective on the relationship between individual, culture and environment. His theory proposes a tripartite interactive systems model of creativity, in which creativity emerges within complex systems. This model is comprised of: 1) the 'domain', which consists of a set of symbolic rules and procedures in the culture; 2) the 'field', or individuals in the society who act as gatekeepers to the domain; and 3) the individual creator's cognitive processes, personality traits and motivation. The model is represented in Figure 4.1.

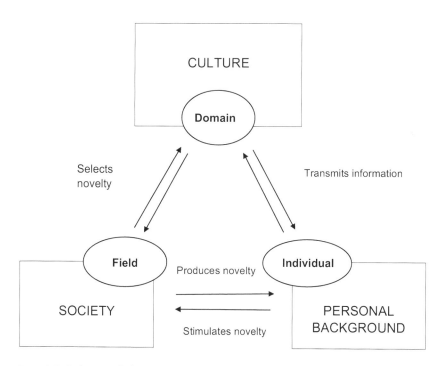

Figure 4.1 Csikszentmihalyi's systems perspective

Source: Csikszentmihalyi, 1996, adapted from Sternberg & Lubart, 1999. Reproduced with permission.

80   *Defining and practising creativity*

Csikszentmihalyi's thesis is that a set of rules and symbols of the domain must be learned by the individual, who must then produce a novel variation in the content of the domain. The experts and/or professionals in the field then judge what will be selected as 'creative'.

Csikszentmihalyi's model is helpful in conceptualising my research because, in seeking to understand what good educators do in university classroom teaching to foster imagination, we are dealing with the domain which in higher education is the disciplinary or subject area in which the skills and knowledge of disciplines and professions are learned by every new generation (Becher & Trowler, 2001, quoted in Jackson et al., 2006). However, Csikszentmihalyi's model of an 'interactive system' under-theorises how such skills and knowledge are constructed or acquired because in-person learning is not what Csikszentmihalyi is concerned with. The focus of the systems perspective is on a macro social-historical process of creativity. The language of an 'interactive system', while not underplaying the complexity of how domains of knowledge are learned by individuals, does not specify *how* the elements in the system interact. The methodology of my research aims to describe how these symbolic rules and procedures are internalised by learners and to begin to theorise it.

Csikszentmihalyi makes the interesting point that 'how much' creativity there is at any given time is not just determined by how many original individuals there are, but also by how receptive the fields are to innovation. He says: 'It follows that if one wishes to increase the frequency of creativity, it may be more advantageous to work at the level of fields than at the level of individuals' (1999, p. 327). His point is well made: If creative and effective ideas are to survive and flourish, those in the field need to recognise which of the ideas are good or productive and support – not impede – them. Otherwise many will pass unrecognised and unused. So how can we influence the field to make it more receptive? If we think about teachers as gatekeepers for innovative pedagogies – new ways of advancing quality student learning (and we can leave the notion of 'quality' open here) – then it is possible to see their ability to take up new pedagogical approaches is affected by the ecology within which they work. And teachers' approaches are influenced by a whole host of institutional and external factors interacting with each other, including, for example, professional learning programs, reward systems and incentives, recognition of teaching, funding for long-term contracts and external regulation, to name a few (Philip, 2013). Done poorly, we risk inhibiting teaching for creativity. However, whole-of-institution strategies to support teaching for creativity are beyond the scope of my study although they point to important areas in which this research can connect to others.

Finally, Csikszentmihalyi's systems theory is important for highlighting the interaction of the three areas – individual, domain and field. He focuses mainly on domain and field, which he argues are underdeveloped in theory and research, but my research focuses on the nature of what is represented by the arrows in the figure, as it were, which symbolise the two-way interaction of knowledge and learning between individuals and domain and how imaginative

Defining and practising creativity 81

approaches to disciplinary learning are cultivated there. This gap is one reason why, by emphasising forms of imagination, semantic innovation and agency, Ricoeur's theory (as discussed in Chapter 2), offers a fresh way to look at learning, particularly how to learn something new, which is so germane to higher education.

In the following section we consider how creativity (in the overarching sense) can be enhanced and discuss the foundational elements and approaches to doing so.

Can creativity be enhanced or encouraged, and if so, how?

The different definitions or characterisations of creativity, imagination and innovation discussed earlier are responsible for the divisions in the literature on whether 'it' can be enhanced or cultivated, but as mentioned earlier, the terms are often used interchangeably. The considerations in the psychological and educational literature that researchers have found are instrumental to enhancing broader 'creativity' are:

- Establishing purpose and long-term intention towards creativity.
- Encouraging the acquisition/mastery of domain-specific knowledge and skills.
- Simulating and rewarding curiosity and exploration.
- Building motivation, especially internal motivation, and environmental influences on these.
- Encouraging confidence through providing opportunities where success is within reach.
- A willingness to take risks.

These are expanded upon in the following.

Taking an intentional approach to the development of creativity

Spencer et al. (2012) found that, in a school context, a large body of work stemming from the mid-1980s to the mid-2000s focused on pedagogical strategies that foster creativity, without truly exploring the interrelationship between the creative teaching and teaching *for* creativity. Jeffrey and Craft (2004) distinguish the terms, arguing that while creative teaching may involve making learning more interesting, teaching for creativity values the agency of the learner. Jeffrey and Craft's (2004) exploration of findings since that time showed the following:

- Teachers who teach creatively employ both creative teaching and teaching for creativity according to the circumstances they consider appropriate.
- Teaching for creativity may well arise spontaneously from teaching situations in which it was not specifically intended.

82   *Defining and practising creativity*

- Teaching for creativity is more likely to emerge from contexts in which teachers are teaching creatively even if the teacher was not planning to teach for creativity.

(Spencer et al., 2012, pp. 64–65)

In a higher education context, Trigwell, Prosser and Waterhouse (1999) reported links between the ways higher education teachers approach teaching and the ways their students approach learning that can lead students towards surface or deep approaches. This includes complex thinking approaches, such as thinking creatively.

Creativity training programs

Creativity training programs are one technique intentionally designed to foster creativity. Some of these programs incorporate concepts related specifically to imagination as discussed in the last chapter, such as making novel connections and combinations usually in contexts where they are applied in projects that require a whole set of skills to come together.

Jeffrey's (2006a) large ethnographic study involved a creative learning project which sought to find common pedagogical features in primary, secondary and adult learning contexts across nine European countries. His findings stress the importance of agency of the learner in the pedagogy used. He used a common methodological framework across the sites and a criterion of learning and teaching by Wood (1990) involving 'relevance', 'ownership of knowledge', 'control of learning processes' and 'innovation'. The framework compared the context, the situational interactions, the students' cognitive explorations, the students' subjective reactions and what kind of creative agency was released through creative teaching contexts. For Jeffrey, a teaching 'innovation' resulted from a new combination of known factors or from the introduction of a new factor into a prevailing situation. The teaching innovation 'events' involved in these creativity training programs included school environment improvements, coordinated international projects, computer toy constructions for major competitions, business case studies, re-enactments of social issues and local histories and the examination of lives from different cultures. They all passed through well-defined stages of conceptualisation: preparation, planning, divergence, convergence, consolidation and celebration. He found that the common practices used in the projects to teach creativity were strategies where teachers constructed real and critical events, incorporated external collaboration, used spaces innovatively and modelled their own creativity for students. The project findings were that the common characteristics of creative learning were intellectual enquiry (that is, being inventive, experimentation, possibility thinking, manipulation, comparison, 'what if' speculation); engaged productivity; bringing their own experience and imagination to knowledge-based engagements; taking ownership and control of learning; using imagination with intention; risk-taking; co-participation; acting recursively (starting again and patterning); and deliberately developing competence after reflection in process and product reviews. Jeffrey stresses the meaning and joy, pride and ownership, in the way the students experienced knowledge and the products of their labour, which fostered a sense of belonging and social identity (p. 410). An interesting finding was that contestation of knowledge was seen as a legitimate aspect of knowledge (p. 409). As the research was on special cross-disciplinary programs, not on everyday learning, it arguably undervalues the creativity-enhancing possibilities of everyday disciplinary curriculum and pedagogies and de-emphasises domain-relevant skills and concepts, but the effects on students' experience of their learning highlighted aspects which were useful points of comparison with my fieldwork observations.

Encouraging the acquisition / mastery of domain-specific knowledge and skills

Creative contributions presuppose expertise in domain-relevant skills. The extensive literature on expertise emphasises the acquisition and mastery of domain-relevant skills and knowledge and, if appropriate, materials. It follows that fostering the ability to make a creative contribution in a field requires the cultivation of foundational expertise in related techniques, knowledge or skills. This is of great importance in higher education, which is educating the next generation of professionals and researchers. This point refers to the obvious fact that one is not likely to make a contribution, for example, to an understanding of disease, unless one has acquired knowledge of cell biology; one is unlikely to write good plays without deep engagement with theatre. Likewise one is unlikely to be able to design prosthetic limbs without knowledge of forces, chemistry of materials, kinesiology and experience of patients' needs (Csikszentmihalyi, 1996; Gardner, 1993; Amabile, 1983). My overall point is that expertise is a necessary but not sufficient condition for creativity; expertise in domain-relevant skills has to be balanced with a contribution from imagination for there to be a creative outcome.

Stimulating and rewarding curiosity and exploration

Csikszentmihalyi (1999) has identified the stimulation and reward of curiosity and exploration as important to enhancing creativity. In higher education, offering choice in student assignments is often seen to be the place where opportunities for exercising personal choice and discovery can be built into the learning and teaching program. When practised, it also offers students some experience of *problem finding* and of the personal rewards that can ensue.

Other teaching considerations, techniques and strategies that facilitate imagination and creativity include modelling creative personal attributes like inquisitiveness, openness to evidence, concentration, persistence and sometimes putting problems aside for a time to gestate. Striking a balance between challenge and support is also an important consideration in offering chances to explore a topic. Many of these attributes were observed in the teaching sites of my research.

Building motivation

Building motivation, especially internal motivation, as opposed to external or extrinsic motivators such as rewards or incentives like grades or awards, for which the evidence is mixed (Collins & Amabile, 1999), is an important theme in the psychological literature on enhancing creativity. Amabile's definition of creative attributes includes motivation as one of four main aspects which combine cognitive and social-cultural aspects: domain-relevant skills, creative processes, intrinsic motivation and the 'creativity relevant skills' of the individual (Amabile, 1983). In addition, because creative people need to be able to persevere in the face of complexity and unresolvability, the matter of how they maintain motivation is important (McWilliam & Haukka, 2008).

Another strand in the literature on building motivation focuses on environmental factors where creativity is normalised and the organisation of schools and other organisations to develop habits of mind conducive to creativity. (Claxton, Edwards & Scale-Constantinou, 2006; Amabile, 1983, 2010; Collins & Amabile, 1999). A progressive example in relation to the school sector is the Creativity, Culture and Education's Creative Partnerships Program in the UK, which developed a Creative School Development Framework (CSDF) including a detailed planning form, to assist schools to systematically develop and support an environment conducive to creativity (CCE, 2010). The planning form focuses on five dimensions: leadership; curriculum; staff learning and development; and environment and resources which includes different learning spaces and the public display of products of learning. The purpose of the tool is that school leadership uses it to monitor their progress from year to year using level descriptors, with the involvement of staff and pupils.

Encouraging confidence

Encouraging confidence is important to enhancing creativity through providing opportunities where success is within reach. Because creativity can involve daring to be different, a certain level of self-confidence is necessary to be comfortable with uncertainty and sensible risk-taking (Lucas et al., 2013, p. 17). This factor is linked to attitudes to risk-taking, discussed in the following.

Risk-taking

A willingness to take risks, including by promoting beliefs that creativity is subject to effort, persistence and motivation and is not dictated by genetically determined capabilities beyond our control (Nickerson, 1999), is a consideration in the literature on enhancing creativity and is related to enabling personal attributes such as confidence (as discussed prior) and persistence. Learning how to manage risk, rather than simplistically taking risks, will be more important in some fields of higher education such as surgery, patient care or finance.

Imagination and higher education teachers' views

The four aspects of 'creativity' most congruent with a surveyed group of United Kingdom national teaching fellows' definitions of creativity were 'imagination', 'seeing unusual connections', 'original ideas' and 'combining ideas'. Responding to a dearth of knowledge about teachers' views of creativity, a report entitled *Facilitating creativity in higher education* (2006), commissioned by the United Kingdom Higher Education Academy and conducted by the Creativity Centre, discussed the views of national teaching fellows in England. National teaching fellows are academics who have won national teaching awards. The study involved an email survey of 94 national teaching fellows and 21 interviews. Key findings were that teachers believed that creative teaching facilitates creative learning. The four aspects of 'creativity' – 'imagination', 'seeing unusual connections', 'original ideas' and 'combining ideas' – align closely with Ricoeur's conceptualisation that we saw in Chapter 2, confirming its usefulness as an underpinning theory. Once again, the findings illustrate the interchangeability of these terms as understood and used by higher educators.

The UK study also reported that approximately 92 per cent of surveyed fellows saw creativity as a capacity that could be developed rather than as a rare gift and that over 90 per cent of respondents aimed to develop students' creative capacities. They reported using a range of approaches to do this, including stimuli for imaginative thinking or heuristic strategies; the provision of a suitable context for creative work; supportive factors, such as the relationship between tutors and students; encouraging the development of personality characteristics; learning skills for use in creative work; setting tasks that require creativity; and developing students' motivation.

An interesting but not surprising finding was that 60.6 per cent of respondents did *not* believe that the most academically successful students were the most creative (McWilliam & Dawson, 2007), perhaps indicating you can still usually rote learn your way to academic success. Assessment of creativity was identified as a vexing issue by the participants. In contrast to their overwhelming agreement on the importance of students' creativity and that it should be developed, only *one quarter* of fellows undertook some form of formal assessment of it and only *one third* undertook informal assessment of creative achievement. Given what is known about the impact of assessment on where and how students direct their attention to learning, and their study time (Nicol & Macfarlane-Dick, 2006; Boud, 2006), the fact that creativity is generally not included in assessment probably sends a clear message to students that it is not important in the domain studied and not relevant to course learning outcomes. The assessment of creativity and imagination matters because, for better or worse, in the twenty-first century, evaluation has developed into an unquestioned arbiter of value, whether of students' achievements, institutional quality or national educational competitiveness (Broadfoot, 2000, p. xi). So how are we to interpret higher education teachers' responses here? Might it be that teachers are responding to their students by reducing the risk-taking associated with creative thinking by separating creative

86 *Defining and practising creativity*

tasks from the high-stakes assessment (assessment that is worth a high percentage of marks in terms of the total grade)?

An Australian project mirroring the UK study was conducted in 2007 by Erica McWilliam and Shane Dawson for the Carrick Institute (the equivalent of what was later called the Australian Learning and Teaching Council and, later still, the Australian Government Office for Learning and Teaching) entitled *Understanding creativity: a survey of 'creative' academic teachers* (2007). The Australian study involved a survey of 37 national teaching award recipients. It found that teaching award winners' views largely reflected those of their UK counterparts, not least in their belief that creativity was a skill or attribute that could be developed. Similar to their UK colleagues, over 90 per cent said that through their teaching they aimed to develop students' creative capacities and reported using much the same range of approaches to doing this. Interestingly, slightly more – 64.8 per cent – thought that the most academically successful students were *not* the most creative. In addition, 77.8 per cent agreed that encouraging students' creativity does enhance their academic performance.

McWilliam and Dawson (2007) describe the UK and Australian educators' conception of creativity as containing a mix of what they term 'first generation' and 'second generation' creative products, ideas or objects. Characteristics associated with each generation are shown in Table 4.1.

McWilliam's notion of two traditions of thinking about creativity has been picked up by others. 'First' generation refers to the tradition that construes creativity as an outcome of individual processes of intuitive, or subjective, ideation; 'second' generation understands creativity as an outcome of social processes with generic applicability (2009). She argues that assessment tasks that ask students to engage with cultural productions that might, for example, combine words, images, sound, artefacts and ideas in new and meaningful ways and then to work in teams to evaluate them in terms of their perceived usefulness build on second generation ideas (McWilliam, 2007, p. 8). McWilliam, Dawson and Tan's (2008)

Table 4.1 First and second generation creativity concepts

First generation creativity concepts	*Second generation creativity concepts*
Singular, an individual capacity	Plural, team based
Serendipitous, non-economic	'Hard' or an economic driver
Spontaneous, arising from the inner self	Environmentally derived or supported
"Outside the box"	Requiring rules and boundaries
Arts based	Trans-disciplinary
Something out of nothing	Something to something else
Natural or innate	Learnable
Not amenable to teaching	Teachable
Not assessable	Assessable

Source: McWilliam & Dawson, 2007, p. 4.

Defining and practising creativity   87

research tried to evidence creative processes (specifically cognitive playfulness and team orientation) empirically by tracking students' networking activity (the way they 'flock together') as they used digital tools to work in creative teams. Her emphasis on second generation notions reminds us to value pedagogies that engage communities of learners in social processes to produce ideas.

This perspective proved useful in my data interpretation and analysis of classroom practices, such as when individual educators or the faculty/institution were found to enhance students' learning communities, as well as for noticing what students do with domain-relevant imaginative ideas in practical forums. It led me to ask questions like: Are there opportunities to communicate, share and embed new ideas among peers, key players and stakeholders? This also takes seriously Csikszentmihalyi's argument that it may be more productive to foster the receptiveness of gatekeepers in the field to new ideas. Developing students' receptivity to new ideas means they may be more likely to be open and receptive in whatever fields they work in, in the future − whether as generators or part of the field of gatekeepers − which may lead to innovative applications of those ideas.

Similar to the United Kingdom, higher educator teachers thought that assessment regimes acted as constraints on developing creativity. Reasons given included that it was not the process of creativity that was being assessed but rather the product of inspired or imaginative thinking. Other factors identified as inhibitors to creative teaching and assessment were large classes and poor teaching, institutional policies on workload, teaching environments and the amount of time students engage in paid employment and their reduced study time (McWilliam & Dawson, 2007). Lack of time to plan teaching, devaluation of teaching because of an emphasis on research, concerns about plagiarism, disinclination to take risks because students often respond negatively to novel forms of assessment and teachers being disinclined to risk poor student evaluations of teaching are other possible inhibitors. McWilliam and Dawson reason rightly, I think, that regardless of how it is interpreted, the findings reinforce the need to address the assessment of creativity in higher education and to examine the relationship between creative ability and academic achievement (2007, see also Looney, 2009). The way in which the academic teachers not only provided opportunities for imaginative engagement by their students, but also included it in assessment, became important points of consideration in my interpretations of data.

While these studies raise important issues related to teaching in higher education, the problem with focusing on educators' views is that there can be a gap between what is espoused as valuable and what is practised. For example, some teachers may not realise they are fostering imagination because in their eyes they are just practising good teaching; they might therefore fail to articulate how they do it. McWilliams categorises teachers' approaches to encouraging imagination as including activities such as role plays, scenarios, writing stories and discussion forums; teaching strategies, such as problem-based learning and reflection tools; student support, such as a balanced mix of challenge and scaffolding approaches;

88 *Defining and practising creativity*

provocation; and team work. It is not clear from the discussion exactly how these involve imagination. The list does not distinguish between imaginative synthesis and critical review and reflection and conflates team work with collaboration (team work can sometimes be several people tackling different tasks on a problem and involve no collaborative development of ideas). By studying cases, my research sought to provide some exactitude about what is imaginative, how the approaches cultivate imagination and some nuanced detail about how it is related to disciplinary learning. The examples of the physics class group thinking through a difficult concept together, and the purposive support of collaborative learning by having a physics student common room, are both cases in point.

McWilliam frames imagination as the cognitive component in a wider social activity of creativity that involves the creation of something new and useful out of something received from the culture or social setting. This is a commonly accepted definition (Klausen, 2010). While the other insights provided by McWilliam are valuable, her preference for second generation creativity is problematic. It appears to me to set up an inside/outside dualism as the theoretical basis from which to approach the question of the role imagination (assumed to be a purely inner, mental force) can play in student learning within higher education. Could it be that the social or outer properties of creativity are given greater stress in the definition of the entity 'creativity' because they are more easily measurable? The dichotomy also obscures the 'outer' resources of language, disciplinary concepts and 'mindtools' that structure and transform imaginative activity into which – in Polany's language – we extend our minds, as well as the dialectical interaction of the inner and outer processes when learners recognise demands in tasks and use those tools to think and approach/solve problems (as discussed extensively in Chapter 3).

Creative imagination and disciplinary learning in higher education

One progressive development in curriculum in higher education aligns closely with the design of my research. The UK Higher Education Academy's 'Imaginative Curriculum Project' created 'a network of practitioners who believe that designing a curriculum is a creative process in which knowledge, skill, imagination and passion for a subject, come together'. They recognise that creativity is generally unrecognised and undervalued in undergraduate higher education in the UK despite its pervasiveness in institutional statements of graduate attributes. Its proponents say, 'If creativity is central to being, then higher education needs to understand what it means to be creative in the many domains it embraces, for example historian, biologist, lawyer, engineer or any other disciplinary field of endeavour' (Jackson & Shaw, 2006). It calls for the 'need to raise awareness of what creativity means in these different contexts and encourage educators to support forms of learning that will enable students to develop the forms of creativity that are most appropriate for their field(s) of study and future careers' (p. 2). This reflects the strong disciplinary focus that is a common reflection of academic identity. My research study falls well within its remit by seeking to illuminate what imagination and creativity look like in four cases of non arts-based disciplinary or professional domains – the 'hard' science of physics; a key humanities discipline – history; an applied professional course, finance; and an experimental health science subject, pharmaceutical science – in a qualitative study of classes using the methods of ethnography.

The Higher Education Academy Imaginative Curriculum Study, 'Subject perspectives on creativity: a preliminary synthesis' (Jackson & Shaw, 2006), uses a definition of creativity from Csikszentmihalyi's systems theory as socially and culturally constructed. It took two approaches to elaborating the particular meaning of 'creativity' in higher education and how it is 'operationalised' in each discipline. Firstly, 18 subject benchmarking statements were examined using an evaluation tool to identify aspects of student learning that could be described as directly or implicitly 'creative'. They found that creativity was not something with which the subject benchmarking groups were much concerned (p. 5). The exceptions to this were: acknowledgement of the need to operate in complex and ambiguous settings; systematic processes of inquiry; and activities that had potential to nurture creativity, such as project/assignment work, personal development planning and reflection.

They sought to dig deeper into the omission of creativity from subject benchmarking statements and so surveyed, by email, academics in four disciplines, history, earth and environmental sciences, engineering and social work, and asked them six questions: What does it mean to be creative in your discipline? What is it about your subject that stimulates teachers and students to be creative? How do higher education teachers in your field enable students to be creative? How do teachers in your field recognise or assess creativity? What are the barriers to creativity? And, is creativity valued in your discipline? Central to their findings were that while the nature of problems in each discipline differs, finding, formulating and working with problems in their discipline and communicating their solution was the key focus for creative thinking and action in all disciplines. This was particularly the case where problems were new, unpredictable and emergent (p. 13). Jackson and Shaw developed a framework representing the use of the imagination in disciplinary problem-working contexts. The framework was a 'generate-explore-synthesis-solution finding' cycle that is enacted iteratively (p. 14). The researchers say the use of 'imagination' – which they define as the faculty or action of producing ideas, especially mental images of what is not present or not been experienced – took on special meaning in disciplinary contexts. Imagination as a thinking process was understood as a source of personal inspiration, something that sustained motivation throughout a work project; it generates ideas from which creative solutions are selected. In their opinion, imagination facilitated interpretations which cannot be understood by facts or observation alone. Knowledge also provided the context for the working of imagination. They said the concerns and interests that both academics and non-academics encounter stimulated imagination.

These notions share key ideas with Ricoeur's notion of imagination. First, imaginative constructs are conceived as non-existent models/constructs for

90   *Defining and practising creativity*

things (the production of ideas or images that are not present or have not been experienced). Second, it appeared that curiosity and depth of interest ignited the imagination, which motivated forming analogies, which can lead to answers, and so on. However, Ricoeur emphasises the novel combinatorial activity of the more generative 'productive imagination', which offers a model or an image which schematises the *relations* between things. This is a stronger, more precise notion than a 'mental image' *of* things, which is closer to the 'reproductive imagination' that he was moving away from. Ricoeur's distinction between reproductive and productive imagination allows his theory a more complex relationship to knowledge, to theory and, therefore, to learning in higher education than is to be found in the higher educators' views.

The evaluation tool used in the Imaginative Curriculum Project research contained four categories for 'support for creativity in students' learning' – student thinking abilities; student ideas; student imagination and originality; and student activities with the potential to promote creativity – and yet, unfortunately, the student voice is absent from the study. The category 'student imagination and originality' contained the indicators: 'development of new knowledge'; 'development of new practice(s)'; 'making of new knowledge connections'; 'transfer and application of learning in new contexts'; and 'engages in systematic process of enquiry'. Strangely, 'generation of ideas', 'reflection of ideas', 'divergent and convergent thinking' and 'lateral thinking', which one might have expected to be included in 'imagination', were spread across two other categories of 'creativity': 'student thinking abilities' and 'student ideas'. While I agree that 'imagination' can be understood as a subset of a broader, encompassing process of 'creativity', I believe these dubious categories and distinctions are indications of a deficiency with the study that limits its usefulness. It lacked a strong theoretical framework that links imagination with cognition. My research supplies this connection by linking Ricoeur's theory with Clark's extended cognition thesis. In addition, by using observation notes and data from student assignments, my research also tries to close the loop and supply the student learning viewpoint: through consideration of products of learning, such as student assignments, and through focus group interviews. It therefore includes empirical data about a relationship between teaching and its effect on the learning, and learning experience, of the students.

Instruction in imaginative processes: action research reflective studies by higher education teachers

Some action research reflective studies by higher education teachers into their own teaching investigate teaching for imaginative capacity in a disciplinary context. Two studies are relevant to my research findings because they emphasise discovery of the not-yet-known and writing as a technique to promote the personal identifications with knowledge.

Onsman and Paganin (2006) argue that post-graduate research supervision should enable students to be creative in their pursuit of coming to know things that are as yet unknown. They describe examples of their own post-graduate students whose progress on their thesis in quantum physics and neuro-cognition is unblocked through a process of utilising what they call 'perturbative analogies' or distant field analogies. For example, quantum physics students were asked to compare the properties of an orange (or any random thing) to a wave-mechanical problem. Onsman and Paganin's point is that the learner's desire for schema category resolution demands he/she be creative by positing a vast array of relationships – the unfruitful ones can be systematically discarded later. They found that by asking students to consider the two hitherto unrelated things analogically, substantial insights are produced which can move the thesis along. Moreover, it inducts the students into a process of analogical reasoning that will be commonly used in their professional lives. This action research case study is an example of a pedagogy involving metaphoric analogical relationships, which clearly involve imagination and in fact combine imagination and critical thinking. Their pedagogy involved a combination of divergent (imaginative) and convergent techniques.

In a reflective self-study discussed earlier in Chapter 1, Anderson (2010) combined traditional analytical intent with creative writing strategies in her teaching of final year French. She engaged her students in a year-long series of writing assignments (specifically, poetry writing in the form of the French Symbolist poets; journaling; critical comparative work; translation; a creative piece on a freely chosen topic in the style of Roland Barthes's *Mythologies*; accompanying critical commentaries on their work) that, while encouraging precise and analytic judgement as well as a deep knowledge of the resources of language, engaged the students' personal experience, enthusiasm and interest in a way that brought their knowledge into a closer relationship with themselves and their identity. She describes one of her aims, 'Higher education should ideally, as much current thinking argues, enable student learners to take themselves seriously as critical persons in the making'. She argues that disciplinary knowledge and understanding of French language, literature and culture can be fostered through acts of creativity and imagination hand in hand with the more traditional tools of analytical dissection (2010, p. 220).

These studies are practitioner-based action research studies, which have in common educators' attempts to cultivate the creative imagination of their students through blending domain-specific knowledge with imaginative and critical thinking. They do this by 'designing in' to class activities and assessments, creating ways to provoke ideas, finding problems worth investigating, and actively making connections through analogies and writing in different forms. Joining student identity with knowledge was also a theme they share: *bringing students into relationship with their own knowledge* through writing as a research practice. My research, while sharing the aims of these academic teachers – to illuminate pedagogical approaches that attempt to foster the fusion of imagination with learning and (multiple non arts-based) disciplinary competence – differed in that the researcher (me) was an outsider to the educators' discipline and that a de-familiarisation and reconstruction of context may contribute further insights.

92 *Defining and practising creativity*

Beghetto and Kaufman (2009) support the conclusions of these educator-researchers in their emphasis on the simultaneous development of academic knowledge and creativity. They contend that academic learning and creativity should not be split into separate paths. They also argue that theories of learning need to better account for new insights and creative activity (p. 299). They pose a metaphor of 'intellectual estuaries' in which multiple perspectives, and personal interpretations about them, converge in students' efforts to develop new individual insights, deeper understanding of some curricular topic in any discipline and ultimately transformative education. They provide two examples of pedagogical strategies that support intellectual estuaries: exploratory talk and the use of Socratic seminars. Theirs was a school-based study, but it underlined the importance of the mediation of language and a social learning context, which is supported by theorists such as Vygotsky, Ricoeur and Lave and Wenger. Their research calls for a theory of learning that includes creativity and so can account for the creation of new knowledge, not just the learning of existing knowledge, and indeed my theoretical framework sought to supply this. While my research is positioned in this space of pedagogical strategies that foster the fusion of imagination and academic learning, my analysis is unique in that it is informed by Ricoeur's theory of imagination and Clark's thesis of extended cognition to interpret the meaning of what is going on in teaching and in learning. In this way it tries to account for higher education's role in preparing people capable of creating new knowledge and practices.

Cole et al.'s (1999) qualitative study of a naturalistic classroom environment that supported creativity was conducted in a higher education setting. Their data derived from course syllabi, instructor and student interviews and classroom observations which they developed into a four-part framework of key leverage factors. These factors were the student-teacher relationship, the method of assessment, the creative processes taught and the students' responses to these processes. Their findings were distributed across four themes. The first theme was the teacher's belief in the power of teacher-student relationships to enhance students' imagination. (Relationship formation strategies included learning students' names, listening attentively to their opinions and building rapport and making themselves available for consultation.) Second, their chosen method of assessment de-emphasized grades and standardisation because they can be a hindrance to students' risk-taking. Instead, assessments emphasised intrinsic motivation, effort and reflection. The third finding supported the value of a classroom environment in which there was 'no one right answer' and where independence, experimentation and risk-taking were encouraged. Students reported that because they weren't searching for the right answer, they considered many ideas and perspectives than they would have otherwise (pp. 287–289). Fourth, overt instruction in creative processes, such as divergent and convergent thinking, was an essential element. Students were guided in steps and strategies that included brainstorming to generate a wide range of ideas before selecting one for refinement; thumbnail sketches in which they visually experimented with ideas through drawing rough sketches; using matrices to write and juxtapose ideas in cells to help draw relationships between them; and small group work. The researchers found the students benefited from understanding creativity as a process, even a step-by-step process, rather than one spontaneous moment in time (pp. 288, 290). The fourth finding was the most instructive for my research: the use of artefacts/tools to support dialectical blending of imagination and critical thinking and the need for a balance of contributions from both of these. The deployment of diagrams, matrices and language in writing and discussion was supported particularly by my observations of pedagogy in the pharmaceutical science, physics and finance classes where students used multiple modes to compose understanding.

Imagination expressed through narrative in educational and professional contexts

In the literature I critically engaged with, there are a few studies in higher education contexts which refer to Paul Ricoeur's notions of the imagination, particularly his notion of narrative as an expression of imagination. All are connected to the notion of formation of identity, including changes in identity. This suggests that the agency of the learner includes his/her perception of self or identity.

Cole (2009) recommended storytelling as an educational technique to increase compliance to infection control practices among health-care workers. Because stories engaged with the values and identities of staff, Cole found that it was more effective than didactic instruction at modifying behaviour. Cole found it can be a means of encouraging diverse and busy health-care workers to better engage with practices that can remain hidden because they are difficult to discuss.

Three further studies applied Ricoeur's idea about narrative and identity/ies of self in secondary and tertiary classes. McCulloch (2009) used what Ricoeur refers to as narrative's characteristic of reconfiguring chronology into meaningfully connecting events in the personal biographies of teachers transitioning into education faculties in higher education. Solomon-Minarchi (2010) found that authentic storytelling occurred in secondary classroom communities that engaged in reciprocal narrative practices between students and teachers containing both participating storytellers and attentive listeners. The research suggested that engaging in active learning in conjunction with reflective learning provided an ideal scenario for adolescent students to articulate how their narrative identities were changing. Geoff Madoc-Jones (in Egan, Stout & Takaya, 2007) argued that Ricoeur's theory provides language-arts secondary school educators with ways of examining text as reconstituted meaning that take into account historical textual conventions but are grounded in the phenomenon of readers' appropriation of the text and their experience of the self as they read. Education is prospective and looks to the future as well as the past, he says, because the self expresses her/his will, which is in part shaped and formed by the imaginative works s/he has engaged with. 'Studying the works of the past enriches the memory, but the will is tempered in imaginative practices that enable students to express their own projects concerned with tomorrow', he says (p. 77).

How are we to make sense of these studies about the influence of narrative/ stories on the formation of identity in such wide-ranging fields as infection

94 *Defining and practising creativity*

control procedures, developing adolescent identity and language arts? The active work of combining heterogeneous ideas appears to involve many aspects of the whole person, which is, I believe, why it is important to deep forms of learning. That it engages the identity of the learners in these studies seems to be because it engages the whole person. Nussbaum has described this well when she says narrative engages 'the keen responsiveness of intellect, imagination and feeling to the particularity of a situation' (quoted in Barr & Steele, 2003, p. 511). For Arendt, the critical detachment involved in narrative requires one to 'train[ing] the imagination to go visiting' (1982, p. 43). Stories invite readers not only to assimilate different perspectives, but to converse with those imagined perspectives of others and to consider how they differ from her or his own. The power of storytelling is that it can unleash the imagination and engage us with thinking, throwing the reader from what is written about to a reflexive contemplation of its application to present and future courses of action. This is exactly Ricoeur's point, that narrative engages the productive imagination by helping us think about and model alternative possibilities of action and meaning in the practical domain in the world. The implications of these studies are that the identity of students should figure in the teachers' pedagogy if the teachers are engaging students' imagination.

My research seeks to throw light on imagination's teachable aspects in higher education, a system which prepares learners to be capable of developing – and ideally, to have a propensity to develop – new ideas, knowledge and practices. Because these dispositions are needed to find and offer approaches to solving the problems in complex societies and organisations in which citizens operate, we do not want imagination to be perceived as belonging solely to the arts, but for its role in thinking, and in effective action, to be better understood. My research, the outcome of which is found in Chapters 5, 6, 7 and 8, is positioned in this fairly sparsely researched area and seeks to clarify the generativity of Ricoeur's notion of productive imagination and its importance and role to non arts-based higher education disciplines/professions.

In the next chapter, the theoretical lenses discussed in the last three chapters are brought to bear in the first ethnography of a fourth year undergraduate quantum physics class.

Note

1 A word coined by Koestler which the *Macquarie dictionary* defines as 'a whole or individual entity which contains within it entities which also function as whole entities, as the human body which is a complete system but contains within it other systems such as the nervous system, digestive system, etc'.

References

Amabile, T. M. (1983). *The social psychology of creativity*. New York: Springer-Verlag.
Amabile, T. M. (2010). *The three threats to creativity*. HBR Blog. Retrieved from http://blogs.hbr.org/2010/11/the-three-threats-to-creativit/

Anderson, K. (2010). The whole learner: The role of imagination in developing disciplinary understanding. *Arts and Humanities in Higher Education, 9*(2), 205–221.

Arendt, H. (1982). *Lectures on Kant's political philosophy.* Chicago: University of Chicago Press.

Barr, J., & Steele, T. (2003). Revaluing the enlightenment: Reason and imagination. *Teaching in Higher Education, 8*(4), 505–515.

Becher, T., & Trowler, P. R. (2001). *Academic tribes and territories: Intellectual inquiry and the culture of disciplines.* Buckingham: The Society for Research into Higher and Open University.

Beghetto, R. A., & Kaufman, J. C. (2009). Intellectual estuaries: Connecting learning and creativity in programs of advanced academics. *Journal of Advanced Academics, 20*(2), 296–324.

Bosanquet, A., Winchester-Seeto, T., & Rowe, A. (2012). Social inclusion, graduate attributes and higher education curriculum. *Journal of Academic Language and Learning, 6*(2), 73–87.

Boud, D. (2006, August). Aligning assessment with long-term learning. *Assessment & Evaluation in Higher Education, 31*(4), 399–413.

Broadfoot, P. (2000). Preface. In A. Filer (Ed.), *Assessment: Social practice and social product* (pp. ix–ixxx). London: Routledge Falmer.

Catmull, E., & Wallace, A. (2014). *Creativity Inc.: Overcoming the unseen forces that stand in the way of true inspiration.* London: Bantam Press.

Claxton, G., Edwards, L., & Scale-Constantinou, V. (2006). Cultivating creative mentalities: A framework for education. *Thinking Skills and Creativity, 1,* 57–61.

Cole, D. G., Sugioka, H. L., & Yamagata-Lynch, L. C. (1999). Supportive classroom environments for creativity in higher education. *Journal of Creative Behaviour, 33*(4), 277–293.

Cole, M. (2009). Storytelling: Its place in infection control education. *Journal of Infection Prevention, 10*(5), 154–158. doi:10.1177/1757177409341425

Collins, M. A., & Amabile, T. A. (1999). Motivation and creativity. In R. J. Sternberg (Ed.), *Handbook of creativity* (pp. 297–312). Cambridge: Cambridge University Press.

Craft, A. (1999). *Creativity across the primary curriculum: Framing and developing practice.* London: Routledge Falmer.

Craft, A. (2003). The limits to creativity in education: Dilemmas for the educator. *British Journal of Educational Studies, 51*(2), 113–127.

Creativity, Culture & Education (2010). *Change schools CSDF planning form: Guidance, descriptors and form.* Retrieved from https://creativeweb.creative-partnerships.com/.

Cropley, A. J. (1992). *More ways than one: Fostering creativity.* Norwood, NJ: Ablex.

Cropley, A. J. (2006). In praise of convergent thinking. *Creativity Research Journal, 18*(3), 391–404. doi:10.1207/s15326934crj1803_13

Cropley, D., & Cropley, A. O. (1998). *Teaching engineering students to be creative: Program and outcomes.* Paper presented at the Waves of Change: Proceedings of the 10th Australasian Conference on Engineering Education, 5th Australasian Women in Engineering Forum, 5th National Conference on Teaching Engineering Designers, Rockhampton, QLD: Central Queensland University, James Goldston Faculty of Engineering and Physical Systems.

Cropley, D. H., Cropley, A. J., Kaufman, J. C., & Runco, M. A. (2010). *The dark side of creativity.* New York: Cambridge University Press.

Csikszentmihalyi, M. (1996). Where is creativity? In *Creativity: Flow and the psychology of discovery and invention* (pp. 23–50). New York: Harper Collins Publishers.

Csikszentmihalyi, M. (1999). Implications of a systems perspective for the study of creativity. In R. Sternberg (Ed.), *Handbook of creativity* (pp. 313–335). Cambridge: Cambridge University Press.

Csikszentmihalyi, M., & Getzels, J. W. (1988). Creativity and problem finding in art. In F. G. Farley & R. W. Neperud (Eds.), *The foundations of aesthetics, art, and art education* (pp. 91–106). New York: Praeger.

96 *Defining and practising creativity*

Dewey, J. (1958). *Experience and nature.* New York: Dover Publications.

Dewey, J. (2004). *Democracy and education.* Mineola, NY: Dover Publications.

Egan, K., Stout, M., & Takaya, K. (Eds.). (2007). *Teaching and learning outside the box: Inspiring imagination across the curriculum.* New York: Teachers College Press.

Florida, R. L. (2002). *The rise of the creative class.* New York: Basic Books.

Fryer, M. (2006). Facilitating creativity in higher education: A brief account of National Teaching Fellows' views. In N. Jackson, M. Oliver, M. Shaw & J. Wisdom (Eds.), *Developing creativity in higher education: An imaginative curriculum.* Hoboken: Taylor & Francis.

Gardner, H. (1993). *Multiple intelligences: The theory in practice* (2nd ed.). New York: Basic Books.

Harris, A. (2014). *The creative turn: Toward a new aesthetic imaginary.* Rotterdam: Sense Publishers.

Harris, A. (2016). *Creativity and education.* London: Palgrave Macmillan.

Jackson, N. J. (Ed.). (2011). *Learning for a complex world: A lifewide concept of learning, education and personal development.* Bloomington, IN: AuthorHouse.

Jackson, N. J., Oliver, M., Shaw, M., & Wisdom, J. (Eds.). (2006). *Developing creativity in higher education: An imaginative curriculum.* Hoboken: Taylor & Francis Ltd eLibrary.

Jackson, N. J., & Shaw, M. (2006). *Imaginative curriculum study: Subject perspectives on creativity: A preliminary synthesis.* Retrieved from www.palatine.ac.uk/files/998.pdf

Jeffrey, B. (Ed.). (2006a). *Creative learning practices: European experiences.* London: The Tufnell Press.

Jeffrey, B. (2006b). Creative teaching and learning: Towards a common discourse and practice. *Cambridge Journal of Education, 36*(3), 399–414.

Jeffrey, B., & Craft, A. (2004). Teaching creatively and teaching for creativity: Distinctions and relationships. *Educational Studies, 30*(1), 77–87.

Johnson, M. (1993). Moral imagination. In *Moral imagination: Implications of cognitive science for ethics.* Chicago: University of Chicago Press.

Klausen, S. H. (2010). The notion of creativity revisited: A philosophical perspective on creativity research. *Creativity Research Journal, 22*(4), 347–360. doi:10.1080/10400419.2010.523390

Koestler, A. (1964). *The act of creation.* New York: Macmillan.

Lakoff, G., & Johnson, M. (1980). *Metaphors we live by.* Chicago: University of Chicago Press.

Lehrer, J. (2012). *Imagine: The science of creativity.* Melbourne, Australia: The Text Publishing Company.

Looney, J. W. (2009). *Assessment and innovation in education.* OECD Education Working Papers: OECD Publishing. Retrieved from http://dx.doi.org/10.1787/222814543073

Lucas, B., Claxton, G., & Spencer, E. (2013). *Progression in student creativity in school: First steps towards new forms of formative assessments.* OECD Education Working Paper No. 86, OECD Publishing. Retrieved from http://dx.doi.org/10.1787/5k4dp59msdwk-en

Martingdale, C. (1999). The biological basis of creativity. In R. Sternberg (Ed.), *Handbook of creativity.* Cambridge: Cambridge University Press.

McCulloch, M. (2009). *From school to faculty: Stories of transition into teacher education.* (PhD), Glasgow University, Glasgow. Retrieved from http://theses.gla.ac.uk/1273/01/2009mccullochedd.pdf

McWilliam, E. L. (2007). *Is creativity teachable: Conceptualising the creativity/pedagogy relationship in higher education.* Paper presented at the 30th HERDSA Annual Conference: Enhancing Higher Education, Theory and Scholarship, Adelaide.

McWilliam, E. L. (2009). Teaching for creativity: From sage to guide to meddler. *Asia Pacific Journal of Education, 29*(3), 281–293. doi:10.1080/02188790903092787

McWilliam, E. L., & Dawson, S. (2007). *Understanding creativity: A survey of 'creative' academic teachers: A report for the Carrick Institute for Learning and Teaching in Higher Education*. Retrieved from www.altcexchange.edu.au/system/files/handle/fellowships_associatefellow_report_ericamcwilliam_may07.pdf

McWilliam, E. L., Dawson, S. P., & Tan, J. P.-L. (2008). From vaporousness to visibility: What might evidence of creative capacity building actually look like? *UNESCO Observatory, Faculty of Architecture, Building and Planning, The University of Melbourne Refereed E-Journal, Multi-Disciplinary Research in the Arts, 1*(3).

McWilliam, E. L., & Haukka, S. (2008). Educating the creative workforce: New directions for twenty-first century schooling. *British Educational Research Journal, 34*(5), 651–666.

Nickerson, R. (1999). Enhancing creativity. In R. J. Sternberg (Ed.), *Handbook of creativity* (pp. 392–430). Cambridge: Cambridge University Press.

Nicol, D., & Macfarlane-Dick, D. (2006). Formative assessment and self-regulated learning: A model and seven principles of good feedback practice. *Studies in Higher Education, 34*(1), 199–218.

Oliver, B. (2011). *Assuring graduate outcomes*. Strawberry Hills, NSW. Retrieved from www.olt.gov.au/resource-assuring-graduate-outcomes-curtin-2011

Onsman, A., & Paganin, D. (2006, November 27–30). *Perturbative analogies: Fostering creativity in postgraduate research students*. Paper presented at the AARE 2006 International Education Research Conference, Adelaide.

Philip, R. (2013, July 1–4). *Cultivating creative ecologies: Creative teaching and teaching for creativity*. Paper presented at the Research and Development in Higher Education: The place of learning and teaching, AUT University, Auckland, New Zealand.

Ricoeur, P. (1983/1984). *Time and narrative* (K. McLaughlin & D. Pellauer, Trans. Vol. 1). Chicago: University of Chicago Press.

Robinson, K. (1999). *All our futures: Creativity, culture and education (the Robinson report)*. London. National Advisory Committee on Creative and Cultural Education (NACCCE).

Robinson, K. (2011). *Out of our minds: Learning to be creative*. Oxford: Capstone Publishing Limited.

Runco, M. (2010). Education based on a parsimonious theory of creativity. In R. Begetto & J. Kaufman (Eds.), *Nurturing creativity in the classroom* (pp. 235–251). New York: Cambridge University Press.

Saul, J. R. (2001). *On equilibrium*. Ringwood, Victoria: Penguin Books.

Solomon-Minarchi, A. (2010). *Authentic storytelling: The implications for students and teachers*. (Master's Project in partial fulfilment of the requirements of Master's degree), The Evergreen State College. Retrieved from http://archives.evergreen.edu/masterstheses/Accession89-10MIT/Solomon-Minarchi_AMIT2010.pdf

Spencer, E., Lucas, B., & Claxton, G. (2012). *Progression in creativity: Developing new forms of assessment: A literature review*. Newcastle upon Tyne: CCE.

Sternberg, R. J., & Kaufman, J. C. (2010). Constraints on creativity. In J. C. Kaufman & R. J. Sternberg (Eds.), *The Cambridge handbook of creativity* (pp. 467–482). New York: Cambridge University Press.

Sternberg, R. J., & Lubart, T. I. (1999). The concept of creativity: Prospects and paradigms. In *Handbook of creativity* (pp. 3–15). Cambridge: Cambridge University Press.

Taber, K. S. (2012). The natures of scientific thinking: Creativity as the handmaiden to logic in the development of public and personal knowledge. In M. S. Khine (Ed.), *Advances in nature of science research* (pp. 51–74). Netherlands: Springer Science+Business Media B.V., Springer Netherlands.

Tharp, T. (2008). *The creative habit: Learn it and use it for life*. New York: Simon & Schuster.

98 *Defining and practising creativity*

Trigwell, K., Prosser, M., & Waterhouse, F. (1999). Relations between teachers' approaches to teaching and students' approaches to learning. *Higher Education, 37*, 57–70.

Vygotsky, L. S. (1984). Imagination and creativity in the adolescent. In *The collected works of L. S. Vygotsky* (Vol. 4, pp. 199–219). Moscow: Izdatelstvo Pedagogika.

Walsh, E., Anders, K., Hancock, S., & Elvidge, L. (2013). Reclaiming creativity in the era of impact: Exploring ideas about creative research in science and engineering. *Studies in Higher Education, 38*(9), 1259–1273. doi:10.1080/03075079.2011.620091

Weisberg, R. W. (1999). Creativity and knowledge: A challenge to theories. In R. J. Sternberg (Ed.), *Handbook of creativity* (pp. 226–249). Cambridge: Cambridge University Press.

Woods, P. (1990). *Teacher skills and strategies.* London: Farmer.

5 Honours quantum physics ethnography

Introduction

The previous chapter discussed major themes in the literature about how creativity is understood, approaches to enhancing it, and how it is understood and encouraged by higher educators. Various notions of imagination in this literature were compared to Ricoeur's theory of imagination and to his emphasis on the distinction between 'reproductive' and 'productive' expressions of imagination. What distinguishes imagination from creativity was also introduced.

This chapter is the first in the ethnography section in which those elements were applied in an interpretation of a science subject, namely honours[1] (fourth year) quantum physics.

The setting

The scene arranges itself around a plain, rectangular tutorial room with its long side facing north. The Physics building in this Australian research intensive university is a typical 1960s brown brick, three-storey building (now demolished and replaced) with shining linoleum floors, orange solid wood door cases and slightly jaded corridors lined with posters depicting Nobel discoveries, the findings of faculty research projects and photographs of nebulae. There is a reassuring – to me – dry smell of metals and dust, reminding me of childhood visits to my engineer father's office building. The atmosphere is quiet and removed from the rest of the university bustle, despite the fact that 20 metres further down the corridor a practical class is in session, carrying with it echoes of purposeful instructions and the scraping of chairs. Inside the small senior classroom, the wall is painted with whiteboard paint. A strip runs around the room, meaning the lecturer moves along the wall as he writes with the whiteboard marker pen, dividing it into segments. Bi-colour modular desks fit together like puzzle pieces, forming a line facing the whiteboard wall that reflects the bright northern sun.

100 *Honours quantum physics*

The lecturer, Simon, who is an associate professor (he has since been promoted to a professor) at the university, teaches the fourth year honours quantum theory class three times per week. The class consists of seven of the eight physics students and one maths student: a remarkably small number for a large university, but that is on the rise as faculty undergraduate student retention rates improve from year to year. I began my observations in week 5 of the course when the patterns of the class had been established. The ethnography relied upon notes of classroom observations over six weeks, the course learning notes, completed student assignments and transcripts of pre- and post-class interviews with the educator and the same for the student focus groups.

Quantum theory explains the behaviour and make-up of matter and energy at the sub-atomic and atomic level. This is, in Simon's words, 'the vision of logic where everyday intuition, and classical mechanics, breaks down'. These honours students have now had three years of working with quantum concepts to unpick the assumptions given to us by our everyday human experience, which make the quantum world seem 'weird'. In fact, they are told in third year – and I believe they appreciate – that viewed from the perspective of the universe it is our perspective that is odd. In its place, they learn to place the assumptions of the known world in parenthesis, at times, and understand the implications of the change in scale to an understanding of the behaviour of fields and particles at the sub-atomic level. Their task, using their imaginations, is to build models in their heads and reason mathematically so that they can describe and represent the behaviour of quantum phenomena with precision in equations. This will equip them to make predictions of sub-atomic behaviour that can be 'observed', that is, measured in experiments. Simon points out where these principles and methods are currently being used in a whole range of medical and industrial applications, which may offer employment destinations for some of the students. These include – and this is a revelation to me – lasers used in such diverse fields as CD players, lighting and medical instruments, microscopy imaging technology, synchrotrons, semiconductors used in computers, atomic clocks and ultraprecise thermometers. There are also 'quantum wires', 'quantum dots' and 'quantum sheets', all very rich areas of research, he tells them on more than one occasion. The course includes relativistic quantum mechanics and the Dirac equation, quantum computers, the quantum radiation field, the quantum theory of coherence and some elements of the quantum theory of scattering and diffraction.

The language of physics is foreign to me and highly specialised, and the area is bounded by key, or what is sometimes called 'threshold', concepts of energy, mass, field, wave and particle. When I was attending and observing the quantum physics class I would hurriedly write verbatim what was on the whiteboard and try to catch what the students and the lecturer said, without understanding any of it and hoping to discern meaning in it later. It was a foreign language. Endeavouring to grasp onto anything that would help me, I read John Gribbin's *In search of Schrödinger's cat*, I watched Leonard Susskind lectures on YouTube and I read G. H. Hardy's *A mathematician's apology*, which I saw on a poster advertising a Lunchmaths talk given by Simon. I was trying to orient myself. I was aware that I did not need to understand quantum physics to perform my research, but if students were being asked to use their imagination, how would I recognise it if I couldn't follow what they were talking about? Was I wasting my own and everyone else's time? I could tell from the students' sometimes faltering attempts to answer questions in class that this was very challenging material, even for them. I read the weekly readings in the course notes, but the linguistic explanations were almost as opaque as the maths.

Week 5 began with the question: 'How do we describe light quantum mechanically?' This involved developing a notion of photons and deep familiarity with the wave-particle duality of photons.

Dialectical cycling through mathematical reasoning processes

During the first class I observed, the class launched into working through equations which historically follow the Schrödinger and Heisenberg 'pictures' described by the Schrödinger and Heisenberg equations. Simon tells them they are, unusually for them, 'postponing a physical interpretation of what they are doing' while they consider these 'very simple, very rarefied' equations. 'What are some of the things you could do next?' he asks, as they hit road blocks. 'Find the commutator', one student volunteers. One student later explained to me what this meant: 'multiplication is commutative', as in $2 \times 3 = 3 \times 2$; being able to switch the numbers means that 'we calculate the commutator to see if our operators commute in a similar way, and if not, what correction must be made when we swap the order'. So they do and it's off again with completing the maths implied. Working with the *possibilities* offered by the mathematics is one way in which physics offers possibilities to be imaginative. There is no one right way to proceed – a fundamental point that some students struggle with. Simon constantly models the thinking processes of working physicists, and does this with an attitude of self-awareness, as though this is a 'master class'. Watching him, this appears to involve continually drawing from their well of mathematical operations and their physical interpretation of a situation. He even uses the primary school language of 'putting on our physics hats'/'putting on our mathematics hats' – at some points, one is required; at another, the other approach. No one feels condescended to; this is high level work, and though their questions prove they are following, interviews with the students show that sometimes they are teetering on the edge of understanding, and the clarity provided by Simon is appreciated. What appears to be going on is dialectical logic: showing how one thing, for example, experience, and another, say conceptualisation, or in this instance mathematical representation and physical interpretation, are necessary for, and a condition of, each other.

Then they consider two prerequisite pieces of knowledge, which will allow them to continue with their development of a quantum theory of a photon field.

Modelling the use of analogy to put an image to an emerging meaning: an instance of 'reproductive' and 'productive' imagination

The first is a theory of a harmonic oscillator, an 'archetypal object' in quantum physics, says Simon, which was studied in third year, and which, he points out, will be returned to again and again in hundreds of applications during the course of their studies. He says it is one of the most important model systems in quantum mechanics and an analogue of a classical harmonic oscillator, such as a vibrating violin string or hitting a tennis ball when it is connected to an elastic rope. Listening to his analogical explanation, I think of the 'slinky', a play-toy wire spring, which starred in the TV program *Catalyst* recently. Straight away it is apparent that analogies with classical systems which are used to describe the familiar everyday world are still referred to in order to initiate the students' engagement with the concepts. In Ricoeur's terms, this appears to be an instance of what he would call *re*productive imagination – that is, bringing absent but existent objects into mind. But his intent is not simply to *recall* an object which is perceptible by the senses (like the vibrating violin string). The purpose of the *productive* imagination is to be able to help think about the concept's parameters, shape and behavioural possibilities in hypothetical terms or postulate relationships or functions. His teaching illustrates the strong and necessary relationship between reproductive and productive imagination when applied for pedagogical purposes. In Ricoeur's terms, the reproductive imagination is drawing from the students' memories in order to structure, or provide schema for, an image which is an emerging meaning in the sense of depicting relations, rather than necessarily having a mental picture *of* something (Ricoeur, 1979, p. 150).

Simon draws a single vertical y axis, which resembles a picture of a ladder, with steps from zero up, representing 'Fock states' of energy (E^n). The way I understand it, material objects that emit or absorb light often do so in amounts of energy that are *quantized*, that is, they change energy (often) only by discrete amounts. These discrete amounts of energy are represented by an 'energy ladder'. After a long time working through equations, he asks, 'How would you explain equation 210 (in the course notes) in words? Which one destroys?'

$$\hat{N}\hat{a}|\beta\rangle = (\beta - 1)\hat{a}|\beta\rangle \tag{210a}$$

$$\hat{N}\hat{a}^{\dagger}|\beta\rangle = (\beta + 1)\hat{a}^{\dagger}|\beta\rangle \tag{210b}$$

It is something he does constantly when teaching, turning from equations to words to visual pictorial representations to graphs, each form offering an approach to understanding that may appeal to different students but, cumulatively, drawing them into complementary ways of understanding the concepts and, more than that, composing knowledge using these skills.

This time he also asks everyone to think of a mnemonic for the creation and destruction operators. In quantum field theory, a and $a^{\dagger}$ (a and a-dagger) are alternatively called 'destruction/annihilation/absorption' operators and 'creation'

Honours quantum physics 103

operators respectively because they destroy and create particles, which corresponds to the idea of destroying and raising states, or quanta, of energy. I assume that Simon is interested as a teacher in the students' mnemonics in order to share this usual learning ploy, but also to find out if there are any misunderstandings of the physical states that are being described. No one seems to misunderstand. Several students offer their habitual ways of remembering them, such as the dagger looking like a 'plus' sign (so it's 'adding/creating') and the ladder being actually a lift which takes you up and down the scale of energy, with zero being when you can't go down any more. The imagery provides them with a representation of energy states rising and dropping. At one stage, he asks, 'Is this representing a physical state? Is zero obscuring a physical state? That is, it could be anything but you can't know whether or what'.

$$\hat{a}|0\rangle = 0$$

At a point when the prior equation is on the board Simon asks: 'What is the difference between a classical and quantum vacuum?' A great deal of discussion follows: 'Mechanically there's nothing there', the students answer, that is, the classical concept of a vacuum is a featureless vacuum empty of air, matter and light. They continue: 'But in a quantum state, a few things are rising up and being destroyed all the time'. The concept of quantum vacuum is of a dynamic space of so-called vacuum fluctuations of particles and antiparticles that come into existence and move apart and merge together. There is discussion around whether zero in the equation is representing a physical state, or whether in fact it is obscuring the physical state, given the creation and annihilation operators. The symbol of zero by itself (0), on the other hand, implies what appears to be a third state: the complete absence of any system, no universe at all in which the concept of space itself is annihilated. This comparison and contrast is *organising and reorganising* their conceptions of what a vacuum means, what nothing is, in ways that require thinking; that are not given to us in experience – which is the role of all expressions of the productive imagination in Ricoeur's terms. Simon congratulates them that they have got a great deal more out of the description than would be evident from the algebra on the whiteboard.

'Dancing around' a problem mathematically, pictorially, linguistically

Putting language around mathematical and physical concepts is essential in this classroom. Later, in an interview, Simon explains why he does this.

> No one can calculate without conceptualising what they're calculating and conversely, one can conceptualise, but if you can't calculate expressions, then one's understanding is necessarily superficial. I also have in mind that some people think conceptually first and mathematically second. . . . So I go back and forth for a couple of reasons. One is because I think . . . you're

104 *Honours quantum physics*

just sort of dancing around the problem and looking at it from multiple perspectives, which is something I obviously encourage and foster. Secondly, if the pictures are primary and the mathematics is secondary, then if you go around a couple of times, then each, in a sense, has their own favourite starting point and their own favourite ending point if they choose the part early in the cycle and the part late in the cycle.

(pre-class interview transcript)

Putting an image to an emerging meaning is what this teacher is trying to help the students do. The depicted diagram or picture helps prompt the drawing of some other form of representation, such as a different perspective or slice of the first one. The pictures then can act as the basis for making calculations of what it corresponds to, upon which further mathematical reasoning or further imagining can operate. Or the process can be reversed: The calculations prompt the question of what the calculations mean physically. The great difficulty is that they are trying to imagine some reality they have never seen, that cannot be seen, that is consistent in every detail with what has been observed and measured in experiments or which is represented by their calculations.[2] His teaching makes allowance for the fact that some students may have stronger spatial or conceptual ability but weaker mathematical ability, or vice versa, and he points out here it is the teacher's role to find a point of entry for all preferences and, I would add, a real foundation for self-belief or confidence. I notice, however, that in his earlier explanation, if not in his teaching practice, language as the third thinking tool is unmentioned. Linguistic reasoning is as much a step in the dance cycle I observe as mathematical and diagrammatic reasoning.

As the students' questions form, their words are sometimes faltering, and one will almost appear to complete another's question; they add to each other's sentences. It is almost as though they are speaking collaboratively. However, I infer they are individually gaining perspectives on the issue at hand. It is a process in which one is coming to understand the functional significance of the sign system that one has been using all along. Wertsch says that humans use signs before understanding what they are doing, or, as Cadzen (1981) puts it, 'performance before competence' (Wertsch, 2007, p. 186). At a later date, when reading this account of this teaching moment in the classroom, Simon recalls these lines from T. S. Eliot.

> Words strain,
> Crack and sometimes break, under the burden,
> Under the tension, slip, slide, perish,
> Decay with imprecision . . .
>
> (Eliot, *Four quartets*,
> 'Burnt Norton', V, 1944, lines 149–152)

However, there are multiple artefacts and modes of representation involved in the students' endeavour; it is not only words. The work of combining different artefacts or symbols is important to cognition. What I believe I am witnessing is individuals trying to grasp something new, achieved through a social, collaborative extension of their minds (in Clark's sense) into the verbal and mathematical language and pictorial representations ('mindtools') they are using to image and understand the underlying physics.

Simon draws on the board as they speak, asking if what he's drawn represents what they are asking. By cycling ('dancing') around a problem mathematically, pictorially and linguistically, they are combining conceptual understanding in order to grasp or gain insight into the situation. This combinatory process between three modes in which each is necessary for, and a condition for, a more complete understanding of a physical situation is an example of a disciplinary form of 'productive imagination' in Ricoeur's sense. By an imaginative combinatory process, akin to narrative or metaphor, a new relationship between the ideas is established. The resulting redescription can recast their understanding, extending it to concepts which are beyond their direct experience.

Learning by projecting the imagination into disciplinary conceptual tools

I am reminded of Polanyi's work on tacit knowing (1967). I would go as far as to say Simon's teaching method is encouraging a complex, tool-propelled form of intuition akin to the example Polanyi explores of a blind person navigating using a walking stick. Polanyi explains how when we project our minds into a walking stick to navigate a pitch-dark corridor we seem to extend our perceptual awareness beyond the boundaries of our body right to the end of the stick in order to orient ourselves in space. Only in this instance the tools are mathematics, diagrams and language in combination with each other. Together they augment the understanding our minds are capable of, when used in the service of understanding a quantum concept. In my view, Polanyi's explorations are a precursor to the concept of the 'extended mind' developed by Dennett and Clark (Dennett, 1995; Clark, 1997), which builds on work in robotics in which external objects, including diverse tools, symbols and artefacts (e.g., language, lists/pattern arrangements, slide rules or iPhones) are tools co-opted by us in order to perform cognitive tasks. We make them 'our own' through practised use. In Clark's view, the interactive 'coupling' between the objects and the mind *is* the cognitive processing (Menary, 2010). The thinking weaves in, and through, the external objects, or 'tools'. 'Simple external props enable us to think better and hence to create more complex props and practices, which in turn "turbocharge" our thoughts a little more, which leads to the development of even better props' (Clark, 1997, p. 62).

What Simon is encouraging the students to learn is how to blend pictorial, verbal and mathematical reasoning tools functioning as 'proximate terms' (in Polanyi's language) by projecting their imagination and their reasoning through these tools into the situation they are trying to understand. The student's understanding is projected through the cyclical interaction of reproductive imagination in pictures and drawing, mathematical reasoning and language. I draw the conclusion that this is what it means to 'think like a physicist'.

106 *Honours quantum physics*

The students themselves seem to be aware of this conceptual progression:

Student 1: . . . sometimes it also helps to use a really simple analogy that only works a little bit – doesn't capture the totality that you can explore it in different ways. Maybe come up with something different that you need to then explore.

Student 2: I think there's also – it is really abstract because it's layer after layer imaging things. So the mathematics itself requires a bit of imagination. The second layer of mathematics, Fourier transforms, requires a whole bunch of imagination.

(post-class interview transcript)

Learning to be resourceful

While learning tools include conceptual tools revealed in how language or algorithms are used, and in picturing, it is also important to remember that learning how to use them doesn't just happen in isolation. The uses of the tools are *embedded in practices* which increase the students' effectiveness as problem solvers. Interviews with the students revealed they worked through facets of assessment problems collaboratively in the honours student common room – sometimes leaving workings up on the whiteboard for weeks before returning to them to say, 'I don't think that anymore'. They were also actively resourceful, such as by checking library texts for approaches and, on occasions, resorting to discussing approaches with the lecturer (post-class interviews). While these practical learning strategies may seem as obvious as the benefits of learning to breathe, they are part of the initiative needed to learn and apply new knowledge fruitfully and are practices which they can draw on in many contexts in their future working lives. Simon confirms that the collaborations extend to honest and scholarly acknowledgement of the source of ideas from their peers, as follows: 'They'll sometimes reference each other in the assignment, they'll say, "I'm grateful to such and such a person for helping me see this step." So I think a lot of deep learning goes on there' (post-class interview transcript).

Before I began this research, I would have viewed the existence of an honours student room, gifted by the faculty, as no more than a pleasant resource to enhance a feeling of belonging and a place to socialise. It is much more. Edwards (2005, p. 58) points out that cognition, as a process of coming to know, is structured by situations in which it takes place: what those situations allow, what they constrain and the interactions that occur in them. Lave and Wenger (1991) call this situated learning 'legitimate peripheral participation' because it recognises the whole person and frames the agent, activity and world as mutually constitutive. In this student common room, students create a collegiate, collaborative working space in which to do physics, which mimics, as it is designed to, the ways of working of faculty physicists. If we define pedagogy as the careful structuring of learning situations, then this common room plays a part in the pedagogy: It allows the students to experience the social process of coming to know knowledge in concert with others and put it into action. After working together and not understanding something, some students, for example, go off to the library or senior peers to acquire books or ask more questions – which is to act resourcefully (in the rich sense suggested by Vygotsky, 1978) – to help themselves learn. Whether what they do is to produce existing knowledge or produce new knowledge, the process, I would argue, is the same.

The significance of the room goes further. Vygotsky (1984) offers a social-cultural perspective of imagination, suggesting that the cultivation of imagination and criticality in individuals is contingent upon social arrangements. And those social arrangements, as Arendt suggests (1959), must include a commitment to disputation and critical thinking. Investment in student amenities by the faculty sends a message about the value it places on collaborative ways of working that are foundational to physics. Collaboration is how the field of physics works (in the sense of Csikszentmihalyi's [1999] 'systems model'). Like an incubator – of the field – the room provides a forum for the development of skills needed for disciplinary experts who may become the future patrollers of the domain.

This larger frame to what is going on in the students' interaction in the common room is also captured in Engeström's theory of the activity system. A socio-cultural perspective, it builds on Vygotsky's notion that individual learning is embedded in social relations and is represented in Figure 5.1.

Interpreted in the light of this activity theory, 'learning to think like a physicist' is exemplified in the individual subject's relation to the objects of study (for example quantum physics) and is mediated by disciplinary tools, which, as we have discussed, are various mathematical procedures, diagrammatic representations and verbal language. This is represented in Figure 5.1 in the top triangle within the entire triangle above, which, as we can see, is like the tip of the iceberg. It represents, even assumes, an individual learner – an individual cognizing agent. In the lower section are 'Rules', representing the methodologies and practices of disciplines, and 'Community', which represents the disciplinary communities who uphold those cultures and the standards to which they are held. What the educator

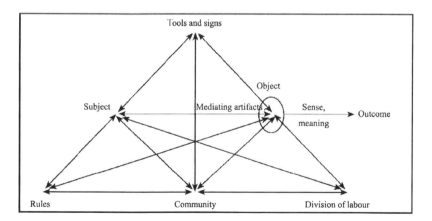

Figure 5.1 The structure of a human activity system

Source: Reproduced with permission of Yrjö Engeström, from *Learning, Working and Imagining: Twelve studies in activity theory.*

108 *Honours quantum physics*

models in his interactions, and what the student common room is intended to mimic, is this wider frame. It offers the opportunity to practice physics more authentically, which is to say, with peers, relatively autonomously, collaboratively *and* individually finding ways of solving problems, using their resourcefulness and the material tools available to them and attributing the steps to knowledge transparently (by citing each other and sources) in a form of legitimate peripheral participation. This is a much wider frame of what learning is, and it encompasses being physicists who build new knowledge in collaborative networks.[3]

Scientific models – examples of productive imagination – involve the making of assumptions

After a lesson on Schrödinger's and Heisenberg's pictures, the next lesson began with the lecturer drawing parameters around the system they were going to consider: a harmonic oscillator. 'Let's assume a vacuum', he says, in order to be clear that the equations they will work with filter out extraneous effects, such as gravity and so forth. Making assumptions is something that scientists do constantly. That is, in dealing with complexity, they set up simplified models with which they can figure out what can be known, and then they re-introduce, step-by-step, aspects of that real-world complexity. It occurs to me that in doing so, they are setting up models, which they are aware do not replicate the situation exactly, in order to hypothesise about the rules under which the new system operates. The terms of the model are, at least initially, more familiar. This assists them to get a better grip on what the effective factors or influences might be in the system they are interested in studying. 'Let's assume' is a scientific and mathematical expression for positing a provisional idea or model – for thinking *with*. This is in tune with Ricoeur's discussion of metaphors and models (as instances of 'productive imagination'). Metaphors highlight an implicit comparison between two unlike things, and theoretical models postulate functional relationships. Both are not necessarily about similarities but rather that they convey the knower's apprehension of a relationship between them. The imagination is active here because it is imagination that enables us to go beyond experience and imagine situations as other than they are, and models help us expand the basis of thinking.

> Recourse to scientific imagination in this regard does not signal a deflection of reason, distraction by images, but the essentially verbal power of trying out new relationships on a "described' model". Thus imagination mingles with reason by virtue of the rules of correlation governing the translation of statements concerning the secondary domain into statements applicable to the original domain.
>
> (Ricoeur, 1975/2003, p. 285)

In Ricoeur's terms the imaginary process happens in that momentary hiatus when provisional rational fictions are momentarily entertained, upon which evaluative thinking can be performed. Imaginary possibilities are 'thrown up' to test relationships or compare characteristics or processes of the model. This suggests imagination may thrive in liminal spaces, or moments, where possibilities are considered before criticality closes them off.

This activity also describes what happens in thought experiments (an imagined scenario which serves to envisage or investigate the consequences of a hypothesis or theory), which are a recognised form of scientific thinking, especially in physics. By testing if nature will conform to previously held expectations, thought experiments can, according to Kuhn, suggest particular ways in which both expectation and theory may need to be revised (Brown & Fehige, 2014).

Teaching for imagination involves teaching openness to future revision or the reconsideration of explanatory possibilities

In another class, emotions are elicited to set in motion the intellectual work of the day. 'Today is going to be an anti-climax', Simon announces enigmatically before proceeding to work through progress from equation 187 in the notes to equation 233, which takes about 20 minutes.

Lecturer: Do you feel disappointed by that?' he asks. 'Is it a kind of sleight of hand? . . . Or beautifully elegant?

Student: Both. [A nice answer since it dissolves the dualism implicit in the question, introducing nuances which can be explored further.]

Lecturer: Can you explain that?

[The student does.]

Lecturer: What do the others [students] say?

Student 1:   We're thinking of this as an infinite collection of harmonic oscillators.

Student 2:   We've got an equation to describe a system.

Lecturer: Let me draw a picture of what's just been said [which the lecturer does]. What is a photon in this construct?

Student: An oscillation in the magnetic field.

Previously, I believe, photons have been discussed as the smallest quantum of light. This new conception defines it as a quantum of excitation of the oscillation, in a particular wave function ('ψ'). Simon then asks a question which asks them consciously to bring this new conceptualisation of a photon together with their prior learning and air the results.

Lecturer: Does this conception of a photon harmonise with your other uses and exposure to the word 'photon'?

The word 'photon' is a tool for understanding. And this word tool now has bivalence. The new meaning they've co-constructed through the class requires that the students' prior concept of what a photon is has to be broadened, has to be more complex. This might entail a shift in their understanding, which is, I believe, the motive behind Simon's question here. This is an example of Engeström's notion of 'object transformation', an important concept in his studies of learning in practice. Engeström calls this process 'expansive learning', and it refers not only to professional practice but to learning to think and act as a beginning historian or mathematician or physicist. Expansive learning comes from repositioning oneself in relation to the object as a result of seeing more in it (Edwards, 2005). The notion of photon is the catalyst for this moment of expansive learning.

Another possible label for the process of learning is 'the development of expertise', where expertise is the capacity to interpret the complexity of aspects of the world and the wherewithal to respond to that complexity (Edwards, 2005, p. 60). Whatever terminology is used, this broadening or problematizing of conceptual understanding cultivates imagination in learning because it shows students that concepts are multifaceted, complex, have diverse meanings in different contexts and are always open to change and reconstruction. This awareness of complexity and openness can overcome the rigid thinking that concepts can sometimes lead to because, if students assume that there is one ultimate, fixed or definite answer, it can prevent them from considering alternative possibilities or alternative perspectives. If, however, they can treat concepts and theories as working ideas that guide and enable inquiry but are always open to future revision, the possibilities opened up by imagination may be more conducive to learning that is of its nature never-ending.

One of the physics students later told me in an email (October 15, 2012), 'Half of the work we do in physics seems to be undoing previous understandings, to add refinements, or outright change them'. (The classical to quantum transition, and especially the wave-particle dual nature of light, are two huge examples that are returned to over and over.)

This openness to complexity and reconsideration implies openness to discovery. In this way, Ricoeur's theory of productive imagination works to unfold the logic of discovery itself (Taylor, 2006, p. 98).

This teaching example conveys to students an experience of this deeper understanding of learning: that learning is not finished with the acquisition of new knowledge, concepts or skills; rather, knowledge has the potential to be reconstructed, or falsified, in the future. This openness to complexity and reconsideration makes the imagination of fundamental importance to education, in particular to higher education.

Abstraction: abstracting from collecting tennis balls in a bucket or photons in a telescope!

The discussion continues.

Student 1: It's not really like tennis balls collected in a bucket, like in a telescope. But they're wave excitations in a field of oscillations.
Student 2: How is it like a tennis ball?
Lecturer: We're thinking of these are being localised as a wave packet.
Student 3: Any localised wave packet can be expressed as a sum of or combination of plane waves.

The 'tennis balls collected in a bucket' is often used as an analogy for the detection of photons by a digital camera attached to a telescope. The class discussion proceeds at some length with Simon drawing a light source, a wave packet seen as a fuzzy ball and a detector on a back wall measuring light. There is discussion about how, instead of considering a single harmonic oscillator, the equations they are working through proceed by finding the total energy of a quantised radiation field, by the more manageable method of adding up all the independent harmonic oscillators in terms of a state with photons, with the relevant factor being wave vectors and polarisation, in 'layers of superposition'. Superposition is the idea that you can describe a complex thing as *the sum of* simple things added together or overlapping. Simon explains to me later that even a brick wall, for example, could be considered the superposition of many individual bricks; air as atoms; light in terms of the seven colours of the rainbow plus x-rays, radio waves, through microwaves, infrared, gamma rays – the many known wavelengths or energies of light. The practice of seeing an array of stars as a constellation is an example of superposition. Even a poem could be considered in terms of superposition: as a series of discrete words, as lines of words, as lines forming a pattern or as a series of individual metaphors that relate to one another to suggest meanings – all analytic constructs can be used to decompose the object of superposition. Superposition is a common mathematical method to ease calculation (I am informed by students later that Taylor and Fourier series expansions are examples of superposition), but it is also used to describe quantum mechanical states. These layers of 'superposition' seem to involve a particular disciplinary form of abstraction which involves the application of a method of decomposing a whole state and reconstituting it as a sum of functions. This method involves considering the whole situation (in this case, a quantised radiation field) *as if* it is made up of a category of components (decomposing it), and then adding or combining together these constructs. This appears to be a highly imaginative process because it involves the mental manipulation of, first, breaking the unknown whole state down into a provisional, fictional arrangement of a simpler situation, and then by recomposing the object by a mental operation that involves combining the 'fictional' layers of the simpler situation. The disciplinary method of superposition therefore involves a cultural trigger to the individual cognizer to imagine performing this decomposition and recomposition process enabled by the Taylor and Fourier series expansions, which require the practice of expert manipulation of these equation tools.[4] Moving myself back into more familiar territory, I ask myself if superposition is an epistemological correlate of Ricoeur's notion of narrative, where fiction recombines elements into a new whole. If so, I believe we see another example of epistemological imagination. One of the students explains:

Student: You're applying the Fourier transform to a physical situation and then . . . the physical situation isn't a regular one it's got this – the wave function is already really abstract. So there's one kind of abstractness and another kind of abstractness. You combine them, it's just so many layers.

Using historical examples to problematise concepts and knowledge and encourage questioning assumptions

The second half of the lecture is spent deriving Dirac's 1927 attempt to introduce a 'phase' operator, missing in the picture constructed by these equations.

$$e^{i\hat{\varphi}} = \frac{1}{\sqrt{\hat{n}+1}}\hat{a} \tag{252a}$$

$$e^{-i\hat{\varphi}} = \hat{a}^{\dagger}\frac{1}{\sqrt{\hat{n}+1}}. \tag{252b}$$

I include this fact only because Simon begins the following class with an announcement that although the equations were accepted, nearly 30 years later, in 1963, they were found to be wrong. Dirac made some unjustified assumptions that his amplitude and phase operators were 'Hermitian' (a mathematical condition meaning they represented observable properties), when they were not. Consequently, this rendered all further arguments contained in his equations invalid. I duly find this time lag amazing. The students seem to take it in their stride – perhaps they've read it in the course notes. The way Simon explains it, Dirac was far ahead of his time, so it was not until much later in the 1950s, when quantum thermodynamics was more developed, that the significance of it was understood. 'Why didn't they find out it was wrong sooner?' he asks.

A constructive pause follows in which the students are given time to think about the many possible reasons for the delay. And the inevitable question arises (even to me): If Dirac's operator was found to be wrong, what other maxims could, upon closer examination, be found to rest on false assumptions? It is a pregnant moment! The implications are clear. Those same assumptions that serve to push the boundaries of thought can simultaneously obscure alternative insights. Simon points out, 'You don't need fancy maths to win Nobel prizes. You need insights and the breaking of hidden assumptions'. He constantly urges the students not to believe what he says or his equations, but to work them out for themselves. 'Don't languish in assumptions!' This real historical example serves a profound pedagogical purpose.

This is exactly Lakoff and Johnson's (1980) and Reddy's (1979) point about the rigidity in conceptualisation that ensues from uncritical use of habitual metaphors (see Chapter 2). This is a reason for not taking assumptions for granted. And it is why Ricoeur has the y axis of his theories of imagination representing the degree of a human subject's critical consciousness of the difference between the imagined and the real (see Chapter 2). Productive imagination entails an awareness of the fictiveness of the creation. There seems to be almost a poetical and tantalising 'lightness' being asked for here: Physics of its nature requires the making of assumptions and cannot advance knowledge without making them, yet being open to reconsideration and questioning those assumptions on the basis of other possibilities asks for an attitude of mental flexibility because it can underpin critical consciousness. Once again, this point is being reiterated in another teaching situation: that imagination is important to education because it entails an openness to revision and questioning of assumptions. Saul (2001) makes the point that the idea of purpose in imagination is always incomplete – it is always drawing us forward by further dissatisfaction, questions, further frames which can model new meaning.

Modelling internal standards of knowledge attempts and using error as an impetus to learning

Simon uses the moment to explore the notion of error further with the students. 'Dirac was wrong but in a useful way – what do you think of that statement?' The class notes say that in the following year, 1964, researchers Susskind and Glogower found a way to answer the objection. Many questions follow, with students' attitudes to the notion of Hermiticity as a 'useful but not sufficient condition' being probed; one comment about 'how weird to go from trigonometry to adding operators'; and Simon receiving a range of questions about bra's (a notation <I) and ket (I >) (that is, bra[c]kets on the sides of equations that are symbols representing a state inside them): 'Is it like having two systems?' 'Yes, when you have two systems they can start interfering'.

Dewey recognised error as one of the benefits of his fallibilist notion of knowledge – it justified further inquiry and learning (Bleazby, 2011, pp. 73–75). The place and importance of error-making in physics is not something new to the students. In fact, that error-making is integral to doing physics is almost a refrain in Simon's third year class, which I visited prior to joining the four year honours class:

> Ask yourself, "What are the things I could do?" If it fails, try something else.
> I want you to be unsystematic and exploratory.
> Don't be afraid to be wrong. We physicists work on a problem for 9 months or 15, even 30 months, so we spend 90 per cent of our time being wrong! In fact it's necessary to be wrong, often. [I see he's not exaggerating!]

We see from these comments that the educator sees creativity in physics as an iterative and imperfect process. In my pre-class interview, Simon talked about how this class might play out (before it had happened). It illuminates his view of how creativity can be stimulated, which involves a complex relationship between error and creativity.

> I'll try and get some discussion from them about why it took 30 years for this error to be discovered. Then I'll turn the point to the fact that he was actually wrong in a profound way. . . . Sometimes superficial reasoning can lead to profound things and sometimes one can be wrong in a profound way. I do that because I want them to see some of the history, I want them to never take anything on authority and never, in a sense, feel that they can't

114 *Honours quantum physics*

be creative just because some Nobel Prize winner has said such and such should be so . . . it gives them permission to dismantle previous theories and try and seek to build upon them.

(Pre-class interview transcript)

This stance to the development of knowledge is supported in the literature on creativity as discussed in Chapter 3. For example, Cole, Sugioka and Yamagata-Lynch's (1999) study found that classroom environments that support creativity are ones in which independence, experimentation and risk-taking are encouraged. It is also endorsed in studies by Amabile (1983) and Nickerson (1999) which highlight the role of beliefs about creativity: that is, that creativity is subject to effort, persistence and motivation and not dictated by genetically determined capability or 'giftedness' that is beyond our control, which is implicit in Simon's view. He pointed out the value of these skills and abilities to students' future employment. In the pre-class interview, he talked about modelling error in his own teaching in order to model an openness to revision and rethinking.

As a second example, I'll often criticise my own notes and/or solutions, in a sense that I'll very often say I was coming in on the train this morning thinking about this morning's lecture and reading what I'd written in preparation for today's class and thinking there's a better way to do this. So let me read against the grain of my own text. Let me deconstruct my own text and present an alternative perspective. That process of self-criticism is a natural thing, for me it's also an essential part of creativity: the rigor of always applying scrutiny to one's own understanding with a view to deepening [their knowledge].

This is repeated in the post-class interview:

If they don't make sense or they find a better way to picture it that works for them, then that's better and actively to be sought. Not just, if they find an error in my solutions please let me know, but if they find a fundamentally better way to work something out, then post that to Moodle.

Doing good work and making a contribution, in spite of error-making – or more radically, because of it – is something within the reach of all. But what makes some attempts better than others? What does the process of self-criticism in creativity consist of? Qualitative evaluation of problem solving is also part of the picture being conveyed of physics thinking: a voice in the head that acts like a witness to the steps in thinking – what we might term teaching metacognitive thinking. He urges them to judge for themselves, 'Always ask, "Could I do this better? Could I do this more elegantly? Could I do it in a way more meaningful for me?" Every problem can be solved in many different ways'.

His teaching is far away from just transmitting the contents of a textbook; he's modelling a certain kind of knowledge and standards for making use of that knowledge. But those standards involve an internal locus, where alternative perspectives and operations are considered and where 'meaning' and aesthetics have a part to play. In terms of imagination, this approach is supported in the creativity literature because it emphasises internal motivation and the importance of allowing choice, which implies agency (Amabile, 1983). Dewey pointed out that all experience has an aesthetic dimension in the sense that human beings tend to seek experience towards some kind of fulfilment. The aesthetic makes it possible for us to have relatively unified, coherent experience. Imagining new possibilities in this way also negates the conventional opposition between aesthetics and reason, which has been criticised by Dewey and by Johnson (1993).

Feelings about knowledge

Of interest to me was the observation that attitudes of surprise or bafflement, even offence, to emerging knowledge are common in this classroom. And it is not only students who have had emotional reactions to emerging knowledge. Simon's teaching included occasional anecdotes of the human figures who were responsible for the development of quantum physics. In this way, having *emotional attitudes to knowledge* was modelled by this pedagogy.

Quantum concepts were intellectually confronting in their time even to the physicists who gave birth to them (e.g., Max Planck, Albert Einstein, Edward Schrödinger). These people were not detached from what they were discovering. It infused their being.

> If we are going to stick to this damned quantum-jumping, then I regret that I ever had anything to do with quantum theory.
>
> (Erwin Schrödinger)

> God does not play dice with the universe.
>
> (Einstein)

> Hitherto the principle of causality was universally accepted as an indispensable postulate of scientific research, but now we are told by some physicists that it must be thrown overboard. The fact that such an extraordinary opinion should be expressed in responsible scientific quarters is widely taken to be significant of the all-round unreliability of human knowledge. This indeed is a very serious situation.
>
> (Max Planck)

As we saw in Chapter 3, writers such as Dewey, Nussbaum and Johnson agree that emotions are part of purposeful behaviour in relation to our environment (Dewey in Bleazby, 2013, p. 97; Nussbaum, 2001; Johnson, 1993) because they are part of how and why we act and what we want to achieve. We can hear, in these statements, these historical figures weighing the probable effects of their knowledge proposals on their societies. By displaying the evolution of

116 *Honours quantum physics*

quantum physics as a human voyage of discovery, and not even by the story of a heroic struggle to achieve it, the students are not presented with knowledge as something flat or simply given. Instead, at least in this case, what is conveyed is a story of the development of knowledge by people who were in some respects dismayed by the confronting nature of quantum concepts which they were themselves unfolding. These historical figures are being used as models in a pedagogical sense. They were people doing something risky by challenging certainties. The learning that appears to be on offer here is that there are attitudes to knowledge that touch on emotions, that knowledge is indeed personally felt.

In the pre-class focus group, one of the students said: 'Creativity in physics, I'll think of Dirac and really, really clever people. Because there must be a huge amount of creativity in just putting things together in a way that no one has thought of doing before . . .' (pre-class interview transcript). Another commented that he found creativity in the process of discovery, as well as in learning: 'The other thing is just in the linkages that are involved in discovery. I think we all make them whenever we're trying to just learn a new topic because we're going, that topic links to this one and that one' (pre-class interview transcript).

Lifelong learning: the eternal return of the same

A little while later there are two classes on quantum coherence theory which I will discuss. The first class begins with Young's pivotal two pinhole experiment.

Simon alludes incidentally to the repeated return of scientists to this form of experiment by using T. S. Eliot's oft-quoted 'We shall not cease from exploration/ And the end of all our exploring/Will be to arrive where we started/And know the place for the first time' (*Four quartets*, 'Little Gidding', V, 1944, lines 239–242). As an aphorism, it encompasses the wonder and never-endingness of all learning. He takes examples, each of which he draws on the board, of sunlight, candlelight and laser beams passing through the slits, and discusses the wave functions' fluctuations in terms of 'coherence' – or the ability to form what is termed 'interference' – as the waves bounce and reflect off each other when they pass through the multiple holes. Hence, 'incoherence' is also a technical term which refers to the *in*ability to form interference (for example, candlelight). Apparently laser light has large correlated oscillations in the wave function and is coherent and so will show fringes of interference on the back wall; candlelight, by contrast, is incoherent and will show no fringes when detected; and sunlight is partially coherent and will show visible fringes on the back wall.

In order to get a handle on the difference between classical and quantum statistical mechanics, he then draws a glass of water and says the volume, temperature and position can be known in this classical mechanical system but the huge number of atoms which makes it up cannot be calculated precisely. Another thing which cannot be known is the position of a given particle, so it's a partly random system and can only be determined through statistical probabilities. They work through equations that describe a set of microstates corresponding to the macrostate. Then, as usual, the students are invited to put language around these concepts, which a few of them do: 'Some set of wave functions will describe some microstate'.

Simon asks them if they have any questions or if they are comfortable with the two levels of probability – two levels of indeterminacy. Discussion follows on what is a 'pure state', a precisely defined quantum state, such as a Fock state, as opposed to an ensemble of possible states, a 'mixed state', as he refers to it, which involves a statistical mixture describing an ensemble of wave states any of which may be a particular wave function. I find this mindboggling. However, the students appear to tackle this abstract conceptualisation just fine. I am once again reminded of how John Dewey conceived of the imagination, as involved in making inferences from what is given to what is possible – from what is present to something absent – and of Ricoeur's notion of imagination as semantic innovation, created by fictions which model possible aspects of reality. The concept of two levels of indeterminacy seems to describe this imaginative thinking. Dawkins argued similarly, calling the process 'setting up a model in your head', which is what we see here in mathematical modelling (1989, p. 59).

Productive imagination and creatively linking-up diverse things

However, one question Simon poses in class is particularly interesting in a pedagogical way. He asks, 'Why is this obvious in retrospect?' – an extraordinary question. It emerged in my interview with him at the start of the teaching session in relation to the same question he sometimes includes in assignments.

> I'll ask . . . [them] to tell me why such and such result is self-evident if you think about it from an appropriate perspective – tell me why this result is obvious. When I use the word 'obvious', I don't mean some sort of genius just says this is obvious, but rather someone thinks about something deeply enough until they realise that, at the risk of sounding narrow-minded, that it can't be otherwise. It's a challenging question to ask because . . . we calculate so much in physics and yet here I am asking them to explicitly not calculate – you know, calculate nothing, just tell me why this equation, this law of physics, this result of physics can't be other than it is. It's fundamentally a creative thing that it robs them of the ability to hide behind mathematical manipulations, because that can help of course, but it can also hinder. I want to liberate them from needing to think through mathematical logic because it's also about concepts which can, in some sense, exist independent of the mathematical expression rather than just as a thought, it can exist independent of language. . . . It gets them thinking along new tracks. It's also very difficult to assess that kind of thing as well, so one can't write answer sheets for this kind of thing, but again, that's kind of deliberate because I want to encourage that creativity while giving them the – I don't like the word, but the rigors of an intellectually challenging and mathematically sophisticated course.

> (pre-class interview transcript)

118 *Honours quantum physics*

He is asking students to describe their emerging explanations and deepening knowledge about the physical nature of the systems they are deriving using mathematics. The maths describes what is real, but in terms of physics it is incomplete as it still needs to be connected to an understanding of what it tells about the physical system. Yet he says it polarises many physicists – some would view it as self-evidently true and others as self-evidently the opposite. Whichever way of you think of it, the task shows how much importance he places on connecting up knowledge when encouraging creativity and imagination, as he provides what appears to me to be a wide array of opportunities for linking hitherto discrete forms of knowledge.

If we pause to recall Ricoeur's discussion of both metaphor and narrative (in Chapter 2), it will allow us to understand a theoretical basis for forms of learning tasks that involve synthesis. It reminded me of what happens in metaphor when we have experienced the insight precipitated by the semantic shift (in Ricoeur's terms) entailed by making a new metaphor intelligible – and once seen, it is hard to un-see it, and we tend to see it as obvious. It appears to me that a task that asks someone why something is obvious destroys any complacency by asking them again to reconstruct how that explanation was derived. This is congruent with Ricoeur's contention that the imagination, as we see it in metaphor and narrative, involves a combinatory activity – not a lumping together, but a combining of elements into some cohesive whole that may produce a flash of insight that illuminates a reality it describes – which Simon describes as inherently creative. The danger of complacency is referred to in Chapter 2, illustrated by clichéd metaphors that have entered into ordinary parlance and dull the mind to the fiction of the construct. As a teacher concerned with encouraging his students' capacity for creativity, Simon seems to contrive multiple opportunities in class tasks for the students to form and re-form connections that prompt them to construct their own understanding. For the physics discipline this is essential to its way of knowing: to learning to think like a physicist. On the basis of Ricoeur's theory, I would expect to see a teacher devising learning tasks that involve forming connections, which is what is happening.

> I've known students who are brilliant in the sense of getting superb marks throughout their undergraduate and yet the creativity is dead. They're completely inflexible and unable to creatively apply their ideas and that would be an example of a failure of the education system, certainly for them.
>
> (pre-class interview transcript)

I would argue that the process applied to the quantum problems involving the drawing of pictures, graphical representation, dialogue about them and mathematical calculation – all of this process is fundamentally a way of solving problems, serving to combine information in ways that give a purchase on the problem. The process is analogous to the mental work of making metaphor intelligible and, applied to narrative, to combine settings, character and episode into meaningful wholes. It is not as though imagination leads us away from the details, the facts of the situation or the way they can be represented mathematically. My point is that the imaginative processes of forming connections is the same even if the structures or materials differs.

Importantly, in both cases, the forming of connections is directed towards a purpose, whether that be combining metaphoric elements to come to a fresh understanding of a situation or a combinatory process involving diagrams, graph-making, language and mathematics to solve a troubling problem. As Lipman argues, 'What matters is that those who explore the realms of possibility must retain as much as possible their sense of fact, just as those who explore the perceivable world must keep their imagination about them' (2003, p. 245). The point also underlines the fact that in the case of this physics class, imagination is just one facet of the creation of new knowledge – new for that learner, or new perhaps for the domain. It could be seen how these moments of combination were interspersed by sustained periods of working through mathematical equations. Developing fluency in maths working was regarded as underpinning the possibilities for being creative in physics[5] because practice and fluency build a quickness in using the symbols and an intuitiveness about what mathematical reasoning may be fruitful.

Teaching for imaginative learning is teaching how to learn new things (not just existing things)

A similar pedagogy focused on forming connections informed the second class on this topic. The class was on fringe visibility and its relationship to correlation and coherence. Simon once again drew the two-pinhole experiment (see Figure 5.2).

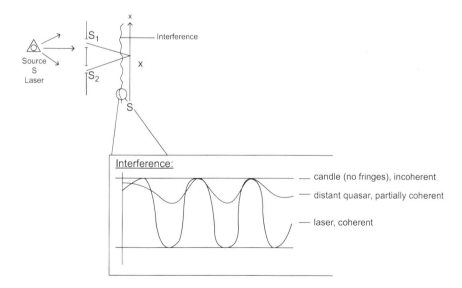

Figure 5.2 Diagram of a two pinhole experiment with a breakout diagram representing the interference incoherent, partially incoherent and coherent waves indicated but not illustrated in the top diagram

120   *Honours quantum physics*

'We're talking about the correlation between two points, and the correlation of two times, t_1 and t_2, the correlation between space-time points.' First, a couple of long equations are derived. The first of which I think is a quantitative, precise description in maths of coherence. He then introduces a discussion about the relation of three things: quantum coherence function, quantum correlation and quantum degree of coherence. He says, 'I want to play a game. Does someone want to pick any two functions on the board which tell us how they link with each other? Turn off your maths brains and turn on your physics brains'. This is interesting pedagogically: The task once again explicitly urges the students to make connections. Just as metaphors forge a relationship between two hitherto unconnected notions, and narrative asks us to figure out from the unfolding events of the plot what is the overall point or theme/s of the story, so this task asks the students to forge links between concepts to see how they relate to one another. This will produce deeper forms of understanding. As I witness this in action, it occurs to me that if this is always the case, that whatever 'learning' is, it is inextricably linked to activating our imagination if it is about forming connections (connections that 'structure understanding' in constructivist terms) or prompting us to see alternative possibilities. It also seems to me to show how non arts-based disciplines do not necessarily have to adopt the usual imaginative formats – role plays, narrative, assigning metaphors – in order to encourage imagination, *although they may well do so*. I find myself asking the question: Is this the reason teaching for imaginative learning allows students to learn practices that lead to new knowledge, and not just existing knowledge?

A student asks whether 'g' could be all imaginary, and Simon answers that yes, it can be, meaning in the technical/mathematical sense of a so-called 'pure imaginary number',[6] which is the same as Ricoeur's 'productive' sense, rather than in the sense of 'illusory'.

Correlation tells you how well correlated the two physical wave function phases are, he says, while moving his hands rhythmically and oppositely up and down.

Embodied cognition: forming analogical relationships between body and concept

A student asks a question that Simon interprets in a drawing on the board, but the student says she doesn't see it like this and points to the initial drawing of laser light, candlelight and light from a distant quasar, from which they continue the discussion and elucidation. Another student asks what is the case if $g = 0$. After several more calculations, Simon draws a graphical representation on two axes of the real oscillations between -1 and $+1$, with one student pointing out that when $g = 0$ the circle that is drawn collapses to a point and expands to the outer edge of a circle when the fringe is at its maximum. For example, candlelight which is incoherent, meaning it has no fringes, will always have 'g' as zero. There is much discussion, with the students now answering each other's questions. All the students are laughing at one point, doing rhythmical movements with their hands and bodies to show different correlation relationships. Using his hands once again to illustrate the correlation, Simon says, 'the disturbance being created means if I know where this is [one hand in one position], then I know where the other is'. He jokes that if someone wants to write a paper on coherence, they should talk to the class because no one expresses it as well as they have.

In this example the body is being used, manipulated in fact, by educator and students to represent, physically, the nature of correlation. This is yet another example of how students learn cognitive practices. Here it involves teaching them the capacity to manipulate representations – in this case bodily manipulation of limbs – and thereby transform how they can conceive, and think about, phenomena. From a Vygotskian developmental perspective, this appears to demonstrate how reasoning appears first on the 'intermental' plane, or plane of social interaction, before being internalised into and shaping the 'intramental' plane, the plane of individual cognition (Menary, 2010).

It is interesting to me that in spite of the ineffability of 'understanding' quantum mechanical microstates, there is a persistent attempt to construct physical understandings of it through analogues to physical systems and bodily experience – reproductive imagination – which duplicate something original, but which are used to model aspects of the quantum world and so manifest an understanding of the nature of its physical reality.

In an interesting and related ethnographic study of protein molecule modelling, which offers support to the idea of the pedagogical efficacy of embodied imagination, Natasha Myers (2008) showed that becoming an expert crystallographer, and making sense of intricate objects, had researchers using their bodies as a resource to learn about, work with and communicate precise molecular configurations. Her field observations suggested that, in the process of building and manipulating protein models, crystallographers sculpted embodied models alongside parallel digital renderings they crafted onscreen. Crystallographic modelling at the computer interface was therefore not only a means of producing representations of proteins, but a means of training novice crystallographers' bodies and, in her view, imaginations (p. 163).

> In other words, through an interactive practice of sculpting molecular models, the models themselves can act recursively to sculpt and reconfigure the modeler's body. Crystallographic model-building is thus a practice of learning through incorporation, of drawing the model into one's body as it is sculpted piecemeal onscreen through a graphics interface. In this sense, molecular embodiments are generated by 'infolding' the model into the 'flesh' of the modeler, where it comes to reside as a part of the modeler her- or himself (on 'infolding' see Haraway [2006] and Merleau-Ponty [1968]). Inflected and informed by the embodied models that get embedded in their tissues, expressive researchers' bodies become expressive media for the expression of molecular forms.

(p. 190)

122 *Honours quantum physics*

At the same time as manipulating physical analogies for learning concepts, the students in the quantum physics class showed they were well aware of how analogies, while illuminating, would have limitations and could break down, and that other analogies would have to be used. For example, in the interviews, one particular student frequently used the resources of objects in the room to explain things to me in the pre-class focus group.

> [*Moving objects around on the table.*] So this [*while gesturing*] is the event horizon of the black hole and the black hole is this mass because you get particles here that don't exist, and because physics is weird, two particles start existing. One of them goes into the black hole. One of them goes into the universe. Now that particle in the universe is an extra particle. So because it's got mass, this black hole has to shrink. Just using whatever is around on the table. Your metaphors – you often tend to use a lot of metaphor, which often really does simplify the situation.
>
> It also forces you to think of the situations where the metaphor doesn't apply. Especially as I got into more advanced physics.

This student's illustration demonstrates an internalised competence in a dialectical process of imaginative and critical thinking. Both are used to think about something which is as yet unknown and thus, I argue, has transformed their capacity to learn how to learn.

Conclusion

The case study of this honours quantum physics class raised interesting issues about Ricoeur's theory of imagination. Primary among them was the relationship between reproductive and productive imagination. Pedagogy in this physics class pointed to what appeared to be a contingent and step-wise relationship between reproductive and productive imagination – something which Ricoeur himself does not expand on, although he does speak about memory's role in anticipation or rehearsal and its interaction. Memories rest upon people's embodied experience of the world. Embodied analogies and other metaphors were used by the teacher and students to model systems upon which further forms of reasoning, such as mathematical, diagrammatic and linguistic reasoning, could operate (as in using body rhythms to 'model' correlation). This was interesting because quantum concepts and the quantum world cannot be experienced or understood directly and even the notion of 'measurement' raises complex issues of interference by the observer/experimenter. Nevertheless, Newtonian notions were combined with diagrams and mathematics to hypothesise about the nature of the physical systems they were studying.

The essential role of the combinatory power of imagination applied in metaphor and narrative that connects disparate things by combining them into new wholes was applied in a pedagogy designed to promote the imagination in physics. As we have discussed, Ricoeur contends that metaphors and narrative

Honours quantum physics 123

redescribe in ways that can produce semantic shifts, and this function is not restricted to structures in literature and the arts. The combinatorial activity appeared to explain the pedagogy in which students were led in a 'dance' cycle of diagrammatic, mathematical and linguistic forms of reasoning (which the educator said mirrored the work of physicists). Each of these skilful forms – or tools – offered an approach to understanding, but, cumulatively and in combination, they appeared to synthesise the students' understanding of the concepts – in this case quantum concepts that cannot be understood directly but can only be constructed indirectly through the mediation of these cognitive tools. This comparison and contrast between the three seemed to be designed to *organise and reorganise* their conceptions of the quantum notion being considered. Blending figuration and verbal and mathematical reasoning as tools functioning as 'proximate terms' (Polanyi's term) composed new knowledge, which is the role of all expressions of the productive imagination in Ricoeur's terms.

Finally, this ethnographic case displayed the active role of imagination in the provisional nature of knowledge. On multiple occasions in multiple ways – through the attitudes to error, to the admonition to question assumptions and approach problems in ways that were meaningful to the individual students, to embodying the hypothetical representation of the nature of correlation – concepts and theories were treated as working ideas that guided and enabled inquiry but could be reconstructed or falsified in the future (Bleazby, 2013). This is captured in Ricoeur's theory by the productive imagination, including the human subject's critical consciousness of the difference between the imagined and the real. Productive imagination entails an awareness of the fictiveness or constructedness of the creation. For learners, this means an openness to reconsider how knowledge may arise in the future. This suggests that imagination's importance for opening up possibilities has an important role to play in the renewal of knowledge and for inquiry, and learning, to be never-ending. This point about the role of imagination was also made by Dewey. The importance of openness to complexity and reconsideration (Bleazby, 2012) makes the imagination of fundamental importance to education, in particular to higher education.

The following chapter considers an ethnographic case from the humanities, namely a first year medieval European history subject.

Notes

1 An honours year is an optional fourth year on top of a three year degree, for students with distinction averages, which is focused on research education and confers an honours degree.

2 I am indebted to Richard Feynman for this form of expression, which is taken from a different context and loosely adapted from *QED: The strange theory of light and matter* (1985).

3 The 'Division of labour' in Engeström's diagram represents the division of labour that is characteristic of workplaces rather than classrooms or teaching contexts and is beyond the scope of this book.

4 This interpretation is implied by Hutchins's (2014) excellent article on the cultural system of human cognition, in which the individual cognizer is seen as a 'local network' from the perspective of a distributed cognitive system, where the teacher in the classroom improves the ability of the predictive mind to ascertain meaning.

124 *Honours quantum physics*

5 The imagination's role in mathematics, which seems to be itself fundamentally a way of talking about understandings of mathematical relationships
6 An imaginary number is a number whose square is less than or equal to zero.

References

Amabile, T. M. (1983). *The social psychology of creativity*. New York: Springer-Verlag.

Arendt, H. (1959). *The human condition*. New York: Doubleday Anchor Books.

Bleazby, J. (2011). Overcoming relativism and absolutism: Dewey's ideals of truth and meaning in philosophy for children. *Educational Philosophy and Theory, 43*(5), 453–466. doi:10.1111/j.1469-5812.2009.00567.x

Bleazby, J. (2012). Dewey's notion of imagination in philosophy for children. *Education and Culture, 28*(2), 95–111. doi:10.1353/eac.2012.0013

Bleazby, J. (2013). *Social reconstruction learning: Dualism, Dewey and philosophy in Schools*. New York: Routledge.

Brown, J. R., & Fehige, Y. (2014, Fall). Thought experiments. In E. N. Zalta (Ed.), *The Stanford encyclopedia of philosophy*. Stanford: Stanford University.

Cazden, C. (1981). Performance before competence: Assistance to child discourse in the zone of proximal development. *Quarterly Newsletter of the Laboratory of Comparative Human Cognition, 3*(5), 5–8.

Clark, A. (1997). *Being there: Putting brain, body and world together*. Cambridge, MA: The MIT Press.

Clark, A. (2010). The extended mind. In R. Menary (Ed.), *The extended mind* (pp. 27–42). Cambridge, MA: A Bradford Book, The MIT Press.

Cole, D. G., Sugioka, H. L., & Yamagata-Lynch, L. C. (1999). Supportive classroom environments for creativity in higher education. *Journal of Creative Behaviour, 33*(4), 277–293.

Csikszentmihalyi, M. (1999). Implications of a systems perspective for the study of creativity. In R. Sternberg (Ed.), *Handbook of creativity* (pp. 313–335). Cambridge: Cambridge University Press.

Dawkins, R. (1989). *The selfish gene* (Second ed.). Oxford: Oxford University Press.

Dennett, D. C. (1995). *Darwin's dangerous idea: Evolution and the meanings of life*. New York: Simon & Schuster.

Edwards, A. (2005). Let's get beyond community and practice: The many meanings of learning by participating. *Curriculum Journal, 16*(1), 49–65.

Eliot, T. S. (1944). *Four quartets*. London: Faber and Faber.

Engeström, Y. (1990). When is a tool? Multiple meanings of artifacts in human activity? In *Learning, working and imagining: Twelve studies in activity theory* (pp. 171–195). Helsinki: Orienta-Konsultit Oy.

Feynman, R. P. (1985). *QED: The strange theory of light and matter*. London: Penguin Books.

Gribbin, J. (1984). *In search of Schrödinger's cat: Quantum physics and reality*. London: Black Swan.

Hardy, G. H. (1940/2004). *A mathematician's apology*. Cambridge: Cambridge University Press.

Hutchins, E. (2014). The cultural system of human cognition. *Philosophical Psychology, 27*(1), 34–49. doi:10.1080/09515089.2013.830548

Johnson, M. (1993). Moral imagination. In *Moral imagination: Implications of cognitive science for ethics*. Chicago: University of Chicago Press.

Lakoff, G., & Johnson, M. (1980). *Metaphors we live by*. Chicago: University of Chicago Press.

Lave, J., & Wenger, E. (1991). *Situated learning: Legitimate peripheral participation.* Cambridge, UK/New York: Cambridge University Press.

Lipman, M. (2003). *Thinking in education.* New York: Cambridge University Press.

Menary, R. (2010). Dimensions of mind. *Phenomenology and the Cognitive Sciences, 9,* 561–578. doi:10.1007/s11097-010-9186-7

Myers, N. (2008). Molecular embodiments and the body-work of modeling in protein crystallography. *Social Studies of Science, 38*(2), 163–199.

Nickerson, R. (1999). Enhancing creativity. In R. J. Sternberg (Ed.), *Handbook of creativity* (pp. 392–430). Cambridge: Cambridge University Press.

Nussbaum, M. (2001). *Upheavals of thought: The intelligence of emotions.* New York: Cambridge University Press.

Polanyi, M. (1967). *The tacit dimension.* Garden City, NY: Anchor Books.

Reddy, M. (1979). The conduit metaphor. In A. Ortony (Ed.), *Metaphor and thought* (pp. 284–324). Cambridge: Cambridge University Press.

Ricoeur, P. (1975/2003). *The rule of metaphor: The creation of meaning in language* (R. Czerny, K. McLaughlin, & J. Costello, Trans.). London: Routledge.

Ricoeur, P. (1979). The metaphorical process as cognition, imagination and feeling. In S. Sacks (Ed.), *On metaphor* (pp. 141–153). Chicago: University of Chicago Press.

Saul, J. R. (2001). *On equilibrium.* Ringwood, Victoria: Penguin Books.

Taylor, G. H. (2006, Spring-Fall). Ricoeur's philosophy of imagination. *Journal of French Philosophy, 16*(1 & 2), 93–104.

Vygotsky, L. S. (1978). *Mind in society: The development of higher psychological processes.* Cambridge, MA: Harvard University Press.

Vygotsky, L. S. (1984). Imagination and creativity in the adolescent. In *The collected works of L. S. Vygotsky* (Vol. 4, pp. 199–219). Moscow: Izdatelstvo Pedagogika.

Wertsch, J. V. (2007). Mediation. In H. Daniels, M. Cole, & J. V. Wertsch (Eds.), *The Cambridge companion to Vygotsky* (pp. 178–192). Cambridge: Cambridge University Press.

6 First year medieval history ethnography

> Imagination is rather unnerving for most historians. Imagination seems to demand that they loosen their grip on the reality that makes their histories different from fiction. But imagination need not be unnerving. Imagination need not be fantasy. Imagination is the ability to see those fine-lined and faint webs of significance. Imagination is hearing the silence because we have heard some of the sounds. Imagination is seeing the absent things because we have seen so much else. Imagination is an act of human solidarity, or rather imagination is an act of solidarity in our humanness. . . . Imagination is our capacity to see ourselves as somebody else.
>
> (Dening, 1998, pp. 208–209)

Introduction

I arrive at the Rotunda at the Clayton campus of Monash University in Melbourne, Australia. It is Monday morning, in the first week of the academic year, in early March, and for most of the students crowded into the central waiting area, this is their first class at university. On my way over, just moments before, I overheard one student tell another how excited she was. These are first year students, and the newness of their experience hits me: the university campus is new; 'lectures' and 'tutorials' are new; and their expectations are high, mixed perhaps with trepidation. I remember myself on the same threshold, but I also witness myself as an interloper, albeit one returning to one of my 'home' disciplines: unlike physics, history along with English literature are *my* disciplines. I should know my way around, I tell myself, although I know next to nothing about medieval history.

In the 10 weeks I attend lectures, and the 7 weeks of tutorials, I come to appreciate that this class focuses on establishing the skills and conditions for being a good historian. It does this by systematically developing the students' skills in working with 'primary' historical sources: the ability to interpret, question and analyse primary works from the period (Hughes-Warrington, 2009), such as letters, speeches, literary works and maps. Expertise in wielding the skill of working with primary documents is requisite to their imaginative and creative application in history. This is the view of history which emerges from the medieval European history class over the semester: History is not just the

First year medieval history ethnography   127

transfer of information *about* the past; it is *a way of working*, and the foundational skills require development and practice.

In this sense, the first year class is an introduction to what an historian does. Each week in the tutorial, the students are required to read at least one primary and one 'secondary' source (that is, the writing of other historians). Those students who are leading the tutorial for that week read far more and are expected to locate evidence from a number of primary sources and incorporate it into their presentations. And the questions that the primary source can illuminate are endless. Each source contains such a wealth of detail that, depending on the focus of the historian's interest, it is possible to look again and again at the document to 'see' or infer telling evidence about a myriad of issues about the period. This entails developing the ability to forensically read the primary sources. The point is that what is revealed by this careful reading is used by the historian to build an argument about what the source can show about the (social, economic or artistic) past. The interesting discovery for me was how a seemingly mechanical teaching of the skills, which included using a framework of questions to problematize the primary sources systematically, became an instance for observing Ricoeur's 'productive' imagination in play and Vygotsky's 'tool mediated action' at work in language and processes – when they are pressed into service to consider possible interpretations about the past and to begin to build an argument.

In my account to follow, I illustrate the pedagogical approaches taken by the teaching team represented by the participant lecturer, whom I will call Cecelia, and the highly experienced head tutor, whom I will call Jennifer, in this first year unit. The student participants were from one of the tutorial (breakout) groups. The ethnography relied upon the following kinds of data: descriptions of classroom observations, course documents, completed student assignments, the textual thread from the weekly online discussion forum and quotations from interviews with the participating professor, head tutor and student focus groups conducted before and after the class observation.

The starting point is the historical sources. The table of contents in the course reader reveals the extent of the primary sources – and these are just the jumping-off point for students: 'The Beatitudes' from the Gospel of St Matthew, *The rule of St Benedict* (c. 530), Einhard's *Life of Charlemagne* (circa 817–837), Pope Urban's account of crusading speech: 'Speech at Council of Clermont' (1095), Abelard's *Historia calamitatum* (1134): Heloise 'First Letter' (1135–6), the *Magna Carta* (1215), Thomas of Celano's *First and second lives of St Francis* (1225–6), Catherine of Sienna's 'Letter 31' (1375), Hildegard of Bingen's Letter to the prelates of Mainz (1171), Eleanor of Aquitane's Letter to Pope Celestine III (1193), Boccaccio's Prologue to the *Decameron* (1351) and Chaucer's Prologue to *The Canterbury tales* (1392–95). In addition, there was at least one secondary source to read each week. As said earlier, the students who led the week's tutorials were required to read more widely, from both primary and secondary sources.

128   *First year medieval history ethnography*

How to read forensically

In week 1 of the unit, in a jammed lecture theatre in the Rotunda – a circular building with theatres around the outside, like pineapple segments – the lecturer, Cecelia, addresses how to read a primary source. She has selected a key episode in Matthew's gospel in the New Testament that Christianised the Western world during the Middle Ages: Jesus's Sermon on the Mount, known to Catholics as 'The Beatitudes'. In a secular society, as Australia is in the twenty-first century, I assume many will be unfamiliar with it, but it will be familiar to some who have attended church schools. Cecelia urges them:

> From whatever way you approach the text, you have to be imaginative. If you know the Bible, you have to try to imagine you've never seen it before. I want us all to come at it with fresh eyes.

I am struck by this seemingly radical statement. Cecelia is overtly talking about imagination. But this lecture is about how to read.

> You already thought you could read, but listen, you need to do it differently from usual . . . if you are already familiar with a source, you have to approach it as though it's new and for the first time.

Cecelia seemed to be suggesting that imagination has something to do with defamiliarising yourself.

> You may think you know how to read. But go slow. Texts are meant to be confronting. Our job is somehow to leap from here to there. And why do we need to? Because our world is built on this. This comes from a place very different from us.

She appears to be suggesting that care needs to be taken not to assume similarities between the present and the past. The challenge of educators is to create engagement with the past while avoiding ahistoricism.

Later I asked the teaching team to expand her explanation of this in the post-class interview.

Tutor: Because it's so foreign. One of the ways I see imagination playing out here is students have to come to terms with twin facts: 1. people were still people who you can rely on to act like humans with their own rationality etc., but also that that rationality is not ours and it's so different and so has to be respected within its own parameters. Some weeks particularly challenge this for students, so the week where we did the mystics and Catherine of Sienna's letters, some students just could not cope with that. They either just wrote her off as a complete nut job, or they just reduced their discussion to

First year medieval history ethnography   129

the safe boundaries of the political relationships that she had and the execution of the young man that she was talking about. Perhaps it's partly also because our world is not a religious world in the same way that theirs was. So even those students who are people of faith, of whatever faith, they still find it really different and weird. And that's a really genuine challenge. To realise that the world can still be a human world, a human society, operating logically and yet nothing like what we think it should be like – and coming to terms with that is challenging.

Lecturer: I imagine that students who do anthropology and sociology have to do the same imaginative work where they are encountering difference and they're trying to respect the logic of it while enumerating the ways that it feels profoundly different. And I think that's great ethical work. And it's one of the things I'm proud of teaching medieval history and I think it makes them better people.

(transcript, Interview)

These comments suggest that historical empathy is not about being seduced into a sympathetic portrayal of the past; it is the act of embedding historical actors in their context. The *discipline* of history is required to help us to overcome what we cannot instinctively feel or see (Griffiths, 2009). Becoming aware of the past's difference from the present is also a point made by the ethnographic historian Greg Dening, who, similarly, saw history as involving imagination:

The humanness we share with the past is at the one time the same and different. The most unhistorical thing we can do is to imagine that the past is us in funny clothes. Our imagination has to allow us to experience what we share with the past and see difference *at the same time*.

(1998, p. 209, my italics)

We can see from their comments that at least some history educators think that history involves both imagination and critical thinking and that the relationship between them is dialectical. Also that the imagination involves holding ideas in our heads that may feel contrary to our own, that this is difficult and that it somehow involves ethics. This recalls Ricoeur's axis of critical conscious of the fictiveness of imaginative products. The ability to conjecture and to imagine alternative explanations or ways of understanding the past implies also becoming aware of, and checking, assumptions. Doing this involves engaging critically with the past and present. Students of history need to be awake to the unquestioning assumption that to imagine the past is like the present is to simplify the problem, falling into the trap of 'reproducing' the present – in Ricoeur's sense of the reproductive imagination. These views represent at least the views of some historians. Given the different traditions within history, as with any discipline, I do not argue that this represents a 'typical' historical view, but that is not our concern here.

130   *First year medieval history ethnography*

Cecelia then demonstrates how students of history would 'read', in this deep historical sense, the declarations of Jesus in The Beatitudes. She commences reading it aloud, quite slowly.

> Blessed are the poor in spirit, for theirs is the kingdom of heaven.
> Blessed are those who mourn, for they shall be comforted.
> Blessed are the meek: for they shall inherit the earth.
> Blessed are they which do hunger and thirst for righteousness: for they
>   shall be satisfied.
> Blessed are the merciful: for they shall obtain mercy . . .
>
> (*The Holy Bible*, King James Version)

Cecelia asks the students what strikes them about this text. She talks about the rhythm, recalling and comparing the passage with Martin Luther King Jr's famous speeches, and reminds them that King was, like Jesus, a preacher who delivered his sermons orally. Oral delivery required him to capture and hold his audience's attention through a variety of devices. Another rhetorical device it uses is repetition, and she reminds them of others who do this whom they may be familiar with: Barak Obama, Ronald Reagan, Paul Keating and Gough Whitlam. Another device used is working with opposites to create paradoxes, on which she says: 'Jesus was expressing an idea about perfection that was counterintuitive'. She says the text seems to demand a literary analysis to understand the rhetorical and literary power of the oratory. But, she stresses, as historians we have to *find the context*. As historians we have to interrogate the text using the following questions: Who wrote it? When? Where? Why? (What motivated them? What did they want the text to achieve?) What does it say?

In the next section, I argue that questioning forms the prerequisite critical skill that is foundational to imaginative engagement in history. The questioning shapes opportunities for thinking and interpreting afforded by the sources. What, then, are the imaginative opportunities opened up by this emphasis on working with primary sources?

Interrogation of primary sources: the five 'W' framework

The technique of interrogating a primary source through the well-recognised lexicon of sequence relations (and therefore a kind of cultural mnemonic), the five 'w' words – who, what, when, where, why – is based on the idea that the history student (and the historian) never encounters the past, except insofar as it exists in 'primary' sources, texts or some 'remains'. The texts themselves may be something written down in a letter, or a hagiography; they may be drawn in a map or constructed in architecture; they could be bones or fossils; they could be oral traditions transcribed in some way, such as a song or a myth; or they could be material objects like a painting or a fashionable dress that enclose their narrative in a material or a design. It doesn't matter which, but one thing historians can never do is to observe the past directly. Whether it is 'a story caught in a letter', a dance or a tattoo' (Dening, 1998, p. 207), it can reveal insights about gender, power, social organisation, wealth or government in the period in question. Interpreting primary sources requires students to actively use higher order thinking skills by engaging in the processes by which history is constructed (Hughes-Warrington, 2009, p. 11). Along the way they internalise the 'facts', the memorisation or rehearsal of which are too frequently the goal of methods of teaching history in secondary (high) school systems, which rely on textbooks and other secondary sources (Burenheide, 2007, p. 57), which flatten the act of reading. In textbooks, with their privileging of the secondary interpretation over practical apprenticeship of skill development, history is presented as unproblematic, finished interpretation.

The long shadow Christianity cast on Western cultures in the Middle Ages justifies applying these questions to Matthew's gospel, Cecelia says. In this first week of the course she demonstrates this historical questioning technique as well as the way historians rely upon 'secondary' sources to deepen their historical understanding. The 'who' question is dealt with first. She says the author of Matthew's gospel was not the disciple Matthew, a fact established by dating techniques that place the text about 80–100 CE; and it borrows from Mark, which was written first. It was written by a Jew who would have been a convert of Jesus. She continues, saying that other historical work shows that in this period there was conflict among Jews over the interpretation of Jewish Law, and its writing coincided with the period following the destruction of the temple in Judea in 70 CE by the Romans, a devastating act, akin – for us – to the destruction of Federation Square in Melbourne or the Menzies building for Monash Arts students. In this period of persecution when the text was written, the writer was depicting a radical Jesus. The 'Jesus followers' movement, as she calls them, used the gospel as further evidence that Jesus was the messiah referred to in Isaiah in the Old Testament, and they used that interpretation to support a radical Jewish diaspora. So if we read this document *as if* Matthew's gospel is a campaign document, she suggests, then the gospel becomes a conversation with other, as yet unconverted Jews, many of whom had fled Roman violence to cities in the Roman provinces of Syria and Antioch. This 'as if' form of expression indicates to me that she is proposing a hypothesis. Hypotheses generate testable ideas and are a form of productive imagination, in Ricoeur's terms. But other authorities suggest the text was addressed to gentiles (as non-Jews were called by Jews) and was a missionary document, spreading the Word of Jesus to the wider non-Jewish population and conveying a universal message. There was lots of debate in the period, she says, about what Jesus meant when he said to 'spread the Word'.

The last interrogative question is 'Why?' Why did Matthew write down the text when he did? Her answer is that the old traditions of Judaism were failing and this was an attempt to capture the meaning of Jesus for a religious renewal: If you are going to do active missionary work over a large area you need a script of proselytising words to help you do it. Hence the 'gospels' ('good news') were written.

132   *First year medieval history ethnography*

Having set the scene for the course, Cecelia finishes this first lecture with the question she first raised at the start of the day: What was *the argument* presented in the lecture today? I duly do as she suggests and write down what I, thinking as a student, think her argument is: that texts need to be contextualised if they are to be understood historically; that an historical approach includes careful, close reading, interrogating the text with the questions – who, when, where, what, why? (in no particular order). Asking questions of sources means you need to consider their context. In this way, these questions lead to other questions: Who was the audience envisaged by the source writer? To what purpose was its rhetoric directed? What action was it designed to incite? Answering the questions means you need to delve in to the sources and resource your opinions with other historians' arguments mounted on their encounters with yet other sources. The significance of her repeatedly asking the students to revisit the question 'What was the argument presented in the lecture today?' is dealt with later in the section, 'The synthesis exercise and – what is an essay anyway?'

In my account to follow, I illustrate the pedagogical approach to teaching the handling of source material by discussing one week's lecture and tutorial. My principle of selection here is random, as I could have taken any number of lectures and tutorials and explicated a similar purpose in the pedagogy. My selection is also based on the individual students who consented to full participation in the research. The reader of this account should realise that the week-by-week sequential learning path laid by the lecturer in her definition of terms, periods and the accumulation and progression in knowledge, if not in skill development, is lost in this method of recounting – and in my opinion it was an excellent introduction for first year students. My ethnography is therefore not an account of the course, but of how the pedagogical approaches built a conception of the role of creative imagination in history.

Example of 'lecture' that models the historical treatment of a primary source

The illustrative lecture explored here models what the students are expected to do when they interrogate historical sources as historians do to determine critically its relevance to their area of interest. It is taken from the third week of the subject. It demonstrates they are taught from the start how to build historical knowledge: to be producers of history, rather than simply consumers. This is later reinforced in my interview with the lecturer and tutor at the conclusion of the course. The lecturer said: 'Coming to know the data is a rhetorical, hermeneutic process in itself. The data is never just there. You're always inventing the data' (Interview transcript).

There is a difference between the source evidence and historical 'data'. The data is not 'out there' but is formed in reciprocal relationship to the questions asked of the sources and the historian's interpretation of how the source evidence answers those questions. In other words it is a kind of fluid subset of the sources. This is something these educators recognise distinguishes historians

First year medieval history ethnography   133

(and the humanities) from natural scientists, who often speak about data and findings separately, as in the statement, 'Here's my data and in the next chapter I'll talk about it' (transcript, Interview, 13.12.13; Maxwell, 1992, is interesting on this point also).

The theme of the third week was 'Invasions and Centralisation' and was to cover the period of the Dark Ages, from 450–750 BCE, to the reign of Charlemagne. 'I'm trying to get you into the intellectual, imaginative and the social space of Medieval Europe', Cecelia explained. She began by talking about the medieval state in the period of contraction of the Roman Empire and incursions by Germanic invaders from the east of Europe; related the importance of the 'tribe' and its values of chivalry, honour, masculinity and fighting; covered the archeological evidence about Childeric, a 'barbarian' (in Latin 'bearded man') who made a treaty with the Romans and built a small kingdom; Clovis, his son; the predominance of Arianism – a form of Christianity which did not accept Jesus's divinity – in the area we now call France; before finally coming to Charlemagne in Aachen in 814 CE. She showed a YouTube video of a Blondie song about the life and achievements of Charlemagne. Having set the scene, she then illustrated how to apply the five W's to Einhard's *Life of Charlemagne*.

Einhard (775–840 CE) wrote a history of Charlemagne, an unusual subject in a period that for three or four hundred years had produced few secular literary works, the preferred material being saints' lives. The 'why' question in the guiding interrogation framework emerges first. *Why* did the source writer write this work? At the start of *Life of Charlemagne*, Einhard compares his *Life* with Cicero, writing his work into history by self-consciously positioning himself in relation to the great Roman philosopher. Cecelia argues that you can infer from this how the glorious classical period of Rome cast a long shadow of influence on medieval scholarship, as well as also how high Einhard's aspirations were, despite his modest origins from a 'barbarian' tribe. 'It's about legitimacy', she declares. Einhard's mannerly modesty, by comparing his endeavour to Cicero, disguises *an ambition to highlight the greatness of Charlemagne.* This interpretation highlights the need in historical analysis to discover what I might call, after the philosopher John Austin (2003), the 'performative' function of a primary historical source, that is, what influence or action the author intended to achieve by it, what rhetorical choices the author made in producing the source and whom he or she was trying to convince of what. The possibilities opened up by this conjectural, projective process of imagination would then need to be checked by further reading of the sources.

Who was Einhard? (The 'who' question). From other secondary sources, it emerges that he was born a peasant, educated in a monastery in Fulda, but evidently did not become a priest. He went to work in Charlemagne's court in Aachen (or Aix la Chappelle), where he became a private secretary to Louis, one of Charlemagne's sons. His public service career illustrates a new career path for young men who had learned to read and write in Latin, something which had not existed earlier. Charlemagne employed administrators to keep records while he established and governed the first empire since the break-up of the Roman

134　*First year medieval history ethnography*

Empire. Aachen Cathedral – and she shows a photograph of it – is evidence that he set his capital there, that he had wealth and could source skilled stonemasons and other specialised craftsmen to build it, which is itself indicative of a nascent stability and growth of civility in the kingdom.

The 'what' question then comes into its own. To go beyond knowing that the source is a history of Charlemagne, Cecelia delves into some of the details in the text of Einhard's *Life of Charlemagne*. Citing what were called *missi dominici*, dedicated envoys – or messengers – of the lord, she elaborates on the historical implications of the meaning of the Latin words – *missi*, or messenger or envoy, and *dominici* in both senses of the Lord God and lord, ruler. 'How many ideas are being synthesised into an argument about the machinery of empire, governance and legitimacy!' she exhorts. She is right. It is the kind of link I will hear the tutor point out many times in tutorials throughout the semester. Even the existence of the role of *missi dominici* in the Carolingian Empire, as a position of employment, implies a great deal about what an 'empire' is, its ways of governance and how it founded its legitimacy in religion. This fact alone forces the historian to re-examine what might be current, taken-for-granted 'obvious' notions of society and government in order to understand what civil society and governance were like in a different period – the similarities and the differences. It also opens up for examination the structures of society and how they function. Looked at through the lens provided by Ricoeur's theory, we see that the imagination is synthesising new connections, which create a complex and layered understanding of how an empire operates.

'You can't manage territory of this size by charisma and power', Cecelia says.

The 'why' question re-emerges here: Einhard wrote his *Life* between 817 and 837, after Charlemagne's death, under Louis's rule. Although Louis was Charlemagne's son, this was a period when automatic inheritance by the eldest son was not the norm, so he had to legitimise his claim to the throne. For example, there was a question whether the oaths the vassals made to Charlemagne needed to be remade all over again to Louis.

So what does this form of questioning have to do with imagination? Recalling Ricoeur's notion that metaphors and narratives function as models for trying out relationships, we can say that the historian projects a past by manipulating models about how things like power and governance work. The projective nature of historical knowledge means imagination is fundamental to a practising historian. Historians do not believe they simply reproduce the past in their accounts of it. There is no way of recovering the past in its wholeness, telling audiences 'what happened' and how 'it' was experienced by all the people of the past. That simple notion has to be unmasked. In its stead is a temporal and process-orientated and perspectival notion of history. In every period, individual historians rework what is known about the past by asking questions of interest to themselves.

The observation of classes and history assignments appeared to show that the interrogative process of reading and making sense of the primary sources does not involve a linear process of acquiring and applying knowledge. Rather, it involves making connections discursively and discerning patterns or webs of meaning in the sources that answer those questions – that becomes the argument (or a segment of the argument). This implies the ability to think about alternative explanatory possibilities, be they different values held by people in the past, their internal logic, the context in which people move, reasons for events and so on. Drawing on Ricoeur's (1975/2003, p. 285) and Dawkins's (1989, p. 59, p. 200) suggestions that imagination mingles with reason by modelling explanatory possibilities, history involves conjecturing, considering alternative explanations, checking if that possibility is supported by interpretation of more instances of evidence in a continual interplay between past and present and engaging in imaginative and critical forms of thinking. The critical thinking part of the dialectical operation involves engaging critically with those connecting webs of meaning and testing and comparing the validity of the links. To use a spatial analogy, it suggests that there is not much 'distance' between analysis and imagination in historical interpretation. Imagination is involved in the dialectical imaginative-analytical operation of evidence formation – the process of transforming inert data in primary sources into evidence laden with meaning. That this is understood by students was confirmed in the post-class interview when two students spoke about the relationship between fact and imagination being part and parcel of their 'immersion' in the primary sources.

Student 1: . . . you can have an informed understanding, we don't really know what [the facts] are so let's try to find some answers . . .

Student 2: I quite enjoyed researching too. There's that little buzz you get when you make a connection.

(post-class interview)

Introduction to history and gaining confidence: 'No one comes out of the womb reading Latin'

As discussed in Chapter 1, Lucas, Claxton and Spencer (2013, pp. 16–17) proposed a model composed of five 'creative dispositions' when they devised a formative assessment tool for assessing pupils' creativity in schools. Being imaginative was one of these dispositions, and the others were being inquisitive, persistent, collaborative and disciplined. Confidence is related to persistence in the form of tenacity as an important habit of mind. We can rephrase this to say that confidence can provide individuals with the power to persist with an idea, even though it might be met with doubt, opposition or resistance. Without it, new ideas may not be translated into action. It is this idea that gave significance to another teaching moment I observed. Was this a deliberate pedagogy adopted by the lecturer? A psychological element underlying imagination seemed to be at work here. It involved a form of creative pedagogy involving the student identifying and/or empathising with another person's previous life experience.

On the first day of the course, Cecelia took to the lectern. As a way of inviting questions in lectures, she stressed that 'no question is too stupid' and preceded to tell an anecdote about preparing for her first day of class at Johns

136   *First year medieval history ethnography*

Hopkins University in Baltimore as a PhD scholarship student. She described how she read and re-read *The Machiavellian moment* by J.G.A. Pocock without comprehending it and had convinced herself that 'students were cleverer here in America, that texts were harder here in America'. As she made her way to her first class on campus in this defeated mood, she asked directions of someone. This person inquired what she was doing and, upon receiving her answer, commented what a hard text that was. The feeling of relief. Cecelia encouraged them with the following empathetic words:

> No one comes out of the womb reading Latin. Just because the person beside you in the [tutorial] knows something you don't, it doesn't mean that your own questions or confusion makes you stupid or wrong. We all have a different past.

She showed an apt medieval painting of students in pews listening to a lecturer in a raised pulpit, one student dozing, a few chatting, a couple daydreaming, and she asks them to think of a lecture as the lecturer *making an argument for two purposes*: first, that it is somehow important for the student to know; and second, that it is about the nature of the past. The reason this is important, she says, is because this is what they have to do in an essay. So she is saying the lecture is in one way modelling what the students need to do – particularly what is required to demonstrate their learning. She asks them to ask themselves the following prompt – 'Here's what she's saying. I have to work out why this matters'. This is an overt clue to an important metacognitive skill, which must become a habit of mind for learners, something only they can perform during and after the lecture (and, I would add, not only the lecture, but to be autonomous and reflective citizens and workers in the societies of the knowledge era). It is not only what is said and how, but *what you make of why* it is said. Harking back to the point made earlier, confusion is also held up as a signal for a learner: 'I want you to start thinking: whenever you're confused, *that's* the time you are ready to learn. *Use* the experience to explore ideas'. This is a nice inversion. Confusion for a first year student – or perhaps anyone – can cause anxiety because it can imply ignorance, possibly even stupidity, and that's embarrassing. There is a generosity about this philosophy. What she is saying is that as historians as well as, I think, learners, being confused can be *the start of something* much more interesting. It can lead to questions. And questions can open up worlds of new knowledge if we notice and listen to them. The potential for learning occasioned by the confusion at the root of questions, she suggests, is that it prompts closer examination of documents or, when pooled and discussed with peers, feeds curiosity and further inquiry. Bits of information start to be connected to each other, extending their understanding. Armed with this attitude, she encourages them to voice their confusion and explore ideas afforded by it. To gain confidence that confusion is positive!

This is an interesting attitude that links an emotion to a cognitive activity. It will enable the students to consciously recognise an internal signal which can help them become independent learners – important for higher education.

First year medieval history ethnography   137

But, most important for my research, it is an opportunity for imagination. It is strongly mirrored in the literature on problem *finding* in the creativity literature (for example by Csikszentmihalyi and Getzels, 1988, as discussed in Chapter 4) – the formulation of new problems that are meaningful to the person posing them, which spring from a feeling of dissatisfaction with previous attempts to understand an issue or arise from questions prompted by a feeling of confusion. At the same time, Cecelia appears to also situate this learning approach in social terms: historical exploration is not necessarily a solitary intellectual labour. She urges the students that they are 'a great resource for each other' because articulating the problem that is the source of the confusion can broach opportunities for discussion and collaborative exploration with their peers. No one comes out of the womb reading Latin: With persistence and hard work, meaningful interpretations can be made; more close reading and discussion need to ensue.

There is real subtlety in the approaches to learning she is modelling and urging here. She acknowledges the role of emotions that often instigate curiosity and exploration, which provide the energy that impels someone to persist in finding answers (Csikszentmihalyi, 1996). The open-endedness of this search and the need to make new connections are what make constructing new knowledge imaginative. There is also the role modelling given by the master historian to the apprentice – through sharing her discovery that if you pay attention to the source of the ignorance causing embarrassment or anxiety, and instead of giving up or avoiding it, delve into sources in detail, you can come up with potentially rich questions and interpretations that answer them. In effect: 'This is what a good historian will do'. The domain-specific knowledge and skills (what Lucas et al. termed the 'Disciplined' disposition – developing techniques, reflecting critically and crafting and improving your work [p. 17]) have to be melded with the personal attributes of hard work and persistence. Her message is that if you do the hard work and read the sources closely, you will be rewarded! This building of motivation and persistence is well supported by the creativity literature (see, for example, Amabile, 1983; Nickerson, 1999) as we saw in Chapter 4. In this teaching moment, self or critical awareness of emotions are being intelligently linked to the higher order thinking skills by which new historical knowledge is constructed.

The approach is also underpinned by the educator's personal commitment to feminist and equity principles. This emerged in the interview.

> I tell the stories to convey that there are many ways to be an academic. And many ways to own this knowledge. . . . It's a very personal style thing but all of it is encouraging an imaginative leap into which they can be in this world too.
>
> (transcript, post-class interview)

There is also an educationally profound aspect to the approach we see here which goes beyond the skilled making of new connections that create new knowledge because it implicates how they form their identity. She is talking about learning *to imagine yourself as* an historian. This imagining yourself as an

138 *First year medieval history ethnography*

historian happens, she says, by imagining a relationship between self, practices (or methodologies) and material. Learning is meshing with *learning to be*. It is about imagining yourself as someone other than you are. 'When you're asking them to think like an historian, you're actually asking them to imagine themselves as an historian – to imagine a professional identity – So how would an historian approach these sources?' (transcript, post-class interview).

The plasticity of identity was touched on in one student's laughter in the final interview when he commented that one source of fun he derived from the course was the 'buzz when I went into the library. I was a uni[versity] student now. I was a real academic!' (post-class student focus group).

I would like to suggest that this imaginative process is akin to the process of imaginatively straddling the distance between past and present when history asks us to see the humanness of past figures who may deeply challenge our sensibilities by their difference.

Having practised some skills and personal attributes for thinking and working historically, in the next section our analysis turns to what opportunities for using imagination were offered to the students in the assessments for the class.

The development of historical skills in assessments

Assessment is the process of identifying, gathering and interpreting information about students' learning for the purpose of providing information on student achievement and progress and set the direction for ongoing teaching and learning (NSW DET, 2008–9). For teachers, '[g]ood assessment means we must focus unerringly on our educational goals' (Boud, 1998, p. 2). This is because assessment does more than measure what a student knows, it influences what skills students acquire, where they focus their time and attention and study habits (Boud, 1998). My account focuses particularly on what opportunities the history assessments offered, if any, to use imagination.

The assessment, in order, consisted of a short test (10%); a synthesis exercise (25%); an oral tutorial presentation (10%) including participating in the online discussion forum; a research essay based on the presentation (30%); and a final in-class test similar to an exam (25%) (ATS1316 Medieval Europe, Unit Guide). I will focus mainly on the 'synthesis exercise' and the essay (which developed the tutorial presentation), as these formed the bulk of the marks and, for that reason, can tell us what capabilities the educators were most keen to develop. I will consider what was being asked of the learner by each task and also what kind of achievement was considered successful.

The synthesis exercise and – what is an essay anyway?

The essay is the principal form of assessment in the humanities, especially in history. Why? What is it about an essay that is so integral to the understanding,

First year medieval history ethnography 139

forms of thinking and evidentiary base the humanities seek to foster? Contrary to received understandings, does imagination play any role in writing a research essay? Is it just a tired, traditional form of assessment? These questions led me to wonder about the purpose of the synthesis task, which was the first major task of the course. How did it help develop the foundation skills needed for the essay, and did any of these skills involve being imaginative? Could the synthesis task and essay present students with opportunities to ignite semantic innovation?

Interestingly, Ricoeur argues that imagination underpins the rhetorical techniques of metaphor and narrative that organise new connections and produce 'semantic innovation' (shifts in outlook). Narratives and metaphors have in common their ability to synthesise heterogeneous elements. Just as metaphors affect a displacement of an overall meaning at the level of the sentence, so plots combine agents, circumstances, action, goals, causes and chance into a meaningful, intelligible form that is more than a simple succession of events. We are able to see the 'point' of the story – to extract meaning from a configuration of events (Ricoeur, 1983/1984, p. 66). These two modes of 'synthesis', metaphor and narrative plot, can be understood to function as models for understanding reality in new ways – fulfilling the same function as models in science. This led me to ask whether, by actively shaping a coherent and rhetorical argument in an essay based on interpretation of how the sources answer those questions, historians and students of history are being required to unite elements with an internal logic, igniting similar semantic innovation? It seemed to me that the process by which historians shape a coherent and rhetorical argument based on an interpretation of how the historical sources answer their questions is essentially similar: metaphor and narrative plot, and an argument in an essay, model new ways of understanding phenomena.

The synthesis task was to synthesise and interpret Chapter 7, 'Accelerated growth', of Wim Blockmans and Peter Hoppenbrouwers's *Introduction to medieval Europe: Age of discretion* (2007; translated from the Dutch original). It was a lengthy and complex chapter that sought to link population growth in the period 950–1250 CE and changes in food production techniques to changes in the relationship between lords and peasants and their repercussions for culture and social ideology.

According to the Unit Guide, the purpose of the task was to train students in reading and note taking so that they would be able to synthesise various historical sources. It involved writing a 1,000-word summary of the key ideas and evidence in the chapter while at the same time 'critically engaging with the argument'. The following are two examples of opening paragraphs by students. The role of an opening paragraph in an essay is two-fold: to engage the reader in the topic and its significance and to introduce the arguments that will be made.

140   *First year medieval history ethnography*

> Chapter 7 of Wim Blockmans and Peter Hoppenbrouwers's book *Introduction to Medieval Europe* titled 'Accelerated Growth', discusses the economic, political and social changes in Western Europe during the mid to late Middle Ages. They argue that these changes occurred, both directly and indirectly, due to agricultural expansion, emphasising the role of the peasantry and how they were affected by and instrumental in these changes. While they also note the regional differences in these changes and in some cases the literary response, what is most important is identifying how they occurred.
>
> In this article, 'Accelerated growth', Wim Blockmans and Peter Hoppenbrouwers examine the agricultural developments of the Middle Ages, and the political and social impact this had on rural communities. Looking specifically at Western Europe between 950 and 1250C.E, the authors contend the expanding population and growing wealth came as a result of agrarian advances, which in turn fostered the establishment of a new political and social order. For Blockmans and Hoppenbrouwers, these shifts are characterised by the emergence of the banal lords, and the establishment of a courtly culture.

The essay marking rubric categories and descriptors and the marker's written comments illustrate what was expected, as can be seen from three replicated in the following.

> Your piece presents a good paraphrase of the main points of the relevant chapter. You could have improved your grade by giving less detail about the individual points of the authors' argument and spending more words showing your understanding of what parts were most important and how they relate to one another. . . . I would have liked to see more evidence of you imposing your own organisation on the material, rather than observing the order of points in the chapter.
>
> This is an outstanding example of the task. You have noted the main points of argument without simply repeating what the chapter said. More than this, you integrated the material provided in a sophisticated manner with your own interpretation of the argument and showed that there were clear links between the points raised . . .
>
> . . . You can strengthen its impact by focussing on expressing argument/contention as opposed to descriptive narrative. You have begun to do this already, but you can make it even punchier with conscious planning. . . . You can also improve your writing further by dividing paragraphs more clearly into discrete sections of argument, as opposed to the broad thematic division you adopted here (agriculture/lordship/society).

First year medieval history ethnography 141

It can be seen from the grader's comments that the key skills the synthesis task required of students were close reading and organisation of ideas into a written argument, with clear links between points of the argument – skills needed to write historical essays. Like the research essay, the students were learning how to make an argument in prose. The lecturer, Cecelia, described the suite of things to be learned from the task:

> In first year I think formative assessment is really crucial. And then the second assessment – the synthesis exercise: I wanted them to sit down with an article that was challenging and hard and didn't come to them easily and to extract ideas from an article. Because I'm thinking transition, thinking about university skills, the most important thing in an arts degree at uni[versity] is how to think critically about material that's in front of you, so I wanted to build that as a foundation. That just because you read something and it's boring or whatever, that doesn't get you off the hook, you have to go in burrowing and find out, so you have to read slowly. So that's about a technique in reading and note taking and applying knowledge.
>
> (transcript, post-class interview)

For the medieval European history class, the students were required to lead one tutorial. In addition to their weekly presentations, they developed their work into essays that responded to questions provided by the professor. There were four questions for each topic – sufficient to allow first year students to follow up interests and yet not too many (the literature also supports this balance for being conducive to creativity). Examples of the questions are given here, beside their weekly topic.

- Towns: Communes and Universities: Abelard's academic career would not have been possible in the Early Middle Ages. Do you agree? Why?
- Women and Power: The letters of medieval women are an excellent source for an understanding of how women could exercise authority during this period. Do you agree? What sorts of women were able to write letters? Discuss with reference to letters by at least three women.
- Famine and Disease: The calamitous 14th century: "One of the key concerns of the medieval period was social mobility and a defined sense of social hierarchy. This was challenged by the plague and the instability that followed." Discuss the implications of this statement and whether the evidence for instability is compelling.
- Courtly Culture and Literature in the Middle Ages: Pilgrimage sites were places of spatial significance to Christians. What does this mean? Discuss, with reference to at least three pilgrimage sites, the historical foundations that lead to the site being considered sacred.

Studying the completed essays, I note that students who did well, gaining distinctions and high distinctions, generally used seven or eight primary sources and

142 *First year medieval history ethnography*

a similar number of secondary sources. They earned comments by the grader such as: 'You made excellent use of a variety of primary sources which were well contextualised'; 'You assembled an impressive bibliography of well-chosen materials, showing effective research'; and 'Your research . . . identified a lovely range of relevant materials'. The emphasis of the comments, however, were on the students' arguments. To demonstrate this, I will analyse one illustrative paragraph of text from one student's essay.

The essay as a creative pedagogy

This student essay addressed the importance of pilgrimage in the medieval world. It opened with the contention that in all religions there are spaces of spiritual value that are temporally and geographically distinct. It proceeded to argue that, for medieval Christians, the holy sites were considered significant for a range of reasons, the remains of a saint or martyr being a chief one. For that to happen, there had to *be* saints: the number of sacred places for pilgrimage increased from the Carolingian era to the thirteenth century. In addition to Jerusalem and Rome, Santiago de Compostela and Canterbury Cathedral became the destinations of pilgrimages. The student drew a link between Thomas Becket's tomb at Canterbury Cathedral and the Holy Land, the whole of which can be seen, she argued, as a relic sanctified by the humanity of Jesus. To demonstrate how sacred and significant the site was, she cited a secondary source that included evidence that Mt Calvary, in Jerusalem, contained a crevice in a rock that was thought to have opened during the crucifixion of Jesus. The source reported people would 'plunge their heads and faces' into the crevice out of devotion. This student's use of primary sources from the period included a map as a 'testament to the spirituality of the times' – the thirteenth-century Ebstorf map, which literally depicts Jerusalem at the centre of the world. She also blended a written source, which reported that Thomas Becket's tomb had a window on either side through which pilgrims would reach and kiss the sarcophagus, with a painting depicting an example of a similar kind of window in Edward the Confessor's tomb, all showing a similar kind of reverence to the object of sanctification. The grader commented on the excellent clarity of the essay, stating, 'The illustrations you selected complemented your textual evidence nicely, and you expressed your analysis of both with sensitivity to the medieval religious mentality'.

It is clear from the brief outline of this assignment that an essay is a vehicle that structures the development of a number of complex, interrelated skills. These are: formulating an argument (that religions have places of sacred significance); linking smaller arguments – each one with an evidentiary base – to demonstrate the validity of the larger overall argument (pilgrimage was attractive because it could confer blessings, including miracles, from God; there have to be sacred places for there to be pilgrimage; there need to be saints before there can be relics that can exalt places); criticising and making judgements (e.g., that the configuration of the Ebstorf map centred on Jerusalem indicates a Christian worldview); categorising meaningfully (e.g., Santiago de Compostela and Canterbury Cathedral illustrated the growth in the importance of saints and relics

First year medieval history ethnography   143

in the eleventh and twelfth centuries; comparing (Jerusalem with Santiago de Compostela and Canterbury Cathedral); and combining pertinent arguments of others into one's own (the painting of a pilgrim reaching in through a window to Edward the Confessor's tomb illustrates how a written document described the reverence pilgrims had for the martyr saint, Thomas Becket, and for the crevice in the rock at Mt Calvary). Deriving evidence (or 'data') from the sources involves a dialectical form of thinking. Thinking about the possible reasons pilgrimage arose, the religiosity of the people at the time and the centrality of sacred places entails speculation on the one hand and checking against the evidence on the other. The historian's imagination illuminates the reason(s) things are connected; it does the work of combining, linking and sense-making. This ability to combine elements shapes or configures the structure of the argument, confers meaning and coherence to the data. This choosing, combining and constructing *is* the imaginative nature of history. It is constructed because interpreting the evidence located in the sources in order to shape an argument, paragraph by paragraph, involves imposing cohesiveness on sources, where the sources themselves possess no such cohesion – they are about all sorts of things. The rhetorical argument acts as a model for generating propositions about historical reality that interpret for the reader why and how this evidence answers the various question/s posed by the historian.

This places us squarely within Ricoeur's theory as an example of productive imagination (as opposed to 'reproductive' imagination, which sets out to reproduce or mimic the original, as we saw in Chapter 2). History as imaginative construct – or, in Ricoeur's language, its productive, configuring work – receives support in my post-class interview, in which the lecturer said, 'If being a history major means anything, it is mastering that historical style which is arguing through evidence in a rhetorical way' (transcript, post-class interview).

> So that metanarrative or meta-analysis of how historical writing works and actually the emptiness at the heart of it, we slowly inculcate students into that. The emperor has no clothes. The epistemological bareness of it all, we slowly inculcate students into that, and we hope that by the end of third year, we hope they've encountered that existential. . . . So it's not just building historical knowledge. It's also unmasking historical knowledge.
>
> (transcript, post-class interview)

This combinatory work is described by Vygotsky as the basis of creativity: 'It is this ability to combine elements to produce a structure, to combine the old in new ways that is the basis of creativity' (2004, p. 12).

It is telling to hear how the students understand this, in their own words. In the post-class interview one student referred to 'imaginative collaboration with the facts'. Another indicated their recognition thus: 'Reading other people's writing, why not just read a list of facts? What makes a good essay is that imaginative narrative, the story they take you on that makes sense of the facts' (transcript, post-class interview). Another pole of thinking in this dialectical process is that the student historian's critical faculty is continually assessing the argument.

144 *First year medieval history ethnography*

This leads to a closer inspection of the sources and either the development of a different argument or a more nuanced, detailed articulation of the links that forge points in the argument.

Unseen by my study but implicit in the literature and in my interviews is a further factor that gets drawn into the process of historical thinking. Progressively, throughout a degree, this critical process is coordinated by a range of abstract concepts offered by disciplinary terminology, such as what ideology, class, gender or urbanisation suggest about forms of social organisation – without ever losing sight of the detailed evidence in the primary sources. This process of blending imaginative and critical thinking is substantiated in the literature on creativity (Nickerson, 1999; Bosanquet, Winchester-Seeto & Rowe, 2012). Through its lens we can observe Vygotsky's 'tool mediated action' at work in language and processes that are pressed into service to consider possible interpretations about the past and to build an argument.

At the root of this idea that history involves a dialectical relationship between imaginative and critical construction is the provisional, if evidenced, nature of historical interpretation. It is always possible to reconceive/recombine data to form a different interpretation or pattern of significance.

This openness to new perspectives resonates strongly in higher education today. There is widespread recognition of the need to develop pedagogies centred on uncertainty, and what is not known, as much as what is known (Probert, 2014, p. 8). The vision of learner as passive consumer is inimical to what we see here – a view of students as partners with their teachers in a search for understanding – one of the defining features of higher education from both academic and student perspectives (Probert, 2014). This induction into the *practices* of the history discipline is an integral part of learning and cognition. Edwards makes this exact point, when citing Leont'ev:

> A profound revolution brought about by Marx in the theory of cognition is the idea that human practice is the basis for human cognition: practice is that process in the course of whose development cognitive problems arise, human perceptions and thought originate and develop, and which at the same time contains in itself criteria of the adequacy and truth of knowledge.
> (Leont'ev, 1978b, p. 2, cited in Edwards & Daniels, 2012, p. 24)

By positioning the students as producers of history, the students are being induced to engage in practices that transform and complexify their cognitive thinking abilities.

Prompting engagement in historical thinking and avoiding ahistoricism

The next section will consider one week's online group discussion. For 11 weeks of the semester, prior to the tutorial, the students of each tutorial group were required to post at least one comment about the reading. This was partly

First year medieval history ethnography 145

to ensure they did the weekly reading, which would mean full participation in class discussion, and had grappled with the meaning of the documents *before* they turned up for the tutorial and were given the support and practice to deepen how they worked with them.

Each week the tutor would supply a few questions to signal some pertinent issues, thus framing the focus for students. For example, for Abelard and the University the tutor had posted:

> As you read, consider:
>
> - What is the nature of Abelard's troubles? Are they intellectual? sexual? political? personal?
> - How does Abelard's experience fit with the rise of the University as an élite place of learning?
> - Do you sympathise with Abelard or his detractors? Can you articulate how and why you feel this way? Reflecting on your response, to what extent do you think you have judged him on medieval terms or modern ones?

The online discussion board provided a fairly informal learning space. It appeared to me that it allowed the students some space to get some opinions off their chest. The questions posed asked them about their emotional reactions. For example, they made comments such as,

> From a modern perspective, he comes across as quite arrogant; assuming that everyone was jealous of his intellect, appearance and success;
>
> It is difficult to sympathise with Abelard and his decision to commence a sexual relationship with Heloise, as he does so out of deceit; however, it is curious that Heloise's father gave 'complete charge' of his daughter to such a young and 'exceptional'' looking man';
>
> Finally, I couldn't help but be ultimately unsympathetic to Abelard and his extensive troubles, primarily due to my perceiving him as arrogant. Moreover, I was irritated by his seeing himself as the victim of unrelenting and unjust persecution . . . , BUT, his predatory intentions if Heloise did not succumb to his charms were a few steps too far in my eyes!

Emotions and imagination

I conjectured that, by articulating their personal and emotional reactions, students were given an opportunity to become aware of the difficulty of disaggregating their contemporary values from their interpretations of the behaviour of historical figures, or social movements, that might impede their understanding of the past – such as in the following comment: 'Of course, this is all from a modern perspective, but I find it hard to divorce my modern morality from historical evidence in this case'.

146   *First year medieval history ethnography*

It was evident that posing the discussion board questions allowed the tutor to hear what emotions students were grappling with that sometimes underpinned their ahistorical reactions. She could then, if necessary, intercede at points to try to steer them towards historical judgements which could be verified in the sources, such as in the following prompts: 'Is it only his desire to teach logic that stirs up enmity do you think? What else – personally or academically – could be at play?'; 'What about if you think of "élite" as in specialised, higher learning (as opposed to a social élite of nobility vs. others)? Does it change your response?'; 'What about in academic debate, setting aside his personal (mis)conduct? Did people disagree with him only because he was a bit of a pain? What was at stake in the "universals debate"? Just academic prestige? The route to truth? Christian orthodoxy? other things?'

The flow of the comments that follow show the students' conjectures as they struggle to interpret Abelard's text, to understand the rise of 'the university' and the germ of a tension between church orthodoxy and what constitutes knowledge.

Student 3:   . . . The notion of the university as an 'elite place of learning' doesn't quite fit with the experiences of Abelard, given that he was intensely involved in the growth of universities, and yet did not come from the nobility. That said, he does contribute to the philosophy of universities – a place exclusively devoted to learning (almost for learning's sake . . . ?).

Student 5:   . . . What was most interesting to me specifically was a small section where he talks about returning to Paris and finding that his position as head of the school had been filled by an ally of his former master and rival, William of Champeaux. The way he describes this whole event is as if it were a battle, using words and phrases like 'set up camp', 'lay siege', William's 'knight', and even referring to arguments between supporters of the different teachers as 'battles' which his students won. This choice of language and metaphor makes me wonder if it is Abelard being egocentric and exaggerating to make himself look a hero, or whether it speaks to the somewhat political and competitive nature of teaching at the time. Does this imply that a popular teacher was a kind of 'general', with an 'army' of students? . . .

Student 6:   . . . In a educationally competitive society, if students really did follow Abelard around, he must have merited that following surely? I think the cause of all the ill feelings towards him sprung more from his dedication to 'understanding', rather than belief, than from his repellent attitude. In a world that up till then had a high degree of blind faith attached to religious worship, Abelard's work would have indeed bordered on heresy, thus the churches opposition to him, which his undoubtable arrogance only exacerbated.

(reproduced with the permission of consenting participants, April 11–16, 2013, Moodle site, Medieval Europe – ATS1316)

First year medieval history ethnography 147

As discussed earlier in Chapter 2, according to Nussbaum, our emotions are 'suffused with intelligence and discernment' (2001, p. 1). By helping us discern salient aspects of our environment, they play an important role in ethical reasoning, judgement and the ability to respond to the environment in a richly responsive way. Yet in history, emotions can impede an appreciation of an understanding of the logic and culture of past societies. In this ambiguous situation, imagination is important in helping historians straddle the differences between the present and the past. Johnson (1993) argued that how we frame a situation will determine how we reason about it, and how we frame it will depend upon our imaginative capability. If we are caught in an emotional reaction of our own, it can hinder sense-making from an historical source. I recalled the educator's comment in the interview (transcript, Interview 13.12.13) that in history this was 'great ethical work' because it involves openness to, and tolerance of, otherness. It suggests, once again, that imagination is critical to the ability to open up a liminal space, a hiatus, for critical distancing in which we can hold different logic and values in consciousness, our own and others'. In this space, new possibilities of sense-making – of semantic innovation – open up that can bridge the present and the past. This is why Ricoeur's notion of critical awareness as a defining factor in productive imagination is so pertinent (see the y axis in Figure 2.1)

Conclusion

The pedagogical approaches in the course engaged the students with the disciplinary tools and practices to mediate their understanding of the past. What I would call their developing expertise involved the systematic questioning of primary sources in a close reading of historical sources. Becoming aware of emotional responses to the past, and beginning a process of re-framing historical webs of meaning, was integral to the use of imagination to hold different points of view simultaneously in consciousness and question assumptions. Finally, using a structure (the essay) prompts the configuring work that synthesises evidence from source material into an argument. Configuring work involves a continuous interlinking of imaginative and critical thinking – which substantiates the arguments of Ricoeur, Dawkins and others. Imagining the otherness of the logic of people in history involved ethical thinking because a kind of looking askance at a situation – distantiation/estrangement or awareness of difference – means critical consciousness is part of productive imagination (the y axis in Figure 2.1). Ricoeur's notion of productive imagination provides a language and concepts to interpret *how this occurs* when students of history learn to wield the tools of their trade in this disciplinary culture and the ethical possibilities in traversing the past from our limited, present perspectives. The models of past reality this produces are not passive recapitulations of historical reality – reproductively imaginative – and they go beyond direct experience because they involve knowledge construction through social-culturally derived disciplinary manipulations. Each historian practising this form of disciplinary work learns to traverse the past afresh. Each student historian becomes a producer of history.

148 *First year medieval history ethnography*

Ethnographic methodology, with its multiple sources of data and its capacity to observe in depth the progress of teaching strategies and the interlinking of class activities and tasks, and to analyse their effect on learners' creative processes and products, allows us to see the role of imagination in producing history. Ricoeur's emphasis on the semantic innovation involved in combining elements, and constructivist theorists focusing on tool mediated thinking, can illuminate how the creation of knowledge arises and is linked to imaginative processes. The pedagogical approaches and the assignments in the medieval European history course provided opportunities for students to become cultural producers rather than consumers of history, traversing the past afresh. Wielding the tools and techniques of historians involved them in a constant interplay of imaginative conjecture and critical analysis, allowing new syntheses of ideas to arise that were grounded in evidence – the kind of imaginative activity needed to find ways of solving contemporary world problems.

The following chapter considers an ethnographic case from the business and economics professional area, namely a post-graduate class in finance.

References

Amabile, T. M. (1983). *The social psychology of creativity*. New York: Springer-Verlag.

Austin, J. L. (2003). Performative utterances. In J. O. E. Urmson & G. J. E. Warnock (Eds.), *Philosophical papers* (originally published 1979) (Third ed.). Oxford: Oxford Scholarship Online. doi:10.1093/019283021X.001.0001

Blockmans, W., & Hoppenbrouwers, P. (2007). *Introduction to Medieval Europe: The age of discretion* (I. V. D. Hoven, Trans.). London: Routledge.

Bosanquet, A., Winchester-Seeto, T., & Rowe, A. (2012). Social inclusion, graduate attributes and higher education curriculum. *Journal of Academic Language and Learning, 6*(2), 73–87.

Boud, D. (1998, November 4–5). *Effective assessment at university*. Paper presented at the TEDI Conference, University of Queensland, Brisbane.

Burenheide, B. (2007). I can do this: Revelations on teaching with historical thinking. *The History Teacher, 41*(1), 55–61.

Csikszentmihalyi, M. (1996). Where is creativity? In *Creativity: Flow and the psychology of discovery and invention* (pp. 23–50). New York: Harper Collins Publishers.

Csikszentmihalyi, M., & Getzels, J. W. (1988). Creativity and problem finding in art. In F. G. Farley & R. W. Neperud (Eds.), *The foundations of aesthetics, art, and art education* (pp. 91–106). New York: Praeger.

Dawkins, R. (1989). *The selfish gene* (Second ed.). Oxford: Oxford University Press.

Dening, G. M. (1998). *Readings/writings*. Carlton: Melbourne University Press.

Edwards, A., & Daniels, H. (2012). The knowledge that matters in professional practices. *Journal of Education and Work, 25*(1), 39–58. doi:10.1080/13639080.2012.644904

Griffiths, T. (2009). History and the creative imagination. *History Australia, 6*(3), 74.71–74.16.

Hughes-Warrington, M., Roe, J., Nye, A., Bailey, M., Peel, M., Russell, P., . . . Trent, F. (2009). *Historical Thinking in Higher Education*. Strawberry Hills: Australian Learning and Teaching Council.

Johnson, M. (1993). Moral imagination. In *Moral imagination: Implications of cognitive science for ethics*. Chicago: University of Chicago Press.

Lucas, B., Claxton, G., & Spencer, E. (2013). *Progression in student creativity in school: First steps towards new forms of formative assessments*. OECD Education Working Papers No. 86, OECD Publishing. Retrieved from http://dx.doi.org/10.1787/5k4dp59msdwk-en

Maxwell, J. (1992, Fall). Understanding and validity in qualitative research. *Harvard Educational Review, 62*(3), 279–300.

New South Wales Department of Education and Training. (1998–9). *Assessment K-12*. Retrieved from http://www.curriculumsupport.education.nsw.gov.au/consistent_teacher/assessment.htm

Nickerson, R. (1999). Enhancing creativity. In R. J. Sternberg (Ed.), *Handbook of creativity* (pp. 392–430). Cambridge: Cambridge University Press.

Nussbaum, M. (2001). *Upheavals of thought: The intelligence of emotions*. New York: Cambridge University Press.

Probert, B. (2014, May). *Why scholarship matters in higher education*. Australian Government Office for Learning and Teaching. Retrieved from nla.gov.au/tarkine//nla.obj-310527272/pdf

Ramsden, P. (1992). *Learning to teach in higher education*. London: Routledge.

Ricoeur, P. (1975/2003). *The rule of metaphor: The creation of meaning in language* (R. Czerny, K. McLaughlin, & J. Costello, Trans.). London: Routledge.

Ricoeur, P. (1983/1984). *Time and narrative* (K. McLaughlin & D. Pellauer, Trans. Vol. 1). Chicago: University of Chicago Press.

Vygotsky, L. S. (2004). Imagination and creativity in childhood. *Journal of Russian and East European Psychology, 42*(1), 7–97.

7 Finance ethnography

Strategy – skilful management in getting the better of an adversary or attaining an end; the science or art of combining and employing the means of war in planning and directing large military movements and operations; a method of conducting operations especially by the aid of manoeuvring or stratagem.

(Concise Macquarie dictionary 4e)

Simulations . . . are open-ended evolving situations with many interacting variables. The goal for all participants is to each take a particular role, address the issues, threats, or problems that arise in the situation, and experience the effects of their decisions. The situation can take different directions, depending on the actions and reactions of the participants. That is, a simulation is an evolving case study of a particular social or physical reality in which the participants take on bona fide roles with well-defined responsibilities and constraints.

(Gredler, 2004)

Introduction

'Money, Market Dealing' is a post-graduate finance subject taught at the university campus, a campus that specialises in post-graduate business degrees in a faculty that attracts a high number of international students as well as local industry people upgrading their qualifications. The lecturer in charge, whom we shall call Jeff Kent, won a national teaching award partly for instigating Simulated Teaching and Research Laboratory (STARLab), which simulates a bank's treasury dealing room. Simulation has been defined by Fanning and Gaba (2008) as 'an imitation of some real thing, state of affairs, or process'. It refers to 'the artificial replication of sufficient components of a real-world situation to achieve specific goals' (p. 459). Simulation as a form of experiential learning has strong roots in aviation and anaesthetics and, at least since the Romans practised lancing techniques on the quintain, has used technology to achieve its aims (p. 459). Models of simulation education are widespread in high hazard industries, such as firefighting, transportation, health care and beyond, where the stakes are high and safety is paramount. Role play, of much broader and older lineage than simulation, broadens the definition to include not only trying out new activities, but rehearsal for activities or roles, learning behaviours, operating as a team and interacting socially (p. 459).

The origins of role play and simulation may be traced to the psychology of play, in which children imitate or emulate adult behaviour to learn how to interact with their world. When I first walk in to the STARLab, it reminds me of the trading floor of the stock exchange I have seen on TV with its electronic display board and shouting and arm-waving, except that STARLab functions remotely and so is quiet.

I am attracted by the idea of including the unit in my case studies of imaginative university teaching and learning for two reasons: first, finance is not generally regarded as an imaginative enterprise,[1] which is an assumption my research seeks to investigate; second, because the whole semester is run as a simulation – a high tech, simulated financial environment in which groups of students take roles in an imaginary bank, trading currency in the first module of the semester and managing loans and deposits in the second. What opportunities for fostering imagination – the subject of my research – are afforded by simulation, and – a separate, although linked, question – what opportunities are offered by simulation pedagogy? In some quarters, using technology in the twenty-first century is equated, almost by default, with innovation and hence creativity. My expectation is that, by allowing the acting out of staged scenarios, simulation as a pedagogy seems, on the face of it, to provide students with a licence to combine pertinent information in personally meaningful ways. It allows you to put your understandings to work by acting on them in ways you think appropriate. This synthetic process certainly appears to connect it to Ricoeur's theory of imagination, particularly in his discussion of narrative (see Chapter 2). However, perhaps perversely, I argue with myself that simulation may not 'qualify' as imaginative. How does the simulation provide opportunities for students to imaginatively project new proposals for action in the future? If imagination enables us to anticipate consequences or find novel perspectives about problems, doesn't simulation plug that gap in some sense, *standing in for* or *replacing* the imagination? Because in simulation learners play through various set scenarios and experience the signs of consequences of various actions. By providing software and a simulation laboratory which mimics the workplace, and allowing the students to apply prior learning, could the simulation *discourage* the students' own mental enactment – their imagination? Or is the key point *the way* the technology *is used* in the teaching approach either to foster critical and creative thinking or shut it down?[2]

In this ethnographic case, I draw attention to creative teaching and the opportunities for fostering imagination in a non arts-based professional subject, a subject where that capacity is not obviously considered part of the curriculum. This chapter aims to offer a new and productive way of thinking about these referents. Chiefly, this requires analysing what is involved in learners manipulating different abstractions of knowledge and thinking strategically. The analysis of this case will seek to clarify and possibly extend Ricoeur's theory of imagination by connecting it to other theorists' ideas about imagination and thinking 'tools', as well as to pedagogies that help foster both imagination and the interlinked dispositions of creativity: inquisitiveness, persistence, imagination, collaboration and discipline (Lucas, Claxton & Spencer, 2013, pp. 16–17; see Chapters 1 and 4 for this discussion). The ethnography relied upon data from class observation notes, completed student assignments, course learning resources, quotations from interviews with the participating educator and the transcript of the post-observation period student focus group.

152 *Finance ethnography*

Background and context for the case study

STARLab is a high tech, purpose-built facility in a large room with circular tables for six or so people, upon which sit computers for each student equipped with market simulation software. The laboratory functions as a 'capstone' subject, meaning students bring theoretical knowledge they have learned previously in their degree and apply it in their final year to demonstrate they can put their learning into practice before they enter the workforce. A university promotional video says that STARLab exposes students to situations and events that demand they draw on prior knowledge and engineer financial strategies using a variety of financial 'instruments' to hedge risks and seek profits in competition with other students (other traders). Figure 7.1 shows the set-up of the room, illustrating an environment conducive to active and socially interactive learning.

The promotional video has the coordinating professor conveying his teaching intentions, with shots of students interacting with the learning environment. The seniority of those interviewed suggests the video is a marketing drawcard for prospective international students. The university depends financially on international student enrolments. The video is also used to showcase the university degrees for the purpose of accrediting its programs with international bodies, EQUIS,[3] AACSB[4] and AMBA,[5] which also helps attract international students.

Figure 7.1 Starlab: a purpose-built, high tech, teaching simulation facility

Setting expectations of learning

In the first class of the subject, Jeff introduces STARLab and its role at the university and provides overviews of the readings and where to find required resources. He sets his expectations by telling the students: 'This unit is unlike any other you will do at university. You are responsible for your own learning. Ask yourself: What is this unit doing for me? How can I learn from it?'; he reassures them that there is 'no such thing as a stupid question'. He introduces a doctoral student and a former student, now post-graduate, who assist him in running the simulation. He jokes that they may give the class a 'hard time' but that's 'their role' but that the students should always ask themselves, 'What is he [the post-grad] trying to teach me?' and, 'What can I learn from this unit?' (and, later, 'Did I take advantage of this unit to learn?'). In this way he explicitly urges them to *be aware of themselves learning* and to see themselves as agents responsible for their own learning – in the short term as students but also in their future lives. He appears to me to be exemplifying an awareness that educators are not 'deliverers' of knowledge or even education. He is pointing out the transformational power of education – the power to be creative *in your own learning*. What is clear is that agency and metacognition are valued by this teacher, and he is modelling the kinds of questions and behaviours that enhance those traits. This is interesting in that Jeffrey and Craft (2004) distinguish between creative teaching and teaching for creativity by saying creative teaching may involve making learning more interesting but teaching *for* creativity values the agency of the learner (Spencer et al., 2012). Metacognition is one way of engaging the agency of the learner. McWilliam (McWilliam, 2007; McWilliam & Dawson, 2007) suggested that higher educators who stimulate creativity value the process of learning, not just the product – which is another aspect we see evidence of in the educator's questions. The idea of students developing a sense of their identity as learners, including as both lifelong learners and professional financiers, is also of interest here because the higher education literature which applied Paul Ricoeur's notions of the imagination, particularly his notion of narrative as an expression of imagination, connected imagination to identity formation and changes to identity (see for example Anderson, 2010; Cole, 2009; and McCulloch, 2009, discussed in Chapter 4). I asked myself what kind of imaginative agency was released through him urging and giving responsibility to the students for their own learning as students and novice professionals.

The students are also informed that they are allowed to ask these teaching assistants anything – so I infer they play a mentoring role as well as roles in the simulation scenarios. He lists the objectives of the unit informally:

- To practice trading.
- To further enhance skills of foreign exchange and trading theory.
- How to write a report.
- Analytic skills.
- How market forces affect behaviour.

154   *Finance ethnography*

The formal objectives listed in the Learning Guide use verbs predominantly from the 'relational' and 'extended abstract' – higher – levels in Biggs and Tang's SOLO taxonomy (2007) and are:

- *Analyse* dealing practices and conventions in the foreign exchange market and cash market.
- *Develop* and *organise* the front office and back office functions of a simulated bank's treasury dealing room.
- *Plan*, *verify*, and *settle* transactions completed in the simulated treasury dealing room.
- *Create* and modify dealing strategies in the treasury dealing room.
- *Plan*, *organise*, *analyse*, *justify* and *report* on positions taken in the treasury dealing room.

The role of creative collaboration

Jeff highlights the participatory nature of the students' learning experience, urging them to learn *from each other*. 'This unit is about networking – go for coffee and talk about issues during break times! (But don't collude!)', he exhorts. A bit later he tells them the trading session will finish by 1 p.m. but 'groups can then use the remaining time to work and plan together'. This appears to show an emphasis on setting up a learning community based on their shared experience of running an imaginary bank and undergoing an active learning process in concert with others. This is evidence of the pedagogy structuring opportunities for collaboration, collaboration being a key characteristic of creativity in the literature (Lucas et al., 2013; Csikszentmihalyi, 1999; Amabile, 1983; Appadurai, 1996), and the literature on learning communities (Lave, 1988, 1996; Lave & Wenger, 1991).

Jeff declares his role is the chief executive officer (CEO) and, as such, that they will be formally reporting to him in a business (not academic) report format. It is clear from this that the pedagogy will involve students not only trying out *new* activities, as simulation is frequently designed for, but rehearsing activities, roles and behaviours, such as operating as a team, report writing and being answerable to a manager. Apparently, so he says, Australian industry have observed that graduates are poor at report writing, and the unit aims to focus on the skills that will prepare the students to be readily employable. He forewarns them, 'What I want to do next week is have a practice trading session – it will be chaos, don't worry, but you will quickly learn'.

Ground rules that release creativity

His method is to use the technology embedded in STARLab to provide students with 'hands on' application through dynamic decision-making simulations, self-reliance and first-hand experience of competitive financial markets. The subject is, therefore, essentially about application – of core finance theory and concepts they have learned in prior subjects in economics, management and finance that they have taken in their degree. Students trade in teams of three acting as banks (named, for example, 'Maybank', 'Bank Negara Indonesia', 'J P Morgan', 'Lloyds', 'Hong Kong Bank', 'Rabobank', 'Wells Fargo'). Decision-making is central to all the activities as students put theoretical knowledge 'to work' while developing their critical thinking, financial numeracy and oral communication skills in order to achieve certain desired ends of the 'game'. There are game penalties with fines: for not following the code of conduct or not answering the telephone to trade. There are rules and conventions of game playing: 'I will trade with you anytime any place subject to price' – this means in the corridor, by email, via the digital university learning management system – not just in the trading sessions. The game also obliges players to follow actual legal regulations and laws. This forces students to revise prior learning in other units. Other rules are about ensuring the game works formally in terms of teaching and learning. For example, there is peer assessment of each team member's performance and contribution for each assessment; if it isn't given, you are fined. Another is that it is possible to get 100 per cent for the unit without making a profit. 'So why *wouldn't* you take risks and make mistakes?' he asks rhetorically – encouraging them to do so (week 2).

Learning agency through risking error

Removing inhibitors to risk-taking behaviour in the assessment regime is interesting in terms of my study on teaching that fosters imaginative learning. It appears Jeff has managed the assessment of the learning outcomes by making it possible to earn top marks in the subject without being the most successful profit maker. Risk-taking is a recurring theme in both modules of the subject: the students are urged to let loose and take risks, trying out different strategies and studying the consequences. Also, trading and managing a balance sheet of deposits and loans itself involves devising strategies to *mitigate* inherent risks, but the simulation manages this in a practice banking environment where the stakes are low because it's a game: 'You can take a risk – without taking a risk! Think about risk mitigation', he urges them. The object of the game is that 'you are trying to gain a market advantage over everybody else in order to make a profit'. The stakes are pretend ones, but, he urges, the learning that emerges from the game is real and, he hopes, enduring as well as fun (post-class interview). The real issue is for students who lose (or gain) money by excessive risk-taking to reflect on why and how this happened with a view to learning to mitigate risk, as well as to ensure they are aware of the pitfalls and dangers of financial strategies prior to gaining employment. He is literally giving students permission to take risks; by keeping the stakes low, the unit offers a licence to take risks. Risk-taking when tackling tasks is supported in the creativity literature as underpinning possibility thinking and experimentation (Craft, Jeffery & Liebling, 2001) and seeking out situations that are complex and ambiguous (Runco, 2010, p. 246). However, it is possible to take risks without being creative or imaginative – they can be stupid or thoughtless risks, without imagining or considering the consequences, and they can be the result of rigid thinking. Good or reasonable risk-taking generally requires creativity and imagination because mitigating risk implies foreseeing consequences and outcomes and judging how these are to be balanced in relation to competing goals you may want to achieve.

156 *Finance ethnography*

In this sense, I do not mean to conflate creativity with imagination, but to tease out some of their distinguishing features. However, as we have seen, the dispositions are interdependent if they are to function well (Lucas et al., 2013), which was also Dewey's argument. As they are interdependent, it is unlikely we would see teaching which fosters imagination without also fostering other aspects of creativity. On a similar note, Nickerson pointed out how taking risks is related to the belief that creativity is subject to effort and persistence and not determined by genetic capabilities beyond our control (Nickerson, 1999) – something we saw in the physics and medieval history ethnographic cases. Once again, the emphasis in Jeff's teaching is on responsibility for one's own learning and adventurous experimentation when learning, reinforcing that the agency of the learner is important.

Imagination as mental flexibility and shifting perspectives

As Jeff speaks to the class, he constantly switches back and forth from the simulation game to what it is *for*: the learning objectives of the game, meaning the game is simultaneously simulation and pedagogical in focus. For example, there is a debriefing each week to clarify the lessons to be had from the day's trading: the trading is not an end in itself. In terms of my research on fostering imagination, this implies his simulation pedagogy offers students two roles and two positions they can mentally assume: banker and learner. It strikes me that assuming different imaginary positions in thinking offers practice in flexibility, in *not* being aligned to just one way of thinking. In this way, I conclude, simulation pedagogy offers rich opportunities to cultivate the imagination, and criticality, of students.

This mental flexibility could also be observed at another stage in the course when the teacher's commentary mentored students in both how to think about the game and how to develop their banking skills: 'The CEOs are not reactive, they act according to a script. But *they* form the market. They continue with their script. They need to develop a series of strategies; just one will not work'. Information about 'the market' is central. He says bankers deal in loans, bonds, money, relationships and, what is often not appreciated, market information. 'If you want a loan, the bank asks you for information about yourself. How do they use that information?' he asks. A third example illustrates the same point: 'We are not trying to make you a trader. We're giving you an *experience of being* a trader – the experience of thinking about the issues, to develop the characteristics of what a good trader will have'. A key benefit to this imaginary taking up of positions (banker and learner) is the flexibility to shift perspectives. The displacement of perspectives exercises the imagination and gives rise to multiple positions from which to reflect and to exercise criticality. Hence the link made in the literature on the interwoven aspects of imagination and critical thinking (Nickerson, 1999; Bosanquet, Winchester-Seeto & Rowe, 2012; Dawkins, 1989).

Imagination in ethics: how surprise ('affect') can trigger reflection in simulation pedagogy

A key part of criticality is developing the ability to act ethically, which in a post–Global Financial Crisis (GFC) world is regarded as a duty of care in finance education. Public attention to financiers who have flouted the law has put the spotlight on the possible failure, and the concomitant responsibilities, of higher education institutions in the ethical education of students. He advises, 'You can't work in financial markets for long without ethical trading practices'. He says it keeps him awake at night – that they may become rogue traders. But he points out that trading ethically is integral to learning how to mitigate risk – and learning to mitigate risk is central to the skill development objectives of the course. He reminds them, 'The good name of your institution is important for markets'. He then asks, 'Who owns the world? You have a chance at postgraduate education to reflect on these questions'. This is a clear invitation to consider the repercussions of financial decisions beyond the bank's narrow financial imperatives – its responsibilities to return a profit to its shareholders – and to consider moral responsibilities. The invitation directs them to reflect and imagine a different world, or a change in perspective *for themselves at least*, through education.

I wondered if the simulation pedagogy would feature an ethical purpose. Could ethical or unethical behaviour alter the course of the game for the participants? One week's dramatic incident in the course of the plot of the foreign exchange module of the simulation shed light on this. Jeff in the role of CEO stood at the front of the room. 'I've got the Federal Police in my office! What are you doing in the dealing room? I could end up in jail! You are potentially financing terrorism or laundering money!'

A buyer for the bank listed on the United Blacklist for financing terrorism and money laundering had bought currency from nearly all the banks at 10 pips above the market price. The bank was on a blacklist, according to a list of approved clients given to them all in the introductory booklet. He tells them that if the bank itself ends up on a blacklist for illegal trading it is bad for business because no one can legally invest in your business' activities as you will lose your licence to trade, let alone the unethical message it sends to the bank's customers. 'See how you have to keep your mind on the wider world. While you are there to make a profit, you have to be aware of ethical issues! It can happen so easily – you get seduced by the price'.

Research by Lucas (2008), an accounting academic, is illuminating on this pedagogical approach and in interpreting how it was that many in the class were seduced by the profit motive, and were caught unaware of the significance of the simulated illegal trade, failing to recognise it as an ethical turning point. Lucas's pedagogy involves creating moments of surprise in which students are 'pulled up short' and propelled to question their taken-for-granted assumptions. She argues that creating moments of surprise in the classroom can precipitate critical reflection. Given that the students I observed were driven by the obvious assumption for banks to make a profit, this surprise trap shocked them.

158 *Finance ethnography*

Dewey (Bleazby, 2013) and Nussbaum (2001) describe how feelings attune us to reality (see Chapter 2); this attunement has ethical and cognitive value because it makes it possible for us to learn from experience. Lucas draws on Mezirow (1991, p. 223, in Lucas, 2008, p. 384) to argue that by integrating moments of surprise in their teaching, educators can help transform students' beliefs, attitudes, opinions and emotional reactions that constitute their meaning schemas. She argues that *critical reflection involves an affective dimension* and that *surprise* can make students become aware of deeply held beliefs. Pedagogically it can then be used to cultivate a disposition to engage in reflection.

We can use these ideas analogically to interpret what is going on in this incident. The finance simulation provided a context in which students are embedded in their roles as bankers for a particular organisation. They mimic collegial relationships in which business values and goals are held in common, which legitimise the 'obvious' good of profit and efficiency (Young & Annisette, 2009). The result: They were seduced into morally compromised territory. We see here how simulation pedagogy can provide opportunities for students to experience contextually relevant ethical seductions, traps and dilemmas. The naturalised setting provided by simulation is important here. Simulation was shown to allow students practice in making mistakes, and affect (surprise) enhanced their 'discernment' of ethical values (Johnson, 1993; Nussbaum, 2001). It gave them first-hand experience in how moral judgement can be affected by the context occurring in the thick of conducting business.

A possible explanation for this learning is that the students' understanding in the sense of reason and affect is expanded as a result of experiencing a contradiction in their appreciation of the goals of the banking system in the immediate and longer term, and also perhaps between their role as players and learners. Bringing both these systems together, as simulation pedagogy does, enables the students to notice and question how the short-term banking motive for profit shapes their own personal actions and thinking. Many of the students were caught out, or surprised, by this contradiction between the systems they were operating in: banking and classroom. This is a good example of Engeström's (2009) hypothesis that contradictions are central as sources of change, expansion of knowledge and development of new practices.

If we recall that predictive processing proposes multi-level generative models of predicting uncertainty, we could infer that the students' pre-existing models or prior assumptions about banking which gave rise to their buying strategy slipped up. In his theory, 'surprise' is operating very much like the nonconscious notion of 'surprisal', which is when a non-correspondence, or error, occurs between the sensory signals encountered and those predicted by the mind. This mismatch drives learning forward, generating a revision or refinement of the students' mental models as the basis for behaviour. The point here is that when problem solving, it can be valuable to shake up your suppositions, to perturb your worldview and thus to force a re-evaluation of your preparatory set of assumptions (Kirsh & Maglio, 1994). Thus, the pedagogical tactic of surprise used by Jeff and by Lucas (2008) could be said to have transformational potential in educational 'designed environments'. Used judiciously, teachers manipulate levels of surprise to shape opportunities for learning – and this includes ethical learning. In this context it is also cautionary to hear that, at least in music, to the extent that prediction is established as a powerful mechanism for conveying musical meaning, affective responses vary due to exposure and culture, and individual preferences influence response to the prediction error. This means that sensitivity to context and audience is important for maximally affective response (Schaefer, Overy & Nelson, 2013).

The incident also provides clues about how, in complex multi-level generative models that characterise human learning, the very roots of motivation, and desire, are pliable because they are subject to dynamic and hard-to-learn social rules involving outcomes that are affected by different time scales, which make the fundamental processes of prediction, Bayesian inference and self-estimated uncertainty challenging for students.

As a result of this surprise event in the simulation game, the (fictional) Australian Prudential Regulation Authority issued a fine. In addition, a self-regulatory committee was set up (comprising all the students involved in the simulation) and met at the end of each week. They asked questions of each team and talked about issues. (However, I was not party to their discussions.) Jeff encourages them: 'This is your chance to see how self-regulation does, or does not, work. The self-regulatory committee is to avoid a central regulator from coming in'. Almost all the student assignments make mention of dealing with the money-laundering bank in the simulation incident. For example:

> Know your customer. In the 2nd session, we traded with a XXX bank. Although the profit made from dealing with this counterparty is highly attractive, this is a clear breach of code of conduct because it is unethical and the bank could have been funding illegal or terrorist activities.
>
> (Student J P Morgan FX Summary Report)

> XXX's lucrative deal made BNI jump on to the bandwagon without looking at the offer's credibility. Only those listed in the approved list of counterparties should be traded with. This brings about another important aspect to be considered as well – ethics. Ethics play a vital role in maintaining good relations with the central bank, regulators, corporates and other banks.
>
> (Student Bank Negara Indonesia FX Trading Report)

> This mistake could have easily caused irreversible damage not only to bank's profitability but also its long term standing reputation in the real world.
>
> (Student Lloyd's Bank FX Trading Summary Report)

160   *Finance ethnography*

The student comments here appear to show an understanding that the reputation of an institution is underpinned by trust between industry stakeholders. The key learning was that ethical thinking has to account for values that guide the performance of professional roles. In this instance the value is trust. The key learning, I believe, is that trust operates between organisations, not only between individuals, and reaches further than simple adherence to law.

Informed by predictive processing theory, what I believe we can interpret here is how the educator has designed a classroom environment in the simulation using plot dynamics that actively draw on students' likely predictions. By guiding the learning through the plot, he can draw on the self-organisation that we can expect of predictive processes of human learning to try to perceptually guide and rewrite that behaviour and value signature and the recomposition of a new enduring time scale model more suitable for twenty-first-century ethical banking. This aspiration might sound risible! But schools, universities and classrooms are not only *determined by* their social context but are designed environments which dynamically contribute to *determining* the social context in which they are embedded.

Loans and deposits module: reproductive imaginary structures and productive imagination in strategy formation

The loans and deposits module was the second module of the course. It began in week 7 and ran for 5 weeks. It was the main focus of the subject according to the coordinating lecturer, Jeff, and was a step up in complexity from the previous currency trading module (transcript, post-class interview, December 2013).

At first glance, the bulk of the activities of this module appeared to be building the foundations for creativity by fostering competence and fluency in domain-relevant skills, such as using mathematical tools, especially graphs and charts, and applying financial theories, as well as learning when (that is, judging) to appropriately apply them and when not to. This involved interpreting what the graphs and theories could convey about the situation.

In an interview, Jeff explains the relationship of the first module on foreign exchange ('FX') to the second one on loans and deposits: 'When we move to the next module [loans and deposits], their capital is strategy now . . . – because you're trying to position your bank for what will happen in the future' (transcript, post-class interview). The key point here in terms of imagination is the emphasis on strategy: 'because you're trying to position your bank for what will happen in the future'. Forming a strategy goes beyond immediate experience and is about anticipating how certain actions are likely to affect the future. However, it is not predicting the future, but weighing the likelihood that alternative courses of action will attain a desired outcome or weighing courses that balance multiple desired outcomes. Doing this involves imagining the ramifications of various plans of action – and then making judgements about them (the critical judgement part of the operation). This is a generative form of imaginative thinking that Ricoeur terms 'productive' because it involves entertaining several provisional constructs in the imagination.

Finance ethnography   161

The key source of data about what the students learned from their trading experience in the loans and deposits module was the final assignment, which was to be written by students as if it was a report to the CEO on the bank (the lecturer), but with the addition of sections for reflection on their learning. Because this module was the key module and represents what is most desirable that students learn, it will be my focus in the next section.

Introducing the simulation game rules of the loans and deposits module

As with the currency trading module, the students acted as a bank in groups of three students. Essentially, the Learning Guide says, they trade with other banks, lending money and taking deposits from other banks as well as tendering with corporations who wish to borrow (loan, from the bank's point of view) or invest (borrow, from the bank's point of view) at competitive rates for certain periods of time. The interest rates each bank adopts, and the rarity of occasions when contracted 'maturity' dates of the loans (which are the bank's 'assets') coincide with the maturity dates of deposits (the bank's 'liabilities'), means this trading activity carries risk. In a teaching situation, this presents a learning moment: thinking about what risks are involved and the ways to mitigate them. For example, if they don't have enough cash they can't meet their obligations to depositors wanting to withdraw money, which would constitute bankruptcy. Having access to sufficient cash to fulfil commitments to customers is referred to as 'liquidity', and it's crucial to maintaining operations (as, I recall, from the rush on the banks in pre–World War I Germany and in Cyprus in 2013 during the Global Financial Crisis). If all the bank's liabilities match with their assets, they add up to a zero sum on the 'balance sheet', which a recommended text for the subject tells me is an accounting statement or table 'that contains a record of assets, liabilities and equity at the end of a period of time' (Gup et al., 2007, p. 540), then the bank is said to have an overall 'square position'. They refer to this as managing their activities on the 'balance sheet'. The rules of the game dictate that each week they are required to square their balance sheets.

The students' banks can also tender to place loans to companies or take deposits from them, usually for quite large amounts. I suppose this to be about companies needing to borrow in order to invest in capital, or the reverse: depositing to deal with large cash surpluses for a period. These transactions could be conducted between the week's trading, but the majority occurred during trading sessions by email or phone with Jeff, and the rule was that banks could only win a maximum of 10 per cent of any tender.

The 'position keeper' (accountant) records trading events on the bank's balance sheet using an Excel spreadsheet, which is one of the financial tools I see groups refer to periodically each week during trading; this person uses it to produce charts and graphs, which track the bank's activities. For example, position keepers could produce a chart containing the quantity of loans loaned to different financial sectors or a spreadsheet to inform themselves of crucial information, such as break-even points for return on investment. The first can provide insight into certain information, such as what proportion of loans are to the corporate sector.

162   *Finance ethnography*

The answer can give insight into the question, 'What, therefore, is my exposure to risk?' One example of a commonly used graph was a 'yield curve', which graphs the various maturity dates of deposits and loans. Interpreting what these graphs describe of the practical field involves imagination – 'reading off' or reinterpreting the data contained in the graph and applying it back to the actual situation one is trying to understand and control, which is how to ensure that the margin between the deposit interest rates and the loan interest rates, and the gaps between their maturity dates, will amount to a profit. This is because it requires imagination to move between such abstract depictions and what they tell you about actual financial prospects. Successful interpretation is the first step to mastery of that situation – it informs the team of the effect on expected profits of changing rates on different maturity dates, as well as on liquidity, and so helps them decide if, and when, to adapt their strategies. Jeff tells the class, 'It is expected you will gain an understanding of yield curve movements, differing maturities, asset and liability allocation, cash flows and prudential regulatory requirements'.

The total budget is 1.5 billion per bank, so the rule is that they can't borrow or loan over this amount. It is clear to me that the graphs are mathematical tools, which help them make profit projections, based on different maturity dates of deposits and loans and, therefore, total ('net') interest rate income and forecasts of interest rate directions. The value of numbers and maths is 'they summarise things', Jeff exhorts. It is how they can track the bank's performance and understand reasons for likely changes of fortune in it. The Unit Guide refers them to 'any commercial bank management textbook for knowledge on capital profitability, performance measures, asset and liability management, liquidity, interest rate risk, models of liquidity interest rate risk, regulation and risk management' to help them understand an apply the concepts (course Unit Guide, 2013, p. 10). The graphs illustrate Dennett's idea of intellectual 'tools' which bootstrap the tool user's ability to reason about what the information means. Appropriate and accurate interpretation of cause and effect, or abstract theory and concrete particulars, subsequently feed the creation of appropriate strategies, which are examples of productive imagination. All these theoretical procedures and concepts will have been learned in earlier subjects in their degree and need to be selected (from memory) and applied constantly in the subject to help them decide if and how current strategies may be modified or new financial strategies tried.

Each week the lecturer makes timed announcements of 'news events', which can be expected to impact on the direction of interest rates and, therefore, the financial strategies the teams may need to adjust. An example from 'Dealing Session 3' serves to illustrate what factors affecting finance these announcements include:

> 10:10 It is time for you to think about the risks you have in your balance sheet and seek solutions to solve the risks and problems you may have.
> 10:15 Trading commences.
> 10:30 Perpetual tender closes.
> 10:30 Quarterly growth figures due. Expectation that will continue current trends. 'Retail sales still low but economists believe that a further

Central bank announcement of cash rates. Possible decrease but

0.75% reduction in interest rates may be as low as rates need to go to get economy moving'.

10:40 Central bank announcement of cash rates. Possible decrease but market uncertain. 'Central bank (RBA) announces a decrease of the cash rate of 50 basis points to 8.0%. All banks required to reduce their month rate by 0.50% immediately'.

10:45 QBE Insurance tender closes.

10:55 'Central bank meeting to discuss interest rates at 12.05am. AMP economist believes a further cut of 25 basis points is likely'.

11:00 News Corporation tender closed.

11:20 AMP tender closed.

(11:30–45 Trading halts for mid-session break)

11:55 Retail sales figures due. Expected to be down on last quarter. 'Retail sales showing signs of increasing but will watch the trend over the next month', says the Retailers Association.

12:05 The Central bank cuts interest rates 25 basis points in cash rate. All banks need to reduce your one month rate by 0.25%. This is the final interest rate cut in 2013.

12:10 Press Statement from the Prime Minister: PM suggests that Australian economy is showing signs of recovery and that further reduction in interest rates will probably see the economy beginning to expand.

12:20 Central bank decides to wait to see if interest rate decreases have kick-started the economy. Next announcement from Central Bank to be made November 30, 2013.

12:25 Book squaring time.

12:35 Trading ceases.

Forming strategies: a productive form of imagination that builds on reproductive forms of imagination – an analysis of student bank reports

On the surface this sounds like a straightforward process of playing out various financial institution events, information announcements and government activities that interact with lending and deposit rates. However, it went further. The simulation game allowed students to accumulate experience of seeing the effect of their strategies and whether the outcomes they forecast eventuated and, if not, to understand why. This second module emphasises forecasting, which reminded me of Dawkins's conception of imagination as a soft technological ability of consciousness to simulate (see Chapter 2).

> You *imagine* what would happen if you did each of the alternatives open to you – you set up a model in your head, not of everything in the world, but of the restricted sets of entities which you think may be relevant. You may see them vividly in your mind's eye or manipulate stylized abstractions of them.

(1989, p. 59)

164   *Finance ethnography*

The difference is that, in this case, the models are not just in your head. Your understanding is augmented by what the graphs and tables suggest about relationships between data and can illuminate how variables affect each other. This informs what plans of action you devise to make up your strategy. Dawkins emphasises the power of imagination to foresee possibilities in the intermediate or long-term time frames upon which judgement can operate. Dawkins's model focuses on providing foresight (powers of prediction) in a similar way to this finance module's focus on forecasting effects of various strategies. The game forced students into planning for contingencies and, in this way, appeared to be an example of fostering a form of productive imagination. How? The forecasting involved in strategy formation does not reproduce reality but projects non-existent future possibilities that contingency plans are designed to meet.

The next section looks more closely at the role of graphs and charts and how the information they display augments and improves the ability to forecast the effects of various courses of action.

Evidence of imagination and formation of strategy in student assignments

The loans and deposits final assignment was to write a report to the CEO on the bank's trading. The proforma or template for their report, which was provided by Jeff, required them to include sections on the economic environment, risk management strategies and 'what we learned'. Although no two reports were structured the same, they each addressed these sections.

Some reports showed limited analysis of the meaning of economic indicators. By limited analysis I mean they *will* note the correlation between an event – such as poor retail sales and an interest rate cut; the Consumer Price Index being lower than expected and accompanying an interest rate cut; news of Greece's withdrawal from the European Union causing global economic chaos with long-term lowering of interest rates – but their graphs are not linked closely to an interpretation of what *those relationships mean for their strategies.* One student group's report, for example, notes these things (p. 3–4), but its graphs and discussion of weekly trading sessions remained at the level of description (p. 4–6). Its yield curve analysis section, too, describes correlations:

> At the beginning, the yield curve was a humped curve. This was due to the 50bp cut at the previous trading session.
>
> During the break and end, the figure did not differ much from the 75 bp and 50bp cut rate. Additionally, it must be noted that only the short-term rate was affected by the rate cut.
>
> (Student Lloyd's TSB report)

Finance ethnography 165

This extract shows use of the yield curve, which graphs the various maturity dates of deposits and loans. Ricoeur's discussion of models in science as *redescriptions* bring us closer to its use in graphs and charts in finance in the sense that models provide a link to metaphor's power to redescribe phenomena (1991). This is because they are models *for* understanding, more than models *of* real things, by which he means they are heuristic constructs that redescribe aspects of reality, opening up new ways of apprehending it. Similar to models, graphs select salient variables and display their relationship to make information easier to interpret. In this sense, like maps, they appear to be derivative instances of reproductive imagination in that graphs, like maps, refer to existing reality. And yet, the conscious extraction of salient characteristics that are placed into relationship to each other renders their representations abstractions, or models, *for* understanding the real situation, which means they are used to generate alternative models for informing action (what action to take). As I have argued earlier, in that slight gap or hiatus is opened up in the learner an opportunity for agency. However, the example of graphs tells us something about Ricoeur's notions of reproductive and productive imagination, and that is the relationship between them. It suggests that Ricoeur's notion of the productive imagination and any transformative fictions like metaphors, models, hypotheses, narrative and so forth must have elements of reproductive imagination, must draw from reality sufficiently so that its productive distance is not too great (Taylor, 2006). This point is supported by Dewey's arguments (see Chapter 2) that inference is a form of imagination and that ideas that ignore facts of the situation are unlikely to be effective in acting on that situation (Bleazby, 2012; Dewey, 2004, p. 52). The instance of the physics students using their bodies to model a quantum concept – in conjunction with other 'mindtools', such as language and mathematical operations in Chapter 5) – was another example. It suggests there is a movement from one to the other. But it also suggests the critical consciousness distinguishing them, that the productive imagination includes an awareness that its knowledge construction is provisional – there is a fictive element to it – and may be reconstructed in the future; it is distinguished from the world-in-itself. In finance the graph is a tool used to summarise information and to simplify an understanding of relationships between variables which have a bearing on the direction of interest rates – this understanding informs strategy and underpins action.

However, in the 'Overall strategy' section of the team's report, the team outlined their understanding of the economic environment that gave rise to their lending and borrowing strategy and the opportunity for profit-making.

> The overall strategy employed was to make long-term loans and funding it through short-term borrowings. Lloyd's main aim was to lend at the two longer maturities and borrow from the two shorter maturities. This strategy was developed based on the falling interest rates environment that was forecasted and assumption that a normal yield curve would exist. In order to improve profitability, we endeavoured to fully gear up to the maximum limit that was

166 *Finance ethnography*

> allowed. However, liquidity needs were always at the forefront of our trading, and we made sure we maintained a buffer over the session (100 million).
>
> . . .
>
> ### Contingency strategy
>
> When the market did not move in accordance to our expectations, our trading had to alter our strategy and use certain contingent strategies to ensure that we react quickly to these unforeseen events.
>
> There were times when the yield curve became humped or inverse, forcing the team to manage the maturity of its loans and deposits, under such circumstances, we kept our trading to the minimum (10 million deals) and waited to see if this was a short-term fluctuation before trading as usual again.
>
> We aimed to transact in large volumes and participate in pre-market deals and tenders, at instances where we were unsuccessful; we immediately dealt with corporations for the same volume at the market rate.
>
> (Lloyds TSB Loans and Deposit module report)

The team initially try to hedge opportunities for profit by lending money over the longer terms and borrowing over the shorter term, keeping in mind the need to maintain a safe level of available cash ('liquidity'). However, conditions changed. The team showed they were receptive and responsive to conditions by minimising trading and trying to manage the maturity dates better. Their rational 'wait and see' response is a fair strategy for action because it allows them time to check for further economic data to indicate likely financial movement. However, they do not articulate a link between strategies in various kinds of scenarios and how each would manipulate possible opportunities for profit-making.

The 'What we learned', 'Concise review' and 'Best aspects of the module' sections of Table 7.1 of the report reflects the insights gained by students as a result of their learning experience.

This table implies the learning of certain principles or rules: the importance of leverage for making profit (the proportion you borrow in relation to equity you put in to make up your total assets); contingency planning for unexpected events; listening closely to changes in market conditions; and the financial advantages of maintaining ethical and civil human relationships during transactions. One student report described how the module made them:

> [T]hink outside of what is written in textbook . . . when trading begins, all these theoretical concepts get cast into the background as we have to observe what goes on in the market, and delve deeper into reasons as to why the market is moving in such a way, and what other banks are trying to play at.

Finance ethnography 167

Table 7.1 Student assignment table

What we learned	Comments
The power of leverage	Important to take full advantage of leverage as it boosts earnings greatly.
Risk management	Must be able to deal with unexpected events through setting out risk management strategies.
Pre-planning strategies	Important to decide on strategies prior to the trading session so that the team will work in unison.
Importance of information	Information is a powerful tool in the marketplace. Without information, strategies could be useless as one would not have an idea of the market in general.
Keeping a good relationship	When dealing with counterparties, important to keep a good relationship as they may be more willing to bargain in the long run.

Source: Lloyds TSB Loans and Deposit module report.

In their minds, reading things out of textbooks is distinct from learning how they would do it.

For this group there is evidence that the pedagogy created a safe experimental environment in which students could test strategies and outcomes, and it encouraged students to take risks, which, as discussed earlier, the literature supports as important to creativity; it encouraged collaboration with peers within the group and outside it to diversify thinking and help make critical assessments. It encouraged students to experiment with rule-governed financial behaviours by applying various theoretical understandings to known economic indicators and deploying financial tools. It rewarded staying alert: flexibly applying various theories in order to respond strategically to a changing environment and being prepared to adapt by having alternate plans should economic indicators signal a changing environment. In this respect, there was space for students to link theory to practice in order to deal with situations. It also required them to make connections between various financial indicators and abstract representations of their financial position. This involved going beyond what is given by linking cause and effect, forming understandings about correlations and forming relationships between financial indicators and abstract graphical formulations.

Similarly, in this section of a report by another student bank, HSBC, the graphs are the tool used to describe a relationship between current events and their degree of correlation with movements in interest rates. This report provides an interesting point of comparison to Lloyd's with clearer articulation of various strategies or opportunities for profit given the particular signs in the economic environment. Risk management strategies in the report are subdivided as follows, indicating a clear delineation of how the team managed different forms of risk by balancing multiple strategies.

168   *Finance ethnography*

Risk management strategies implemented

Liquidity risk
Interest risk

Strategies developed for the trading session

Contingency strategies

The report explains the reasons 'our bank holds a consistent view on falling interest rates based on the overall condition of the economy and our observation of the market each week'. Their extensive list of indicators includes a fall in commodity prices; new car registrations down causing suspended production; construction companies facing insolvency with concomitant unemployment at a 15 year high; executives reporting on low business confidence; and lowering of the exchange rate value of the Australian dollar – indicating competence in understanding the relationships between them and their likely impact on interest rates (Student HSBC Loans and Deposits Report, pp. 5–6). The report of another team, Sunway bank, similarly contains a long list of indicators diagnosed as likely to trend in the long term to a decreasing interest rate environment (Student Sunway Loans and Deposits Report, p. 4). In HSBC's report, this is followed by several graphs depicting interest rate movements over three of the trading sessions and yield curve movements over the trading sessions (see Figure 7.2). These graphs are the tool used to represent the relationship between current events and their degree of correlation with movements in interest rates.

This section of the HSBC report depicted in Figure 7.2 not only summarises how the table and yield curve describe the impact of news and events on interest rates, it then takes the analysis further:

> We noticed that the yield for the next shortest maturity is generally the highest among all maturities and such observation provides useful insights in our strategy making. Also the shape of the yield curves does not necessarily remain unchanged over time or shifts to one direction only. Even though we hold a view of decreasing interest rate, decisions with regards to the next shortest maturity should be made cautiously. Overall, the actual market aligned with our forecast closely thus strategies we developed and implemented should add profits to our bank.
>
> (Student HSBC Loans and Deposits Report)

Finance ethnography 169

Summary of Key Events and Impacts on Interest Rates	
Events	Impact *(Observed Over All Trading Sessions)*
CBA Cash Rate Intervention	Decrease (Certain & Immediate)
Rapid Depreciation in AUD Exchange Rate	Decrease (High Possibility)
Increase in Unemployment Figure	Decrease (Medium Possibility)
Balance of Payment Higher Than Expected	Decrease (Lower Possibility) [1]

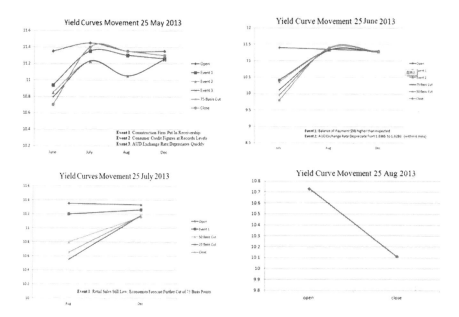

Figure 7.2 Student HSBC Loans and Deposits Report

This discussion (in the box at the foot of p. 168) shows that the representation of yield curves was able to be interpreted by the team in terms of forward thinking, or strategy. The formation of their strategies depends upon, first, the data being meaningfully described in the yield curve graphs and other charts. The graphs and charts model pertinent cause-and-effect values in the situation. Making strategy implies creating ideas for action that take us beyond immediate experience but are suggested by our interpretation of current scenarios. This example suggests, again, that Ricoeur's notion of 'productive imagination', which is about the projection of non-existent or 'fictional' constructs, should be extended to the idea of strategy formation.

170 *Finance ethnography*

Another way of saying this is to say that reasoning is also an imaginative process because it includes imagining the consequences of suggestions if they were applied: these consequences go beyond experience. This aligns with Dewey's point that 'inference is always an invasion of the unknown, a leap from the known' (2004, p. 152). 'Suggestion is the very heart of inference; it involves going from what is present to something absent. Hence, it is more or less speculative, adventurous' (Dewey, 1910, p. 75).

However, Dewey also pointed out that imagining consequences that ignore the facts of the situation are unlikely to be effective in operating on that situation (Bleazby, 2013). Imagination, when applied effectively, is cognisant of the facts of the situation. If I am interpreting the students correctly, they are commenting on the need for constant vigilance of signs of changing conditions that may entail short-term adjustments to the long-term strategy.

The students do not use the language of creativity and imagination: they are not self-evidently aware that their capacity to extract relevant data, to recreate it abstractly in mathematical formulations and then interpret what those models tell them about the original situation they were trying to understand, involves imaginatively making connections. Graphing activity involves them in manipulating data into the form of a diagram that represents a system of connections or interrelationships among two or more values. Manipulating these data using tools augments their understanding, organising or structuring their conceptualization of the financial situation in ways that are not given to them so easily in direct experience. The new picture can then potentially generate propositions for hypotheses and the forming of strategies. As we saw in the physics ethnography (Chapter 5), this appears to show the link between reproductive and productive forms of imagination, in Ricoeur's terms. What is the nature of this link? Are productive forms dependent on reproductive forms? Is it that the makers of each simply have something to say about the world they share? I recall Ricoeur's 'arc of operations' in a literary context. In the first part of this arc, people are routinely involved in the work of decoding the symbolic order of culture. When reading a narrative, they are then involved in a process of re-figuration in which they refer the meaning of the narrative back to their own world, which shapes their reality (Dowling, 2011, p. 16; Valdes, p. 117; Ricoeur, 1991, p. 173). It is the interpretation of the narrative as a model *for* generating proposals about situations (and for acting on them) which makes it a form of productive imagination.

Danger, surprise (again) and learning opportunity: managing the balance sheet

The report continues as the HSBC team go on to describe how in the first two trading periods, their strategy of making as many long-term loans as possible led to the discovery of an unforeseen danger (see Figure 7.3).

> Due to the unawareness of potential liquidity risk, we encountered extremely dangerous opening balance in 25/07/2013. We accumulated $1400 million long term loans which means only $100 million can be made at that time. That is, only 10 standard parcels could force our bank to breakdown. At that point, we were awarded (sic) the importance of liquidity, and carefully managed our balance sheet. The attitude change can be clearly observed in the last period balance sheet (HSBC Loans and Deposits Report, p. 10).

Time Period	Duration Gap
25/5/2013	1.07
25/6/2013	0.57
25/7/2013	0.79
25/8/2013	0

Figure 7.3 Student HSBC Loans and Deposits Report

Their realisation that their profit position was at risk in the event of adverse interest rate movement led to them incorporating new factors in their revised strategy to manage risk better, such as, as they go on to say, the duration gap, which 'indicates the bank need[s] to raise more deposits' (p. 9). Apprehending the complex interaction of these factors will mean they can take more active control of their balance sheet structure as part of the strategy directing their operations:

> In addition to gap and interest rate sensitivity, the duration illustrates that we did not consciously manage our balance sheet as the actual value of the loan and deposit simply depend on dealer's decision.
> (Student HSBC Loans and Deposits Report)

The report articulates their self-critique and what they have learned from the simulation that has allowed them to fall in to a trap of their own making:

> In summary, the balance sheet should be carefully managed. We need to consider liquidity risk, interest rate risk, refinance risk and other risks before transactions and reflect solution of these risks in investment and financing structure. In other words, risk management should be examined before a transaction and then implemented during the transaction.
> (Student HSBC Loans and Deposits Report)

172   *Finance ethnography*

By building in opportunities for trial and error, where students are brought up short by risks and have chances to respond with revised strategies, the simulation pedagogy is here shown to expand the students' learning. This is another example of Engeström's notion of 'object transformation' in his studies of learning in practice and to think and act as a finance professional. Learning as a relational process means that expansive learning comes from repositioning oneself in relation to the object as a result of seeing more in it (Edwards, 2005). We can also see here a number of elements in play that are highlighted in the literature as prerequisite to a learning environment conducive to creativity: making learning personally meaningful by connecting knowledge and emotion, opportunities to tolerate and manage levels of risk.

Contingency strategies and forecasting imaginatively

The report goes on to outline further risk management strategies: liquidity risk and interest rate risk. Liquidity risk incorporates the contingency strategies and actions they took to counter that risk. These contingency strategies are, once again, examples of imaginative thinking (productive imagination) because they are suggested by the mathematical tools and experience but involve reasoning beyond immediate experience.

At this juncture, I think it is important to emphasise that 'experience' here — the learning experience of doing this subject — is an enhanced one. The weekly playing of the simulated banking allows them to learn from repeated experience and develop intuitional knowledge. However, the 'experience' is not a simple, direct one because it is experience augmented by the use of graphical and theoretical tools, which, in Clark's language, turbocharge the possible learning. Imagination is employed in devising contingency strategies which power the agent into foreseeing possibilities in the intermediate or long-term time frames, upon which judgement or decision-making can operate. The strategies that follow show how the banking team proposed to manage the liquidity risk and interest rate risk.

Our bank is exposed to several risks which have adversely affected the operational and financial aspects of our business. Hence, several strategies are implemented to maintain a healthy position of our bank.

Liquidity Risk: Our bank has risk of insufficient capacity to fund increases in our asset (take loan). The risk is inherent in our banking due to the timing of mismatch between deposits and loans. Strategies Implemented:

- Maintaining sufficient capacity to take loans in the immediate term: remained at least 100 million loans to face cash flow obligation over the short to medium term.

> - Maintained strength in our balance sheet structure to ensure long-term resilience in the liquidity as we analyzed balance sheet position after every trading and planned for following week funds allocation.
> - Analyzed and reported our Liquidity Position weekly in order to ensuring our liquidity management in next trading session (Liquidity Gap)
>
> Limited the potential earnings at risk implication associated with unexpected liquidity stress. For example, we had opening loan of 1.4 billion which means we have 0.1billion capacities for loan, so we put a comparative higher rate than other banks to avoid loan hits which limited our potential earnings.
>
> (HSBC Loans and Deposits Report)

They go on in their report to describe how they anticipated and met interest rate risk, explaining it arises from changes in interest rates and as a result of the mismatch between the maturity time of interest-bearing assets and liabilities. The strategy they developed to obviate this risk was to analyse news weekly; identify possible interest rate movements; calculate the 'interest rate gap' against a profile of historical rates; allocate an appropriate amount of millions of dollars to support their expectations based on the previous week's gap analysis, 'as Gap is a direct measure of our net interest sensitivity throughout the time interval'; and regularly consult their balance sheet for interest rate risk. This shows a systematic series of actions, which compose the strategy, that are designed to bring about a desired outcome.

The HSBC bank also demonstrated nimble, opportunistic strategic thinking when it made a decision *not* to carry out pre-market dealing for deposits, as they expected rates to fall and assumed pre-market rates would be higher than rates during the trading session. Their strategy was to wait and see whether the central bank would enforce cash rate reduction, and, if it did, they would astutely take deposits from corporate immediately at a reduced rate for large volumes. Likewise if any tenders were undersubscribed, they would call corporate immediately to take deposits as quickly as possible and negotiate a lower rate.

> We did not rely much on tenders as others did. We acted more aggressively on increasing the deposit from corporate as we knew the tender would not be fully subscribed and we got the chance to negotiate a lower deposit rate with corporate as they were imperatively demanded.
>
> (Student HSBC Loans and Deposits Report)

174 *Finance ethnography*

Feedback on learning provided naturalistically and in real time

This classroom is a place where feedback on the effectiveness of their application of knowledge and skills is provided in situ to the student groups by the action and reaction in the simulation game itself. It does not need an educator to provide the feedback, or a rubric, and in fact to my knowledge no marking rubric was provided on the assignment report. In addition, a great deal of living teacher-student conversation happened in the course as the educator strolled around the groups in class, as well as through one-on-one email communication with the educator (transcript, post-course lecturer interview).

Re-imagining banking: questioning assumptions? . . . or not

It is worth discussing the domain of the practical field in which imagination may be active here. In the previous paragraph I alluded to the purpose of the use of imagination to make profit, and so its domain is arguably narrow. I found the finance class I observed built fluency in inherited, rule-governed skills and knowledge of finance, which include Ricoeur's productive imagination in strategy formation, but it did not appear to question assumptions which may lead to shifts in thinking about banking itself: for example, what banking is, based on a different model of a bank. Imagination is concerned with semantic innovation; it is difficult to anticipate what individual learners will make of the experiences offered to them, and certainly some students may have questioned this assumption privately. Certainly it was not the intention of this finance class, nor were the learners led towards challenging this assumption by the simulation pedagogy in the class. Challenging assumptions itself requires imagination, as I observed and discussed in the physics case study (Chapter 5). There was an unquestioned assumption in the finance simulation pedagogy that the purpose of a bank was to make profit. Certainly, ethical thinking was built into the simulated scenarios such that maximising profit at the expense of long-term viability, or reputation, or illegality led to prohibitions and penalties in the game and the involvement of self-regulation schemes to mitigate the tensions in these conflicting forces. But there did not appear to be events in the simulation game in which to explore or question assumptions, perhaps leading to shifts in thinking about what banking is, based on a different model. For example, I recalled the Grameen Bank founded by Muhammad Yunus in Bangladesh. Based on the idea of microfinance, the Grameen bank challenges the profit motive by lending small amounts of money to the poor deemed by conventional banks as too risky. But these amounts transform their lives (Yunus, 2014). The bank has no branches, visits the borrowers in their homes and loans to women predominantly – in all of which it breaks conventional banking practices. Islamic banking is another example of banking which structures loans differently to that of the traditional Western world and in accordance with religiously derived moral principles. The finance unit did not

Finance ethnography 175

foster imagination in students to the extent of shifting thinking or perspectives about banking itself – but equally it was not designed to. When Ricoeur speaks about productive imagination in metaphor as forming similarities that restructure semantic fields, the elements that are combined can be (to use another metaphor) close or distant. One could argue that the more heterogeneous the elements combined are, the deeper the assumptions it is willing to question or the rules it is willing to deviate from, the greater the levels of imaginative thinking involved. Ricoeur reminds us of this:

> Innovation remains a form of behaviour governed by rules. The labour of imagination is not born from nothing. It is bound in one way or another to the tradition's paradigms. But the range of solutions is vast. It is deployed between the two poles of servile application and calculated deviation, passing through every degree of 'rule-governed deformation'.
>
> (Ricoeur, 1983/1984, p. 69)

This is not to deny that there is imaginativeness in finance or in this finance pedagogy, but to argue that there are degrees of imaginativeness and that some pedagogical approaches demand of students a greater or lesser creative response than others.

Student reflection on forecasting and trading strategy

The assignments asked the students to reflect on what they had learned, which provides an opportunity to gain further insight into their learning. Extracts from this section of the HSBC and Sunway banks include:

> Unlike the FX module, the loans and deposits module is more complex and regulated. The forecast and analysis of scenarios and pre-market news are very important and directly relate to our trading strategy.
>
> . . .
>
> In addition, the total limit of $1.5 billion of loans and deposits that are taken or issued for 5 different maturities. This is not a simply borrow and lend money game. Banks have to manage their risks and returns. For example, liquidity risk is the major exposure that each bank faces. As the scenario indicates a reduction of interest rate, take short-term deposits and loan out at the longest maturity is the way of profits. However, no one can just loan out $1.5 billion at 31/12/2014, and then take deposits at 25/05/2013, because if some did this, there will be no money to loan out for next trading session. And the minimum of $10 million for each deal will destroy this zero

176   *Finance ethnography*

> liquidity bank. On the other hand, banks will not generate more profits if they hold too much liquidity. Therefore, every participant should organize their balance sheet to decide the amount of deposits and loans should take in each trading, and manage their rollover to avoid unnecessary high liquidity that cuts their profits. This module taught me that good and efficient risk management and accurate analysis of pre-market news are the keys to success.
>
> On the other hand, our bank did some psychology analysis to our peer competitors. After the FX module, we realized that other banks performed more conservative than aggressive. The whole FX market was quiet and the participants did not fully and fast react to the market news. People just set their rates among the others to avoid losses. Therefore, our bank decided to take a risk that to hold less liquidity and leveraged up to $1 billion at the first loan and deposit trading, because we believed that we would not receive too many calls from peer banks. Consequently, we won this trading and became the most profitable bank in the class.
>
>   (HSBC Loans and Deposits Module, Final Trading Report)
>
> Secondly, news is related to IR (interest rate) movements, so we must prudently analyze the information and news of market released, because some of these will have a positive or negative impact on rate movement. Because the principal of bank is that they manage and mismatch the maturity of deposits and loans to make the spread at an appropriate rate. Therefore, we need to predict in a correct position, it not only help us generate benefits, but also efficiently match the IR gap and Liquidity gap so that reduce the risk from deposits and loans.
>
>   (Sunway Loans and Deposits Module, Final Trading Report)

HSBC finds that managing risk, particularly liquidity risk, is the main aim of the game. That means learning to manage the balance sheet. However, 'managing the balance sheet' is a mechanistic term which, as we have seen, involves a complex judging of amounts, timing and duration of deposits and loans. The strategies for deciding on these rest on an accurate interpretation of current wider environmental conditions that affect interest rates, fluency in financial knowledge and skills to produce graphs that redescribe the data to emphasise relationships and in that way help them predict outcomes. These then give the spur to the devising of multiple appropriate strategies in what is a form of productive imagination. Sunway, too, shows the importance of monitoring the wider environmental conditions and using the financial tools' redescriptions expertly to be able to respond with an appropriate range of strategies.

Conclusion

Contrary to the scepticism that I brought to my observation of the finance simulation, this ethnographic case study illuminated the potential of simulation pedagogy to develop and enable students' imagination. By mimicking a workplace context, the finance simulation pedagogy provided students with the motivation to apply what they had learned in past courses in the current scenario, to synthesise information and theories and to make learning personally and emotionally involving. In addition, it demonstrated that simulation pedagogy can develop in students the experience of moving imaginatively between two roles or perspectives – their scenario role and their role as learners – encouraging a mental flexibility. Ricoeur's notion of productive imagination implying the conscious awareness of the fictiveness of imaginative constructs (the y axis) captures the importance of this aspect. This hiatus or distantiation is what allows the space in which criticality can occur. In this way, the pedagogy positioned students as agents with influence over what and how much they learned and with incentives to reflect on their learning.

The simulated scenarios were able to catch students off guard and take them by surprise. This emotion was then used by the educator to propel the students to reflect and review past actions. In this interesting process they were forced to reconsider their past action in the light of ethical considerations, specifically the role of trust in, and between, institutions/organisations in society. This was made possible by switching their roles in their imagination – themselves as finance professionals and themselves as learners. The surprise incident in the case illustrated beautifully the potential for simulation pedagogy to make learning personally transformative and its capacity to prompt taking alterative positions and perspectives.

In still other ways, the finance case study challenged the assumption that finance does not involve imagination, most particularly in the way it focused on students forming financial strategies to mitigate risks and envisage the consequences of strategies if they were applied. In this way, the finance case study provided a new context to illustrate the operation of imagination as semantic innovation. We saw, however, how certain assumptions about the purpose and rules of banking were not questioned – so what the pedagogy allowed for semantic innovation was limited or bounded. The simulation teaching approach encouraged productive imagination in that imagination underpins the ability to make a mental leap and project strategies likely to be effective. Graphs were the primary tool isolating certain factors, relating them to other factors, and modelling the problem. In this way they can suggest better interpretations of complex phenomena. Although they are clearly reproductive in Ricoeur's terms, because they are tools for representing relations their suggestions assist predictions and therefore facilitate the formation of strategies that can be integrated with other goal-directed behaviour appropriate in the existing situation. Strategy, as we have seen, is a version of productive imagination, in Ricoeur's terms. This is, I believe, what we would expect from a mind that

178 *Finance ethnography*

integrates socio-cultural tools within an overarching prediction-driven cognitive framework. This case study suggests that by reconstructing the practical field in this way, financial theory and graphic tools provide the grounds to forecast effects and suggest strategic action to bring about intended outcomes – profits usually. Both these phases involve imagination. By providing an authentic environment, the simulation unleashes the motivation for students to want to use the tools fluently and make the mental leap from restructured knowledge to a strategy that is likely to lead to banking success.

Notes

1 Except in the case of the expression 'creative accounting', by which is generally meant illegal minimisations of tax payments by interpreting tax laws 'liberally' to avoid tax. However, this is not an accounting subject. This finance subject is about banking.
2 I am indebted to Jennifer Bleazby for helping me see this distinction.
3 An accreditation program run by EFMD – The Management Development Network, an international membership organisation, based in Brussels, Belgium, with over 800 member organisations from academia, business, public service and consultancies.
4 The Association to Advance Collegiate Schools of Business is a global, nonprofit membership organisation of educational institutions, businesses and other entities.
5 The Association of MBAs (AMBA) is the international authority on post-graduate business education, established in 1967 by a group of business graduates, and aims to raise the profile of business education and MBA qualification in UK and Europe.

References

Amabile, T. M. (1983). *The social psychology of creativity.* New York: Springer-Verlag.
Anderson, K. (2010). The whole learner: The role of imagination in developing disciplinary understanding. *Arts and Humanities in Higher Education, 9*(2), 205–221.
Appadurai, A. (1996). *Modernity at large: Cultural dimensions of globalization* (Vol. 1). Minneapolis, MN: University of Minnesota Press.
Biggs, J., & Tang, C. S.-K. (2007). *Teaching for quality learning at university: What the student does.* Maidenhead: Open University Press.
Bleazby, J. (2012). Dewey's notion of imagination in philosophy for children. *Education and Culture, 28*(2), 95–111. doi:10.1353/eac.2012.0013
Bleazby, J. (2013). *Social reconstruction learning: Dualism, Dewey and philosophy in schools.* New York: Routledge.
Bosanquet, A., Winchester-Seeto, T., & Rowe, A. (2012). Social inclusion, graduate attributes and higher education curriculum. *Journal of Academic Language and Learning, 6*(2), 73–87.
Cole, M. (2009). Storytelling: Its place in infection control education. *Journal of Infection Prevention, 10*(5), 154–158. doi:10.1177/1757177409341425
Craft, A., Jeffrey, B., & Leibling, M. (2001). *Creativity in education.* London: Continuum.
Csikszentmihalyi, M. (1999). Implications of a systems perspective for the study of creativity. In R. Sternberg (Ed.), *Handbook of creativity* (pp. 313–335). Cambridge: Cambridge University Press.
Dawkins, R. (1989). *The selfish gene* (Second ed.). Oxford: Oxford University Press.
Dewey, J. (1910/1997). *How we think: A restatement of the relation of reflective thinking to the educative process.* Mideola, NY: Dover Publications.
Dewey, J. (2004). *Democracy and education.* Mineola, NY: Dover Publications.
Dowling, W. C. (2011). *Ricoeur on time and narrative: An introduction to Temps et récit.* Notre Dame, IN: University of Notre Dame Press.

Edwards, A. (2005). Let's get beyond community and practice: The many meanings of learning by participating. *Curriculum Journal, 16*(1), 49–65.

Engeström, Y. (2009). Expansive learning: Toward an activity-theoretical reconceptualization. In K. Illeris (Ed.), *Contemporary theories of learning: Learning theorists . . . in their own words* (pp. 53–73). Abingdon, Oxon: Routledge.

Fanning, R., & Gaba, D. (2008). Simulation-based learning as an educational tool. In J. Stonemetz & K. Ruskin (Eds.), *Anesthesia informatics* (pp. 459–479). London: Springer-Verlag.

Gredler, M. E. (2004). Games and simulations and their relationships to learning. In D. Jonassen (Ed.), *Handbook of research on educational communications and technology* (pp. 571–581). Mahwah, NJ: Lawrence Erlbaum Associates.

Gup, B., Avram, K., Beal, D., Lambert, R., & Kolari, R. (2007). *Commercial banking: The management of risk.* Milton, Queensland: John Wiley & Sons Australia, Ltd.

Jeffrey, B., & Craft, A. (2004). Teaching creatively and teaching for creativity: Distinctions and relationships. *Educational Studies, 30*(1), 77–87.

Johnson, M. (1993). Moral imagination. In *Moral imagination: Implications of cognitive science for ethics.* Chicago: University of Chicago Press.

Kirsh, D., & Maglio, P. (1994). On distinguishing epistemic from pragmatic action. *Cognitive Science, 18,* 513–549.

Lave, J. (1988). *Cognition in practice: Mind, mathematics, and culture in everyday life.* Cambridge; New York: Cambridge University Press.

Lave, J. (1996). Teaching, as learning, in practice. *Mind, Culture, and Activity, 3*(3), 149–164. doi:10.1207/s15327884mca0303_2

Lave, J., & Wenger, E. (1991). *Situated learning: Legitimate peripheral participation.* Cambridge, UK; New York: Cambridge University Press.

Lucas, B., Claxton, G., & Spencer, E. (2013). *Progression in student creativity in school: First steps towards new forms of formative assessments.* OECD Education Working Paper No. 86, OECD Publishing. Retrieved from http://dx.doi.org/10.1787/5k4dp59msdwk-en.

Lucas, U. (2008). Being 'pulled up short': Creating moments of surprise and possibility in accounting education. *Critical Perspectives on Accounting, 19,* 383–403. doi:10.1016/j.cpa.2006.09.004

McCulloch, M. (2009). *From school to faculty: Stories of transition into teacher education.* (PhD), Glasgow University, Glasgow. Retrieved from http://theses.gla.ac.uk/1273/01/2009mccullochedd.pdf

McWilliam, E. (2007). *Is creativity teachable: Conceptualising the creativity/pedagogy relationship in higher education.* Paper presented at the 30th HERDSA Annual Conference: Enhancing Higher Education, Theory and Scholarship, Adelaide.

McWilliam, E., & Dawson, S. (2007). *Understanding creativity: A survey of 'creative' academic teachers: A report for the Carrick Institute for Learning and Teaching in Higher Education.* Retrieved from www.altcexchange.edu.au/system/files/handle/fellowships_associatefellow_report_ericamcwilliam_may07.pdf

Mezirow, J. (2009). An overview of transformative learning. In K. Illeris (Ed.), *Contemporary theories of learning* (pp. 90–105). Abingdon, Oxon: Routledge.

Nickerson, R. (1999). Enhancing creativity. In R. J. Sternberg (Ed.), *Handbook of creativity* (pp. 392–430). Cambridge: Cambridge University Press.

Nussbaum, M. (2001). *Upheavals of thought: The intelligence of emotions.* New York: Cambridge University Press.

Ricoeur, P. (1983/1984). *Time and narrative* (K. McLaughlin & D. Pellauer, Trans. Vol. 1). Chicago: University of Chicago Press.

Ricoeur, P. (1991). Imagination in discourse and in action (K. Blamey & J. B. Thompson, Trans.). In J. M. Eadie (Ed.), *From text to action: Essays in hermeneutics* (Vol. 2, pp. 168–187). Evanston, IL: Northwestern University Press.

Runco, M. (2010). Education based on a parsimonious theory of creativity. In R. Begetto & J. Kaufman (Eds.), *Nurturing creativity in the classroom* (pp. 235–251). New York: Cambridge University Press.

180 *Finance ethnography*

Schaefer, R., Overy, K., & Nelson, P. (2013). Affect and non-uniform characteristics of predictive processing in musical behaviour. *Behavioural and Brain Science, 36*, 226–227. doi:10.1017/S0140525X12002373

Spencer, E., Lucas, B., & Claxton, G. (2012). *Progression in creativity: Developing new forms of assessment: A literature review.* Newcastle upon Tyne: CCE.

Taylor, G. H. (2006, Spring-Fall). Ricoeur's philosophy of imagination. *Journal of French Philosophy, 16*(1 & 2), 93–104.

Valdes, M. J. (Ed.). (1991). *A Ricoeur reader.* Hertfordshire: Harvester Wheatsheaf.

Young, J. J., & Annisette, M. (2009). Cultivating imagination: Ethics, education and literature. *Critical Perspectives on Accounting, 20*, 93–109.

Yunus, M. (2014, October 11). *Public lecture.* Presented by Monash Business School and Monash University. Robert Blackwood Hall, Monash University.

8 Pharmaceutical science ethnography

He who has imagination without learning has wings but no feet.

(Joseph Joubert)

The chapter focuses on 4 weeks of ethnographic research in first year pharmaceutical science in an Australian research intensive university. I show how the students' independence in learning is enhanced by drawing a diagram or model of the scientific inquiry process and explain this in relation to Ricoeur's notion of reproductive imagination. I call this diagram/model a 'learning artefact' and identify it as a particular form of the class Wartofsky's calls 'secondary artefacts' (see Chapter 3). The picture that emerges from the research is how this diagram is used as a mediating tool for deepening their understanding of what scientific inquiry is, and later, for organising their own performance of science. What the teacher's pedagogy scaffolds over the semester is the building of a link between a social, historical process of science and the individual students' higher mental process of understanding and participating in that process (Wertsch, 2007). This, I believe, is, in Vygotsky's terminology, the *internalisation* process that the pedagogy is designed to facilitate. However, the theoretical framework I use also questions whether the process of learning is captured by 'interiority'. Using Clark's theory of extended mind, I argue the cognitive work to gain competence as well as creativity in science is performed by learning to distribute the thinking across the brain-body boundary and beyond into the artefacts used to think with and also to weave it through the community in which that thinking occurs.

Introduction

Scientific Inquiry PSC1041 is a core first year, first semester subject taken by pharmaceutical science students. On a brilliant, warm day in March I wait with about one hundred students in a courtyard while the students from a previous lecture file out of a stairwell so we can come up. A hundred odd students either way; it takes some time. The campus is in a leafy suburb just north of the city of Melbourne and consists of just one faculty, the Faculty of Pharmacy and Pharmaceutical Science, and has a unique (for this university), intimate campus feel

182 *Pharmaceutical science ethnography*

as well as a strong reputation. (I learn later that it is ranked second in the world in the 2017 QS World University Rankings by Subject, having risen from fifth a few years ago.) There are nearly two thousand pharmacy and pharmaceutical science students including a number of post-graduates, most of whom, however, are off campus.

The cool of the lecture theatre is a relief after the summer sun. I take my place feeling a little out of place as I know this lecturer likes to encourage students to engage with each other in lectures and I don't want to find myself stuck seated between students who are required to interact with each other.

Out front of the theatre, the lecturer, whom we shall call Owen, welcomes the students to their 'very first lecture at university'. He goes out of his way to dissolve the anxiety they might feel as first year students, greeting them, telling them that new students at university often feel anonymous and urging them, 'Come and talk to us!' He asks if they have visited the course 'Moodle' learning management system site. He tells them there will be a lot of discussion in class in small groups and that it might be 'annoying on occasions' to work with others who think differently than you. However, 'Working with each other is absolutely essential to working in the future'. Then he introduces the unit: 'You'll learn by looking at some examples of science, and do your own scientific experiment'.

He also tells them that the subject is different from their other first year subjects – physiology, medicinal chemistry and so forth. That there is less content, which can be deceptive, it appears – there is more *doing* in this subject, 'it's more descriptive' – but that 10 people failed last year. The subject, he tells them, is more process oriented, focused on understanding the scientific method and applying what you understand.

He is clearly clarifying expectations for his students, identifying common misunderstandings before they hurt, helping students smoothly negotiate the transition from school to university. In the first interview, he explained to me why this subject has the active focus it has:

> The model in higher education particularly in health sciences, a lot of the content is taken as established. It's been done. We don't really look at the basis for it. So they'll read textbook pages, and pages of facts about how cells work and how the body works and how drugs work and they won't look at the process by which we *came* to that knowledge, let alone how would we come to new knowledge, you know. We spend so much on the past, and we need to because they need this knowledge base, but I think people fail by and large, either as post-grad students or as technicians, more often because, when someone says to them, 'Go and do this thing'. They say, 'How? Tell me how', and when they're told 'Figure it out' they're like, 'Well I don't do that!' It's a habit of mind combined with having some techniques

Pharmaceutical science ethnography 183

> up your sleeve to be able to solve . . . I think, solving problems at work, you need a rational side to say, I'm going to do this and this and this, but there's a creative step in at least one of those steps. And all of that capability of creating your own path to a solution to a new problem, and implementing it, just needs so much practice, and I think that practice has to be in a safe environment in an undergraduate space – not all the time. . . . At the moment we do little of it, until sometimes in a third year unit people will get plenty of space to do their own experiment or whatever. But I think it needs to start in first year, and to take small steps. Because students will have some of these capabilities, and some more than others. But unless you take small steps, if you get to a point at third year or when they graduate and you suddenly say, 'Here's a complex task which needs really high level creativity', they just fall over it. They haven't seen it, haven't done it, haven't thought about it. And they don't see it as part of their skill set.
>
> (Pre-class interview transcript)

From this statement we can hear his conviction that students need to be educated to take a more active role in the creation of knowledge if they are to be better prepared for work now and in the future. His reasoning also reflects the view that science is not just facts ('content') and that memorising or recalling facts, while necessary, has a disempowering effect if it means learners have not learned the problem-solving process that produced the facts: they don't see creating knowledge as 'part of their skill set'. He is arguing that the activity of science is more accurately understood when it is experienced as a *process* of scientific inquiry aimed at solving problems (which result in findings, which cumulatively constitute established facts). It therefore becomes the educator's role, he argues, to support or scaffold the students' creation of their own paths to solving problems.

He appears to understand 'creativity' as a process transiting multiple stages: conceiving ideas, developing a pathway to solve them and implementation. He sees the educator's role as developing those capabilities in a structured way, allowing time for practice and starting in first year. Trigwell, Prosser and Waterhouse (1999) reported links between the ways higher education teachers approach teaching and the ways their students approach learning that can lead students towards surface or deep approaches, which supports his strategy. It includes complex thinking approaches such as thinking creatively. This is a constructivist philosophy of student-centred, active teaching and learning that he is pursuing (Biggs, 2007; Vygotsky, 1978), and one that is actually adopted throughout the faculty, not in half part because he leads educational innovation in the faculty. His focus on the agency of students is also supported in the creativity literature (Jeffrey & Craft, 2004, in Lucas, Claxton & Spencer, 2013, pp. 64–65). He proposes the curriculum should give them greater opportunities

184   *Pharmaceutical science ethnography*

to construct their own knowledge throughout their undergraduate degree. A move away from textbooks, with their finished interpretations which put a gloss over the hundreds or thousands of research studies upon which their knowledge claims rest, and their limited forms of interaction with knowledge, is therefore necessary. And he is making the argument that to allow sufficient time for practice to properly prepare them, it has to pervade the degree and start in first year.

This view is reminiscent of the findings from other fields of my ethnographic research, particularly of history, which was also a first year subject. Science is far from being inert fact; it is a way of working, and the foundational skills require development and practice. Building expertise in wielding scientific concepts and skills is requisite to their imaginative and creative application – as it was in medieval European history. As this is a first year subject, this seems to me to be an entirely appropriate focus.

Pharmaceutical science graduates gain employment in a range of industries: pharmaceutical, biotech, agriculture, cosmetics, food quality assurance, research – even breweries – all of them in competitive markets that value innovation, for which initiative and being capable of working with the unknown are now pressing. However, this capability rests on actors learning competence in the tools, concepts and modes of scientific practice. I wonder to what extent the lecturer's phrase, 'all of that capability of creating your own path to a solution to a new problem, and implementing it, just needs so much practice' means pedagogies focus on individual actors or agents operating with their own tools, rather than encompassing them nested or being apprenticed within a scientific community. Will the pedagogies, for example, also introduce contexts in which individuals are usually embedded in their professions, which include multi-professional communities? As Engeström (1990a) has pointed out, to be authentic these include the social/collective elements in which there are ways of collaborating, professional rules and also divisions of labour – what he calls the contextual activity systems (see Figure 5.1 in Chapter 5). I wonder what these professional contexts are in pharmaceutical science and, given the diverse nature of graduate destinations, whether the formal education includes at any stage contexts that simulate or actually use pharmaceutical industry or research contexts. (From the second interview, I learned that they do have opportunities to devise products to solve industry issues in third and fourth year.)

His professed goal – that the course should develop skills in problem solving using processes of scientific inquiry, and not a focus on inert facts devoid of the context and origin of the discovery – explains the structure and choice of tasks in the subject across the semester. It asks: *What do scientists do when they set out to make a discovery?* The first tasks and assignment of the subject/unit are for students to develop a diagram or model that represent the processes of the scientific method of inquiry. After drafting their model, the students are exposed to inspirational historical experimental discoveries (through reading and lectures). Following that, a small number of faculty research scientists are invited to come talk to the students about their experimental research. After each of these steps, they are given an opportunity to restructure or refine their diagram/model. They do this in workshops where they compare and discuss models with each other. The next step, not covered by my observation, was that they then think up a testable hypothesis and design and conduct an experiment before analysing the findings (including statistically) and evaluating the hypothesis on the basis of the findings.

My ethnography is of the first four weeks of the Scientific Inquiry subject. This encompasses the teaching and learning involved in understanding the process of scientific investigation and the creation and refinement of the scientific model or representation in the first assignment.

Establishing the learning environment

Returning to my account of the first lecture, Owen now declares that 'the first rule is that these classes are a safe place to be wrong!' In terms of imagination, establishing a classroom environment that provides a safe place to take risks and welcomes learning from errors is supported in the creativity literature. The approach promotes an appreciation by students that creativity is subject to effort, persistence and self-motivation and is not determined by talent or giftedness beyond their control (Nickerson, 1999). And as we also saw in the physics chapter, Dewey recognised error as one of the benefits of his fallibilist notion of knowledge – it justified further inquiry and learning (Bleazby, 2011, pp. 73–75). The students are therefore encouraged to ask questions when they arise, not to leave them until the time-pressured end of semester. Questions are framed as an opportunity to learn. He assures them that any question they ask will usually reflect other classmates' unspoken questions. It is also a way to head off the reluctance which I have heard anecdotally is a common fear among the high achieving students accepted to this university. In this way, I infer, he endeavours to make them feel easier about exposing themselves and appearing stupid or slow in front of others and ushering in a classroom culture of asking questions.

The students also have 'clickers', and Owen also explains how they work. Clickers are a device (given free to all students by the faculty) that allow students to electronically 'vote' for a certain answer to multiple-choice questions that the educators present in PowerPoint slides. The device quickly adds up the votes and converts the 'a, b, c, d and e' options to percentages visible to all. In this way lecturers can quickly identify class misunderstandings; class discussion can also be instigated around the different views expressed by the answers. Learning from these discussions enables students to recognise and self-correct their understanding (if appropriate to that subject) or reflect on differences in conceptions. Clickers can also be used to ask open-ended questions such as, 'What would you like to do in your career? A. Be a scientist, B. Use your degree in business or health area, C. transfer to another degree, D. Not sure right now', which can lead to discussion, disseminate variation of views and

186 *Pharmaceutical science ethnography*

help forge a positive learning environment while decreasing the alienation often experienced in large classes.

The students in this subject are rewarded for clicker responses as they contribute 5 per cent of total marks to their final class grade. Owen tells the students that he has researched the effect of coming to class on student achievement by comparing the grades of students who come to 'nearly all' classes with students who come to 50 per cent of classes and those who 'barely come' to class. It turns out that students who come to 'nearly all' classes do 15 per cent better than those who turn up to 50 per cent of classes and 50 per cent better than those who 'barely come' to class! These effects are significant, and I wonder what effect it has on the resolve of students.

I find myself liking this way of bringing students in to the research cycle by sharing highly relevant evidence with them. It immediately positions them as agents whose choices and actions affect what they learn and takes seriously Vygotsky's dynamic positioning of the learner in relation to the problem – the students in relation to their need to learn for an object or reason. It also forefronts evidence as all-embracing practice in this scientific inquiry subject.

Owen also recommends to them the unit 'learning outcomes', which are listed in the learning management system 'Moodle' site. These may look just like a list, he says, but are a way to keep track of what is expected of them in the semester. He has these learning outcomes in front of him when he writes the exam, he tells them. They are used, then, as a *shared* guide – for unit educators and students – as to what learning is expected.

To close the first lecture as pharmaceutical science students, Owen asks them to write on a piece of paper 'a definition of scientific inquiry. What are the essential elements of a proper scientific experiment?'. Before the next lecture two days later, he emails them via the online learning management system a compilation of the answers they have given. They include the following definitions:

> **Rational and systematic process of forming a hypothesis, testing it, making observations and thus a conclusion.**
> Proper approach to testing or experimenting.
> Fair trials with controls and systematic procedures.
> **Testing the hypothesis or predicted outcome then testing to see if it for or against.**
> Process by which scientific discoveries are made, tested and verified or falsified.
> The way in which scientists conduct an experiment. The steps they take to form a conclusion.
> Following protocol in order to conduct a scientific experiment – hypothesis etc.
> Investigating new knowledge or correcting previous knowledge.

Pharmaceutical science ethnography 187

The structured pursuit of the underlying mechanisms of the universe . . . search for the reason why or how things happen.

The general approach or ways of approaching science. Viewed differently depending on the individual or situation.

The method by which an experiment is run in order to reach a valid conclusion.

A method of scientific discovery which aims to eliminate human bias.

Model scientists use to develop a theory based on a testable hypothesis or observation, reaching a conclusion.

Formulate a way to test variables.

The way in which scientific research is conducted in a methodical, ordered process.

Shared critical reflection

In the following lecture he brings up the prior answers on screen, then leads the lecture-full of students in a discussion about some of them (the bolded ones), walking up the middle of the theatre aisle to cross the social divide that separates the podium from the hall. This transparent sharing of answers appears to me to support the genesis of a 'collaborative' learning practice which according to Lucas, Claxton and Spencer's (2013) framework emphasises the social and contextual aspects of learning and creativity (Lave & Wenger, 1991) – one aspect of which is the giving and receiving of feedback, and another of which says that what underpins creative learning involves moving from novice to more expert phases through an ongoing social and cultural practice of peer critique of one's ideas or practice (Csikszentmihalyi, 1999 – see Chapter 4). He is demonstrating the advantages to knowledge creation of working collaboratively, and this applies to scientific communities.

He asks probing questions: 'Is a theory a hypothesis?' What is the distinction? One – a hypothesis – is about testing variables; the other – a theory – is about a broader explanation; 'What's involved in a proper scientific experiment?' – the key issue being we are 'looking for the effect of one or more variables on one dependent variable'. He raises an issue expressed in the comment, 'Viewed differently depending on the individual or situation', and points out it conflicts with some of the other statements. He then asks, 'Can we ever be fully independent? Can we take out bias?'

Student discussion ensues. One student says: 'Scientists have influence on experiments, to try to prove their own theory'. Another replies, 'Wouldn't *disproving* your theory be counted as a success?' A third student points out that there is a career issue at stake – scientists are valued by the number of papers they publish.

The lecturer agrees that there is no kudos in negative outcomes of experiments so perhaps there should be a journal that publishes negative outcomes. As there are now protocols in place where researchers must declare who

188 *Pharmaceutical science ethnography*

funds their research, this reinforces the importance of taking notice of biases or agendas that may skew scientific inquiry processes. 'If you have developed a drug that's going to go into human bodies, there needs to be rigorous and robust evidence for it'.

The discussion gets into deep territory: It reflects the recognition that science is an epistemic process of scientific inquiry but also a social-historical practice distributed across webs of journal protocols and forms of recognition involving status, profits from products ensuing from research, competition for jobs and resources and ethical issues. Class discussion such as this one models and encourages a practice and the propensity to want to contribute to the ideas of others and to hear how one's ideas can be improved, which is a basis of fruitful collaboration (Lucas, Claxton & Spencer, 2013).

Underlying structure of the pedagogy

The pattern of teaching initially in this subject is that students watch two 20-minute online video lectures by Owen accompanied by a set of slides in the week leading up to the face-to-face lecture. The lecture focuses on richer discussion aided by clicker questions.

Igniting the fire

The stories told in the pre-lecture video convey three striking historical discoveries – landmarks in the field but unknown to me, although they soon draw me in. The first discovery is Arthur Eddington's experiment to test Einstein's theory that light has mass. Using the conjunction of the Hyades cluster passing just behind a total solar eclipse on May 29, 1919, the researchers cleverly realised that star light would be visible due to the darkness of the eclipse, allowing the rare opportunity to take accurate measurements of the star light's gravity-shifted positions. If they compared these measurements with its known actual position in the sky, the margin would show if light had been bent by gravity. In the second example, in 1796 at a time when many people died of smallpox, Edward Jenner noticed a pattern of dairymaids who contracted the mild disease of cowpox and appeared to be immune to smallpox. He took fresh cowpox matter from lesions on the skin of a dairymaid, Sarah Nelms, and inserted it in an incision he made in the arm of an 8-year-old boy, James Phipps. The boy showed signs of infection such as a raised temperature before recovering. Several weeks later, he infected the boy with smallpox, and no smallpox disease symptoms developed, indicating immunity to smallpox gained by the inoculation with cowpox. This risky – and captivating! – example gave rise to lively class discussion (and ridicule of Jenner at the time) and the issue of ethics. The third example was Otto Loewi's ingenious experiment to test two conflicting theories prevalent at the time: that messages in nerves were electrical and so could be measured or that nerve cells were not connected and therefore there must be chemical messages between them. He electrified the vagus nerve of a frog heart bathed in a salt water vat. He then took fluid from the frog heart vat and applied it to a second frog heart, which produced slowing of the second heart, showing that synaptic signalling used chemical messengers.

These examples of scientific discoveries are intended to and do inspire amazement, wonder and curiosity. As pedagogies, they model the idea that creative individuals are inquisitive and good at uncovering and pursuing interesting and worthwhile questions and acting out their inquiries in ingenious ways (Lucas et al., 2013). They also draw attention to the fact that researcher motivation is driven by a concern with problem solving itself rather than its downstream impact or outcome (Walsh et al., 2013, p. 1265). Once again, as we saw in the physics ethnography, historical discoveries are used on the front line of teaching to demonstrate creative work in the discipline. They set an example that demonstrates that unconventionality, persistence and difficulty in problem formulation, such as in research, are an essential part of creative achievement in science (Newell, Shane & Simon, 1962 and Mumford et al., 1994, cited in Nickerson, 1999).

At this point in the semester, my view of the modes of teaching and learning was that they engendered creating certain conditions for creativity, identified by Lucas et al.'s (2013) five dispositions for creativity: inquisitive, persistent, imaginative, collaborative and disciplined. The teaching and learning activities in the first few weeks showed attention to engaging inquisitiveness and building collaboration and disciplinary skills. Imagination, in either of Ricoeur's 'reproductive' or 'productive' senses, has not entered the area at this point.

Identifying key features of scientific inquiry and critiquing key concepts

In the face-to-face class, Owen asks the students via the clicker poll to identify key ideas for each of the prior experiments: the dependent variable, the hypothesis, the control group, the treatment group – if there is one – and what a theory is. To perform this, students need to think critically, distinguishing the meaning of particular features in the narrative and attributing the role each plays in terms of a systematic process of discovery. He then polls the students' responses. The different choices reveal different understandings, which he uses to lead off student discussion as they critique their different choices. He also asks an interesting, and to me unexpected, question: 'Do scientists know what their scientific method is?' This is a surprise to me. Is scientists' knowledge of their inquiry processes tacit? It has not occurred to me that scientists may be so caught up in their habitual ways of doing science that they may not question it. I am aware of jocular rivalry between theoretical and experimental scientists, but that is all.

Identifying the key facets of scientific thinking and experimental procedures emerges as a key learning outcome in the course. It is directly related to the

190 *Pharmaceutical science ethnography*

relationship between creative and critical thinking, which has been the subject of much research in creativity. In the past, creative and critical thinking have been understood as polar opposites. Creative thinking was characterised as expansive, divergent thinking associated with curiosity, exploration and idea generation. In contrast, critical thinking was characterised as focused, convergent, disciplined, logical and constrained. Others argue, however, that they are interdependent dimensions and that education should promote both kinds of thinking (Nickerson, 1999; Lucas et al., 2013). Certainly, science cannot thrive without both. Lucas's disposition of 'discipline' refers to the need to develop knowledge and expertise in the craft related to the domain of creativity in which one is working, which is exactly what is being built here.

In the following week's activity of the subject, which they referred to as the 'Showcase', several scientists from the faculty have been invited to the lecture theatre to speak about their research. Events prevent two from coming, but four scientists present accounts of their discoveries to the students. The subjects are complex but fascinating: intelligent drug delivery and DNA sequencing (which is a 'programmable molecule'); medicines derived from the poison of creatures such as sea anemones and scorpions which can stun their prey – learning about how the actions of these poisons work gives hints about chemical inhibitors of natural processes, derivatives of which can be used to alleviate or prevent symptoms of illness; the development of drugs that decrease cardiac injury; methods for the delivery of drugs to obviate the effect of macular degeneration – something I have given no thought to. When I learn that macular degeneration patients had to endure an injection in the eye once a month prior to this work on an alternative non-invasive process of delivering the drug to the retina, I am right on board! I am frankly bamboozled by much of the unfamiliar language and statistical presentations used, and it is hard, even impossible, for me to discern the key science concepts at work in the experiments during the presentations – what are the hypothesis, independent variable, dependent variable and treatment group. I sit in the theatre during these presentations wondering how the students find these key concepts. But the students have all taken various science subjects in the last year of school. Judging by the questions they ask, not in class but online, they follow more than I do. Many presentations contain experimental terminology and chemistry terms totally unfamiliar to me, such as 'agonist', 'assay', cell 'quenching', adenosine receptor, reperfusion and K1.3 channel. Owen punctuates each Showcase presentation by the invited faculty researcher with his own series of questions that guide the students towards understanding the point. For example, after the drugs from the sea presentation, he asks them:

> Write down *what* he discovered.
> What kind of macro molecule was it?
> What kind of cell do you want to effect?

What kind do you NOT want to effect?
What was the K-potassium channel?

The students do manage to ask some good questions, and their question are posted by the educator on Moodle for all to see later, along with the scientists' slides, which they are told they need to think about and study in more detail. As they are asked to do more research on one selected presentation for their assignment, it is evident that familiarity with the terminology gradually increases.

In the week following the Showcase presentations, students attend a 2-hour workshop. The purpose of the workshop is to prepare them for the assignment, and it synthesises the historical and faculty discoveries featured in the past few weeks of class. The assignment requires students to apply the diagram/model of scientific inquiry process that they were asked to create after one of the lectures to one great historical discovery of their choosing and one Showcase presentation discovery.

While waiting for the workshop to begin, I overhear one student declare his view that the greatest historical discovery was fire. However, I assume because it has left no trace of the process of discovery, it didn't appear in any of the examples given in the assignments I observed. However, it is an interesting student observation simply because it is impossible to underestimate the pervasive impact of fire on human society, but also because it offers an example of a learner thinking about ancient discovery before documented records and the age of science. In their assignments, the students had to recount their chosen, great historical discovery and to identify the hypothesis, the independent and independent variables, the control and treatment groups and the variables held constant. Looking across the students' assignments later, they chose them from different historical periods and from biology, physics, chemistry and psychology: Darwin's theory of evolution in his observation of variations in beaks of finches on the Galapagos islands; Alexander Fleming's discovery of penicillin; Gregor Mendel's discovery of alleles; Michael Faraday's discovery of electromagnetic induction; Ernest Rutherford's gold-foil experiment, which supported the planetary model of the atom; Archimedes's discovery of the principle of displacement in fluid mechanics; Young's double split experiment, which proved the wave-like properties of light; Louise Pasteur's discovery of germs/microbes; Pavlov's dog experiment, which demonstrated learning by association; Hertz's discovery of radio waves; Zimbardo's psychological experiment on the effect of behaviour of roles and status; Copernicus's discovery that the earth revolves around the sun; Galileo's discovery that gravity affects mass; Rowland and Molina's discovery that fluorocarbons break down ozone in the atmosphere; ultrasound to check the health of developing foetuses – a great variety.

Tool-making used to dynamically configure meaning

The assignment instructions were as follows in Figure 8.1.

192　*Pharmaceutical science ethnography*

The diagram should show the typical stages in scientific enquiry. It should be generally applicable, not only for a particular discipline. It should address <u>at least</u> the following elements (you may add other elements if you think they are important):

- A **hypothesis**: a statement of predicted impact of the independent variable on the dependent variable based on inductive/deductive thinking
- An **experiment** to test the hypothesis
- **Experimental approach and design**: Controlled variables, conditions, positive and negative control groups, etc.
- **Discussion and analysis** step(s)
- An **iterative loop**
- An **end point** if the experiment is successful (note: what constitutes a successful experiment?)

An excellent diagram should:

- Capture the sequence of events in **logical order**
- Be **simple** (as simple as possible) and not cluttered

In addition to the diagram itself, write a **description/caption** that identifies the key features of this diagram and states what distinguishes your diagram from others. The description should *not* be a step-by-step explanation and should not be longer than 150 words.

Figure 8.1 Educator instructions for the first part of the assignment

Looking across the 66 student assignments that I had been given consent to view, I become aware that, at their most fundamental, what the diagrams do is transpose the temporal phases of scientific investigation using an analogy with space in the form of a flow diagram. The time period covered by the diagram may be days, weeks or even years in actuality. I also notice that the greatest variation in the students' diagrams is what *begins* the process – *observation* of something unexpected, or seeing a pattern in observations, asking a *question*, devising a *hypothesis* or being influenced by a theory to ask a (new) question. The student focus group discussion yielded a comment from one student which illuminated this variation.

But the one thing I did do differently – the thing that really made me think, was where the idea comes from . . . *in my sleep* I could write a diagram writing down the steps you need to go through for an experiment, but it was what was the starting step, where does the idea come from, inductive and deductive reasoning and the *continuum*

Pharmaceutical science ethnography 193

> between those two. And then the more we talked in groups about it . . . , the more we realised that it always starts with addressing a problem, and when we looked at even classical discoveries, the more we thought about it the more we realised, as much as we might look at it now and go, 'It didn't have a problem, they just thought about it, this must be a thing', there would have been a problem that would have urged them to discover those deeper things. So it's not just 'why does that happen?' It's, 'It impacts me, how can I fix it, how can I change it?'. . . So that was a really interesting discussion.
>
> (Post-class interview transcript)

Another student in the focus group, however, described being 'intrigued' by the potential applications of a cutting-edge technique of using DNA to 'intelligently' target drug delivery to the right cells.

> I chose mine *(his historical discovery)* because I think it's really intriguing that you can do such things. I chose targeted delivery of cancer treatment. They use DNA on the protein to track down where the drug is and track down whether or not it's aiming at the right part of the cell. I found it intriguing that you can use DNA to program yourself to target specific parts of yourself.
>
> (Post-class interview transcript)

Thus the first student describes being persuaded by a felt need to solve a problem that needs solving, but the second student is intrigued by the possibilities new techniques present to rejuvenate approaches to the solving of problems and the fact that these approaches involve biologically created techniques; it is worlds within worlds.

Let us look at one student-created diagram in Exemplar 8.1.

In the reflective writing section in the assignment, this student reflects on his/her choice to begin the diagram with making an observation, or theorising knowledge, because research can develop from either deductive or inductive reasoning. The student muses aloud that it would be improved if 'make observations' and 'think and theorise' *were linked by an arrow* (see Exemplar 8.1) to acknowledge the fact that sometimes research requires *both* inductive and deductive reasoning – as the student found when s/he compared the diagram with actual progress of research in the macular degeneration example (which was one given in a faculty Showcase scientist presentation). Unusually, this student included determining the *aim* of the experiment as the critical aspect for

194 *Pharmaceutical science ethnography*

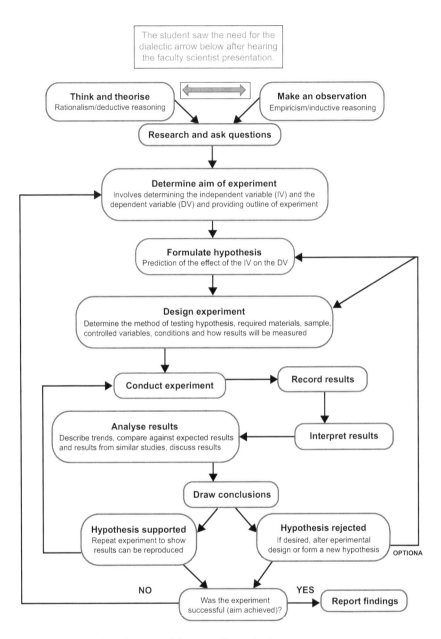

Exemplar 8.1 Student diagram of the scientific method

identifying and separating out various variables. S/he distinguishes this from the detailed experimental design step, which involves determining the method or procedures involved in testing the hypothesis, the materials to be used, the sample, conditions and how the results will be measured. (As an aside, I find only two student diagrams – among those who consented to my analysis of their diagram – which mention ethical considerations in the design of experiments.) In this diagram, whether the aim was achieved determines if the 'findings' will be shared in publications. If the aim was achieved, it is published; if it isn't, there is a loop back to signify redetermining the aim of the experiment. The student notes in his/her reflection, 'It is important to report findings when the aim is achieved, even if the hypothesis is rejected, because the results may prove the basis for further research'. The student diagram clearly shows an understanding that the scientific process is both a matter of *individual* curiosity and questioning and a *social/community* process which must involve sharing findings with scientific peers to advance knowledge. This diagram also has several loops. If the hypothesis is supported, there is a looping back to conduct the experiment again to ensure the results can be reproduced – to 'validate' them, which is a key scientific rule or principle. If the hypothesis is rejected, the loop goes back to either or both – indicating the scientist has to reformulate the hypothesis or redesign the experiment.

On the face of it, it appears that the diagram/model is a form of what Ricoeur terms reproductive imagination. It reproduces, or takes the place of, what the learner understands the scientific inquiry process to be.

Let us take a look at a second example, Exemplar 8.2.

This student in Exemplar 8.2 has the diagram beginning with an observation – something inexplicable which triggers, or, as their written reflection says, 'motivates', a question or ignites a curiosity. In predictive processing terms, the feeling of curiosity is a state that is, I believe, a form of proprioception in that there arises conscious expectations of understanding, and feelings about their non-satisfaction, which give rise to compensatory actions – you could give up and forget it or be motivated to act in ways that seek solutions and influence your chance of finding out the cause or explanation (leading to equilibrium once more). The precipitating series of actions are what science transforms. Curious fiddling around is channelled into systematic and ordered actions. By structuring experimental procedures, scientific inquiry transforms more random or hasty processes of inference. This student has, in order, researching the scientific literature – which provides yet more knowledge-driven inferences (deduction theory-driven reasoning) – and forming the hypothesis – which the student specifies involves forming a causal relationship and hence a prediction. A hypothesis is *in itself* a complex concept of research practice, let alone its role in a complex temporal process of experimentation. (In science it is defined as a testable statement containing a prediction. The prediction needs to specify the measurable effect of one or some independent variable/s on a dependent variable.) As a new step, this student writes 'designing the experiment' – an experimental procedure needs to be devised that involves teasing out the variables' effect on what is trying to be understood and distinguishing independent and dependent variables and treatment and control groups. Results are then analysed, and conclusions drawn from them. The arrows going left and right signify different forms of action depending on whether the conclusions support or negate the hypothesis.

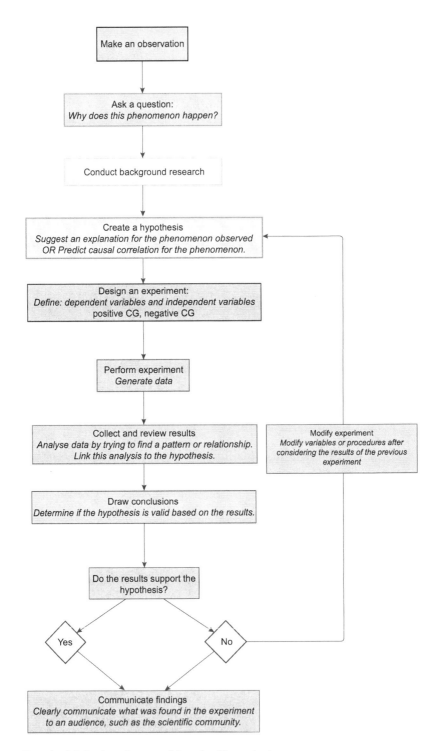

Exemplar 8.2 Student diagram of the scientific method

Pharmaceutical science ethnography 197

These diagrams representing scientific inquiry in effect describe how simple curiosity is transformed and elaborated in ways that shape the scientific creative process. Used as a thinking tool in the pedagogy, it coordinates curiosity with an organised process involving complex skills, techniques used in flexible sequences and critical reflection at different stages. As a pedagogy, it is configuring a form of qualitative transformation in thinking, behaviour and emotions (i.e. the satisfaction of needs) that needs to take place when scientific inquiry processes are adopted.

> By being included in the process of behaviour, the psychological tool (i.e. sign) alters the entire flow and structure of mental functions. It does this by determining the structure of a new instrumental act just as a technical tool alters the process of a natural adaptation by determining the form of labour operations.
>
> (Vygotsky, 1981, p. 137, in Wertsch, 2007)

In this particular student's reflection s/he says that at that point s/he has inserted an iterative loop 'because patience and repetition from adjusting the independent variables and experimental procedure will be needed'. In the marking rubric, the assessor questions why the loop appears to loop back to the hypothesis, rather than to the experimental design. There could be two loops. In this interaction between the student and the teacher's feedback, we see first how the student's model structures the process of inference into one that involves technical manipulations *and* emotional modulation ('patience and repetition from adjusting the . . . variables'). The teacher's comment in the marking rubric questions the location of the loop symbolising repetition of the step the scientist could return to when the results don't support the hypothesis. The feedback is designed to help refine the logic underlying the possible ways of working.

My question here is, if we accept for one moment action-orientated predictive processing as the driving engine of unsupervised learning (in which perception, action, embodiment and imagination co-emerge in order for us to understand a situation), does it help us to then infer how the learning task here is coupling complex scientific logic and procedures within a hierarchical level inferential system? How is the learner learning to use the external structure provided by the self-devised diagram/model? What emerges clearly is that it enables the students to understand the relations of the several parts better – to reflect upon them, to reason about them consciously, to see the progression in time and to note the points where precision can be aided by repetition, doubling back, research, peer dialogue and so on – even to reflect on the emotions that might need to be moderated ('patience') to aid it happening. The diagram-making supports reasoning and imagining about all of that, in relation to the overall goal of investigating scientifically, for which this is a preparation.

The student diagram also includes the journal publication phase – they note the results and conclusions of the experiment are published 'whether it supports the hypothesis or not, since it will benefit the scientific community regardless . . . will allow other researchers to avoid conducting the same experiments and producing the same results'. This student received 4/6 for ideas, content and organisation of

198 *Pharmaceutical science ethnography*

the diagram and 2/3 for presentation, layout and expression. I was not sure what to deduce from the grade.

The third part of the assignment tasks was to analyse one of the faculty scientists' Showcase presentations, identifying key stages in an account of real scientific practice, matching them against a phase represented in their diagram and explaining their reasoning for the match. They were shown to do this in a table. Then they were to write a reflection on the adequacy of their diagram, commenting on how realistic it was and how it could be improved. See Exemplar 8.3 for an example, which represents a truncated version from the number of steps that were included in the student's original diagram.

Not having studied science for years, and despite the preparatory work in lectorials, I found picking out the key science stages and concepts from the welter of detailed faculty scientists' presentations not easy. However, the faculty require school maths and chemistry as a prerequisite, and the students do not appear to find it too difficult.

In the focus group, I asked the students whether drawing their own diagram helped them understand connections between stages in the process of scientific inquiry. There was a variety of responses, with a couple saying that it simply 'consolidated' their existing understanding, one that had been rammed down his/her throat at school so s/he could 'do it my sleep' and another that,

> I'm similar. I've done psychology before so I'm familiar with the whole hypothesis experiment thing. But getting me to come up with my own diagram and thinking about how do I, how is the composition of the diagram, made me re-think of the whole scientific approach, and rethink how science really works and there's all these different ways you can work to make all these different discoveries.
>
> (Post-class interview transcript)

This comment makes clear that forming their own diagram and requiring written reflection encourages conscious reflection on any growth in their thinking. This is metacognition at work. Teaching *for* creativity values the agency of the learner (Spencer et al., 2012), and metacognition is one way of engaging the agency of the learner. McWilliam suggested that higher educators who stimulate creativity value the *process* of learning, not just the product (McWilliam, 2007; McWilliam & Dawson, 2007). The idea of students developing a sense of their identity as learners, including as lifelong learners, is also of interest here because the higher education literature which applied Ricoeur's notions of the imagination, particularly his notion of narrative as an expression of imagination, connected imagination to identity formation and changes to identity (see, for example, Anderson, 2010; Cole, 2009; McCulloch, 2009).

Diagram stage	MIPS* discovery event	Explanations
Make an observation	May's team observed the mechanisms of myocardial infractions and the consequent injuries due to them.	This is the observation which instigated the research into drugs to enable cardioprotection through (sic).
Conduct background research	May conducted background research into the body's mechanism to protect the heart. This led to the unearthing that an Adenosine A1 receptor (A1AR) agonism in the heart, would significantly reduce cell death in the affected areas. The issue with this though, was that heart rate would be dramatically reduced due to bradycardia.	May obtained information necessary to begin planning the experiment beforehand.
Create hypothesis	Biased agonism, the selectivity of a certain signal transduction pathway, is utilized to activate the A1AR receptor. This prompts May to formulate the hypothesis: *"Adenosine A1 receptor biased agonism can trigger potent cardio protection in the absence of adverse effects"*.	Having done background research, May was able to come up with a hypothesis and make aims in order to limit the scope of the experiment. The set aims were: *"to identify drugs that trigger A1AR biased agonism"* and *"to determine whether A1AR biased agonism can enable cardioprotection in the absence of bradycardia"*.
Design/ perform experiment	May's team had to be determine (sic) a drug which produced the desired pharmacological effect without the harmful side-effects. Out of the adenosine-like agonists and atypical agonists, the atypical agonists were selected to be experimented with. The molecules were tested for their signalling profiles in cells containing the A1AR receptor. The cardiac effects of Adenosine receptors were also tested for.	May's team designed an experiment which tested multiple properties of molecules with respect to their effects of their agonism with A1AR. The experiment was carried out which resulted in a drug which is successful in producing the desired effect with minimal side-effects.
Conclusion	May and her team reached the conclusion that drugs could be made which had therapeutic effects without the negative side effects. Their data was displayed as graphs. With this, their research was presented to authorities and pharmaceutical companies, which could utilize their discovery in order to produce treatment for myocardial infractions.	The conclusion and delivery of the results allows the research done to be used to formulate new drugs, and ultimately help people suffering from the consequences of myocardial infractions.

* Monash Institute of Pharmaceutical Science

Exemplar 8.3 The third part of the assignment task required mapping the Showcase presentations by one faculty scientist onto the student's diagram of the scientific inquiry process

200 *Pharmaceutical science ethnography*

As a by-product, of course, the written reflection provides educators an opportunity to gain insight into students' learning. The following is an example of these reflections.

> Upon the analysis of Professor Ben X's Drug Delivery for Macular Degeneration investigation, I *had to re-assess the complexity of the Scientific Method.* My Diagram had initially excluded the stage for additional research and inquiry and the following repetition of; preparation, hypothesis and experimentation. I had previously expected these stages to follow only after inconsistent results, however consistent results also demand further predictions to be made and experiments to be conducted. *My diagram now considers the importance of continuous analysis and development* by incorporating this iterative loop after consistent results. However, *I believe, in reality the discovery process is not restricted to a series of steps, but develops gradually, influenced by many external factors. This came to my attention when researching Michael Faraday's discovery* of Electromagnetic Induction. His discovery developed, surrounded by many other scientist's research and his own experience. Resolving a problem or hypothesizing a theory does not evolve in a closed environment, but develops in an inconstant environment, which either contributes to or hinders the progress of the process. However, I believe the method I have presented provides a logical sequence which maximizes the efficiency of the process by minimizing bias and misunderstanding. This is achieved through extensive investigation stages before and after the experimental stage, maximizing benefit from results.
>
> (my italics)

This student's reflection on his/her diagram indicates the student has reviewed his/her idea of science as a result of studying the historical and faculty Showcase discoveries. The student appreciates more that it is not a neat, linear process but rather involves a process of ongoing analysis, development and research. The student realised the extent to which discovery is dependent on the ground work of other scientists who make up a scientific community. His/her diagram had not taken adequate account of that (did not represent it), and its lack is more apparent to her/him than it may conceivably have been if the student had simply been given a task involving reading and thinking or been told how discovery happens. Missing that factor (the representational error) provided the student with feedback in which s/he can compare and check what his/her diagram shows of the process and what s/he thinks is the reality. Whether, in order to reflect his/her greater understanding, the student chooses to draw a new loop or insert a new step at a particular point, or decides that this will over-complicate the diagram, is his/her decision – but the purpose of the pedagogy has been fulfilled, the power of metacognition to initiate autonomous learning has already kicked in. For our purposes of understanding the growth in learning, this is less important than the possibilities thrown up for learners by the learning task. If learning means changing one's mind then the student's experience of expansion of understanding is just as important as the content of the diagram/model – which is the point, I assume, of the pedagogical approach of this assessment.

Let's recall Polanyi's example of probing with the tip of the stick (Chapter 3). What I am arguing is that, likewise, what this pedagogy allows is for learners to imaginatively extend their minds into the diagram/tool (in Clark's sense). The diagram is like the walking stick – the point of extension. Making it, viewing it and reflecting on it irrigate thinking, allowing elaborated thinking about the complexity of the variations that are the object of thinking – scientific inquiry process in this instance – and that can then be seen to be inadequately represented by the diagram. You can think further, through it.

The critical reflections also nicely demonstrate the criticality which Ricoeur argues is an inherent feature of his 'productive' imagination. However, we begin to see that this criticality applied to the students' self-created models appears to make them more than what is implied by Ricoeur's notion of 'reproductive' imagination (see Chapter 2). Their use as an instrument of pedagogy changes this. More on this in the following section.

The manner in which real scientific discovery departs from the classic pattern was also present in many other students' written reflections (required by the assignment):

> The model is valid for planning an experiment but not for trying to fit a given experiment into the model, as every experiment is different . . .

> The scientific method is not as simple a series of steps. . . . Another area where the depiction does not match complex reality is experimentation. It is not often that proving or falsifying a hypothesis is as simple as performing one experiment . . .

> My diagram is quite simple . . . as in X's experiment, there are usually lots of tests done – for example, isolating different genes to find a suitable one, developing many analogues and testing each one to see what channels they block, animal testings, preliminary tests . . . – all to ensure that the analogue targets the correct channels, and it hasn't even been developed into a proper drug yet! . . . I think looking into a scientific discovery has shown me how much work and how important many little other steps and tests are to an investigation. Therefore the scientific method can be vastly different for every experiment . . .

> Some stages in the diagram are represented in a simplified manner and are more complex in real life. For example, determining the independent variable and the steps of the experimental procedure occurred as a process in May's research.

Tooling active cognition by iterative diagram-making, reflection and social learning

It appears to me that the use of the diagram as the centrepiece of the pedagogy (at this stage of the semester) engages in students a form of epistemic action intended to shape the nature of the students' cognition and guide their behaviour. Their configuration of the diagram becomes the tool or artefact, in Vygotsky's sense, that mediates meaning between them and their developing understanding and competence in the practice of scientific inquiry, in ways that are personally meaningful. The relationship is represented in Figure 8.2.

So how well does it serve that purpose? The diagram is a form of 'reproductive' imagination in Ricoeur's sense because it *refers to* an extant practice. However, for the students its use as a pedagogy transforms it into something not well captured by that description. The basic forms of the students' diagrams act as a heuristic device that helps them identify the pattern of an existing reality – the process of scientific inquiry – a kind of map, if you like.

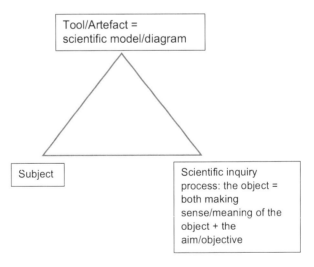

Figure 8.2 Engeström's (1990a) first generation activity theory model, which incorporates as its top level, Vygotsky's mediational triangle

Source: Adapted from Figure 8.2, Yrjö Engeström, *Learning, Working and Imagining: Twelve studies in activity theory*. Reproduced with permission.

However, in learning activities they are explicitly prompted to refer back to it as they are exposed to historical examples of science and scientists working currently. Externalising their understanding by making an object (the diagram), a redescription of the process, makes possible more detailed reflection than would otherwise be the case. While containing the main logic of scientific inquiry, it displays time points where decisions about when a scientist may have to loop back and return and do work at what has been designated (logically) an earlier stage, or to consult the literature on a new point, will have to be taken – the pedagogy is designed to provoke loops of reflection and critical thinking which deepen their understanding of the infinite possibilities involved in scientific practice. Each investigation will have its own unique pathway, even though they follow the pattern – like seeing the wood and also the trees.

As a pedagogical activity that is performed by the learners, then, it functions, to use Wartofsky's (1979) terminology, as a 'secondary artefact', a form of 'representation' that shows the highly evolved ways and rules for performing science – but the complex openness of the process too – thus transmitting knowledge of the process to future generations. In Engeström's terminology of *classes* of artefact, it is both a 'what' artefact – an externalisation in diagrammatic form of the students' understanding of the scientific process – and a 'how' artefact describing when certain concepts and procedures should be performed. The use of such artefacts in education would appear to be a core function of education. For this reason, I call the diagram/model a learning artefact and believe it is a particular form of 'secondary' artefact in Wartofsky's terms. However, its use in the pedagogy in this class is not exhausted by these 'what' and 'how' functions. It goes beyond them in ways that help us understand how it is that higher education teaches learners to learn something *new*, not only to learn existing knowledge.

While the notion of secondary artefacts helps us understand their role in the transmission of important tools and processes in culture, including scientific culture, and the notion of 'classes' of artefacts remind us to think of kinds of cultural tools/artefacts, I believe, however, that Clark's extended mind theory is more useful to helping us understand the pedagogic and cognitive role of the diagram/artefact here. It helps us understand that the pedagogy has provided students with a *tool to think with and through* – which can scaffold or support their conceptions and iteratively deepen reconceptualisations of scientific inquiry practice. They actively engage with the reading and hearing about actual scientific discoveries using their diagram's structure as a resource, and dialectically think about the diagram in terms of the accounts of discovery, and the accounts of discovery in terms of the diagram, in thinking loops that join outer material with inner neural networks.

The pedagogy supports the making, using, reflection, critiquing and remaking of the diagram/model and its efficacy as a tool to represent a living practice. In doing so the artefact stabilises complex ideas (about scientific inquiry), allowing the students to inspect and criticise their own reasoning. It creates a stable structure to which subsequent thinking can attach (Clark, 1997, p. 207). However, also in an important new sense, it complexifies the formation of new connections by also scaffolding the behaviours of posing questions, processes of critical reflection, and anticipating the possible need to moderate emotions and perhaps also the emergence of an identity who does these things. The written reflections use language and the diagram as resources by which the students can describe their own thoughts in a format that makes them available for a variety of new thinking operations. Dialectically, in conjunction with one another, they create a kind of second-order cognitive dynamic. Teaching for creativity values the agency of the learner (Spencer et al., 2012), and metacognitive activity incites agency. Thus, the pedagogy we see in play here by this higher educator stimulates creativity by valuing the agent engaged in the process of learning – which also potentially includes the creation of a learner identity who performs those operations. Although the assessment includes the students' diagram, it is not just focused on the product. This pedagogical strategy is supported in the creativity literature (Jackson & Shaw, 2006; McWilliam, 2007; McWilliam & Dawson, 2007).

In Vygotsky's terms, learning, and an emerging scientific praxis and world-view, is being mediated by the diagram. In Clark's 'extended mind' terminology, it is more than mediated: The students' actual cognitive work – what Clark (2015) refers to as the 'effective circuits of human thought and reason' – that we usually think of as being performed by the brain is distributed across both interior and exterior fields in the doing of the task, the making and reworking of the diagram. In PP terms, by externalising the predictive model of scientific inquiry process, and demonstrating shortfalls, the diagram is refined, and the complex thinking about scientific inquiry is refined/reconfigured to produce a more nuanced predictive model. If imagination is a way of thinking which can be directed towards adapting to, and/or adapting, the environment, it recruits the available tools to do so – in the tools of representation and in the dynamic conceptualisation that guides and shapes actions. It should be remembered here too that subsequent to the period of observation, the students undertook a scientific investigation of their own, proposing a hypothesis and designing and conducting an experiment. Their diagram was used to support their investigation at that stage too. Albeit that the word 'prop' is a bit crude to describe their model of the scientific process, the creating of such a learning artefact enables the learners to think better about science with the augmentation of the prop. As Clark says, 'Simple external props enable us to think better and hence to create more complex props and practices, which in turn "turbocharge" our thoughts a little more, which leads to the development of even better props' (Clark, 1997, p. 62).

In Wartofsky's terms, the 'imagination' is active in modelling the ways that we represent things and that impact on perception itself. In this way, the diagram-making and reflection and researching activity is reorganising the students' ways of perceiving. For a specific feature of perception as a mode of action is that it is mediated (and conditioned) by representation (Wartofsky, 1979, p. 189). In terms of Clark's extended mind theory, it quite literally works by augmenting the learners' horizon of perception through the use of tools though which

Pharmaceutical science ethnography 205

to extend their minds into the systematically framed possibilities of scientific thinking (i.e., it restructures their thinking). What we have learned to re-see in perception is important because it can reshape our worldview, making it available for our subsequent outward practical activity. It is in this way that students are 'inducted' into a way of thinking and working. I am suggesting that because this form of learner-centred instruction involves actively making, seeing and re-seeing examples of science, it will more powerfully achieve the kind of cognitive transformation it is looking to produce.

I am suggesting that if in action perception models, imagination underpins predictive processing by synthesizing top-down models which lend coherence and continuity to our perception and allow us to coordinate action smoothly in the world (Clark & Chalmers, 1998; Clark, 2016), it is also operable in complex thinking such as scientific thinking. By projecting our imagination into representations/artefacts we create, we may similarly extend our perception, through the artefact/representation, thereby augmenting and shaping the explanatory possibilities of the model-making process towards, in this case, the slower, systematic, culture-laden process of scientific inquiry. In both situations, they are led by the same synthesizing drive to learn autonomously by generating models that enable meaningful and coherent action in the world. In the case of the scientific learning artefact, the synthesis is directed towards the symbolic representation and its accounts of science inquiry. In the case of perception, the synthetic model is directed towards the stream of incoming sense data. Both are creative, and both are responsive to circumstances.

In pharmaceutical science, the diagram/model of the scientific inquiry process, which appeared to be a form of reproductive imagination, was used in the pedagogy to anchor reflection on the complexity and variability that were evident in real practices they read about in historical experiments and heard about from the accounts of living scientists. In other words, the model makes a number of assumptions which are inexact. The difference between what is represented in the diagram and the picture that emerges from the stories of practice potentially demonstrates to learners the reason that mental agility is needed at various stages – to remain alive to ways of solving emerging problems during the experimental process.

What this means is that there is a movement from reproductive to productive imagination. Productive imagination generates new models of understandings but draws on elements of reproductive imagination, and this can be aided by pedagogies that scaffold reflection on their created tools/artefact. The pedagogy pulled their thinking to go *beyond* conceptions of knowledge represented by the tool-enabled knowledge. Once again, we are reminded of the y axis in Figure 2.1 representing Ricoeur's notion of productive imagination's critical consciousness of the difference between the created product and the 'real'. This recalls Ricoeur's characterisation of productive imagination as including the human subject's critical consciousness of the difference between the imagined and the real, which I argued was particularly useful to higher education (this idea is expanded in Chapter 2).

206   *Pharmaceutical science ethnography*

Ricoeur emphasises the novel combinatorial activity of the 'productive imagination' – which schematises *the relations between things*, a more precise notion than is implied by the reproductive notion of a 'mental image' of things – and one that speaks to the creation and use of knowledge. He argues that it described more closely the role of imagination in relation to critical thinking and its role in the process of discovery. However, we have seen evidence of the same generation of criticality at work in a pedagogy with its central focus being a mapping of the process of scientific inquiry – in what is ostensibly a form of reproductive imagination.

Interestingly in this context, Amabile (1983) described situations in which *creative* problem solving included a phased step-by-step process or a combination of pathways of steps – which appears to describe the pedagogical approach this pharmaceutical science educator is using. Researchers expounding this view of creativity say that strategies that involve a step-by-step process have much to offer education for a variety of reasons: the learning of a broad range of heuristics or strategies can be used like tools to work through problems to construct solutions. This can be useful as well because many people believe themselves to be uncreative and think that creative ideas come unbidden to the gifted few, which can become a self-defeating prophecy. One qualitative study of a higher education class found that students responded with more confidence to understanding creativity as a structured process rather than as a spontaneous moment because their teacher used pedagogies that framed and supported the generation, as well as the evaluation, of ideas (Cole, Sugioka & Yamagata-Lynch, 1999, p. 288).

However, arguably the pedagogy was not without its limitations. One of the faculty scientists' presentations, for example, reported a chance meeting at a conference with a colleague who irradiated nanorods. Over conference drinks, the question arose in this scientist's mind whether the nanorods could be used to heat liquid (lipid) crystal systems, which would trigger their change in molecular structure, releasing a contained drug. Possibly it could, which was the breakthrough he was looking for. This hypothesis posited a prediction which then required further testing. The analogy he saw was to apply a technique used in one sphere to a new area to solve a problem, and this occurred through a combination of analogical thinking and peer interaction. This scientist's presentation attributed, as features of scientific practice, analogy, networking, collaboration and hard work. Analogy and networking are not features highlighted in the students' diagrams and are not included in the required elements of scientific inquiry process that accompanied the assignment instructions. But analogy is strongly associated with the use of 'productive' imagination, which involves recombination and synthesis resulting in semantic innovation (Ricoeur, 1991, 1983/1984). It is not well captured in the dialectic between deductive and inductive reasoning, which the students were asked to identify. Networking may or may not have been implied in stages that refer to the scientific community in students' diagrams. However, as we have seen in the earlier discussion of the students' reflections, the class tasks and activities did afford the opportunity to observe the messiness and serendipity of techniques in the conduct of real research that occurs over months or years. And a few student reflections do refer to the dialectic between deductive and inductive reasoning, for example, 'Inductive logic can be used to extrapolate this knowledge to a broader pattern – that toxic sea life can produce a way to clock receptors partially responsible for autoimmune diseases, to produce new hypotheses'.

One of the limitations of my study was the limited period of observation – 4 weeks – and there is obviously plenty more time over a 4 year course to introduce and elaborate on subtleties and complexities of the inquiry process in subsequent teaching and learning. It occurred to me that it would be interesting to hear if students revisit their first year scientific inquiry diagram in upper level subjects in order to benefit from opportunities to overlay and elaborate on it with more complex knowledge, experience and reflection.

Conclusion: imaginative synthesis in diagrammatic narrative

Creating and shaping the diagram/model involves imagining and representationally arranging concepts and actions involved in scientific investigation so that the elements (question, observation, hypothesis, variables, etc.) relate to each other meaningfully. The diagram allows a tangible pattern to explore and link individually complex concepts, which is key to creative exploration (Tsui, 2013). However, as the exposure to historical and contemporary scientific discoveries showed, there can be infinite variation in the path of scientific investigations (as there are an infinite number of stories that can follow a few basic patterns). According to Ricoeur, the imagination 'grasps together and integrates into one whole and complete story multiple and scattered events, thereby schematizing the intelligible signification attached to the narrative taken as a whole' (1983/1984, vol. 1, p. x). Similarly, the pedagogy required learners to engage in pattern formation, which made evident that an actual process may diverge greatly depending on the investigation at hand. One of the beauties of the artefact creation is that if a student can create a good diagram, the diagram will display how the process is not linear and encompasses complexity – and flexibility – by arrows and loops to show the necessity to incorporate phases 'out of order', as it were, or a more systematic return to a previous stage. Thus, described in Ricoeur's terms, using the diagram/artefact the productive imagination propels a synthesis, which organises the understanding of the scientific process of investigation. Although there was variation in presentations, there was also a great deal of coherence, indicating the students grasp the logic at work in the combination of concepts and key stages in the scientific process.

In this activity, the learner generates for herself the cultural artefact of scientific procedure and concepts by combining and constructing its elements and makes it a product of her own imagination.

What the ethnography shows is not an educator 'getting ideas across' but generating experiences that trigger understanding of the patterned processes of discovery and learning in scientific inquiry that his students need. If learning,

208   *Pharmaceutical science ethnography*

or understanding, means changing one's mind, then the students' experience of change is just as important as the content of their new diagram/model. The pedagogies afforded students glimpses of the openness to complex new techniques, research, repetition, parallel trials, analogical thinking and so forth that may need to come into play to solve an emerging new problem. If they can treat processes, concepts and theories as working ideas that guide and enable inquiry but are open to future revision and rethinking, then learning will involve imagination, questioning assumptions and the seeking of other possibilities. Underpinning this is the view that learning is not simply a matter of the continuous acquiring of new knowledge, concepts or skills; it is what you do with them. But this is not just about pragmatic use; it is a much richer idea of learning and the kind of scientist identity that might need to go with it than what is implied by the simple idea of 'application', which tends to presume a theory–practice dichotomy. For a beginning first year subject, the learning activity scaffolds grasping an emerging practice involving depth, reconsideration and complexity. The implication of this finding is that educators can foster imagination through pedagogies that build openness to complexity and reconsideration. This educator achieved it through a series of activities centred on learner-made representations/models and structured revision.

References

Amabile, T. M. (1983). *The social psychology of creativity*. New York: Springer-Verlag.
Anderson, K. (2010). The whole learner: The role of imagination in developing disciplinary understanding. *Arts and Humanities in Higher Education, 9*(2), 205–221.
Biggs, J., & Tang, C. S.-K. (2007). *Teaching for quality learning at university: What the student does*. Maidenhead: Open University Press.
Bleazby, J. (2011). Overcoming relativism and absolutism: Dewey's ideals of truth and meaning in philosophy for children. *Educational Philosophy and Theory, 43*(5), 453–466. doi:10.1111/j.1469-5812.2009.00567.x
Clark, A. (1997). *Being there: Putting brain, body and world together*. Cambridge, MA: The MIT Press.
Clark, A. (2015, March 4). *The extended mind: HDC, a history of distributed cognition* [seminar on web]. Retrieved from http://www.hdc.ed.ac.uk/seminars/extended-mind
Clark, A. (2016). *Surfing uncertainty: Prediction, action and embodied mind*. New York: Oxford University Press.
Clark, A., & Chalmers, D. J. (1998). The extended mind. *Analysis, 58*, 7–19.
Cole, D. G., Sugioka, H., L., & Yamagata-Lynch, L. C. (1999). Supportive classroom environments for creativity in higher education. *Journal of Creative Behaviour, 33*(4), 277–293.
Cole, M. (2009). Storytelling: Its place in infection control education. *Journal of Infection Prevention, 10*(5), 154–158. doi:10.1177/1757177409341425
Csikszentmihalyi, M. (1999). Implications of a systems perspective for the study of creativity. In R. Sternberg (Ed.), *Handbook of creativity* (pp. 313–335). Cambridge: Cambridge University Press.
Engeström, Y. (1990a). *Learning, working and imagining: Twelve studies in activity theory*. Helsinki: Orienta-Konsultit Oy.
Engeström, Y. (1990b). When is a tool? Multiple meanings of artifacts in human activity? In *Learning, working and imagining: Twelve studies in activity theory* (pp. 171–195). Helsinki: Orienta-Konsultit Oy.

Jackson, N. J., & Shaw, M. (2006). Developing subject perspectives on creativity in higher education. In N. Jackson, M. Oliver, M. Shaw, & J. Wisdom (Eds.), *Developing creativity in higher education: An imaginative curriculum.* London: Routledge-Falmer.

Lave, J., & Wenger, E. (1991). *Situated learning: Legitimate peripheral participation.* Cambridge, UK; New York: Cambridge University Press.

Lucas, B., Claxton, G., & Spencer, E. (2013). *Progression in student creativity in school: First steps towards new forms of formative assessments.* OECD Education Working Papers, No. 86, OECD Publishing. Retrieved from http://dx.doi.org/10.1787/5k4dp59msdwk-en

McCulloch, M. (2009). *From school to faculty: Stories of transition into teacher education.* (PhD), Glasgow University, Glasgow. Retrieved from http://theses.gla.ac.uk/1273/01/2009mccullochedd.pdf

McWilliam, E. (2007). *Is creativity teachable: Conceptualising the creativity/pedagogy relationship in higher education.* Paper presented at the 30th HERDSA Annual Conference: Enhancing Higher Education, Theory and Scholarship, Adelaide.

McWilliam, E., & Dawson, S. (2007). *Understanding creativity: A survey of 'creative' academic teachers: A report for the Carrick Institute for Learning and Teaching in Higher Education.* Retrieved from www.altcexchange.edu.au/system/files/handle/fellowships_associatefellow_report_ericamcwilliam_may07.pdf

Nickerson, R. (1999). Enhancing creativity. In R. J. Sternberg (Ed.), *Handbook of creativity* (pp. 392–430). Cambridge: Cambridge University Press.

Ricoeur, P. (1983/1984). *Time and narrative* (K. McLaughlin & D. Pellauer, Trans. Vol. 1). Chicago: University of Chicago Press.

Ricoeur, P. (1991). The function of fiction in shaping reality: Reflection and imagination. In M. J. Valdes (Ed.), *A Ricoeur reader* (pp. 117–136). Hertfordshire: Harvester Wheatsheaf.

Spencer, E., Lucas, B., & Claxton, G. (2012). *Progression in creativity: Developing new forms of assessment: A literature review.* Newcastle upon Tyne: CCE.

Trigwell, K., Prosser, M., & Waterhouse, F. (1999). Relations between teachers' approaches to teaching and students' approaches to learning. *Higher Education, 37,* 57–70.

Tsui, C.-Y. (2013). Multiple representations in biological education. In D. Treagust & C.-Y. Tsui (Eds.), *Multiple representations in biological education* (pp. 3–18). Dordrecht; London: Springer.

Vygotsky, L. S. (1978). *Mind in society: The development of higher psychological processes.* Cambridge, MA: Harvard University Press.

Walsh, E., Anders, K., Hancock, S., & Elvidge, L. (2013). Reclaiming creativity in the era of impact: Exploring ideas about creative research in science and engineering. *Studies in Higher Education, 38*(9), 1259–1273. doi:10.1080/03075079.2011.620091

Wartofsky, M. W. (1979). Perception, representation and forms of action: Towards an historical epistemology. In *Models: Representations and scientific understanding* (pp. 188–210). Dordrecht, Holland/Boston, MA/London, UK: D. Reidel Publishing Company.

Wertsch, J. V. (2007). Mediation. In H. Daniels, M. Cole, & J. V. Wertsch (Eds.), *The Cambridge companion to Vygotsky* (pp. 178–192). Cambridge: Cambridge University Press.

9 Conclusion

Introduction

This chapter draws out key lessons or features of my observations of four disciplinary cases in which I was interested in the role of imagination in higher education and the learning experiences educators devised to foster it; how students experienced learning that is focused on engaging their imagination; whether disciplinary thinking and methodologies involve imagination, and, if so, how; and whether Ricoeur's theory of imagination was useful to understand teachers' approaches to encourage imagination as a facet of learning. The substantive ethnographies from Chapters 5, 6, 7 and 8 on physics, history, finance and pharmaceutical science revealed the following features. Teaching for imagination involves:

1   Questioning assumptions, asking What if? questions and openness to knowledge being reconstructed; openness to change.
2   The making of new meaningful connections, discerning patterns or webs of meaning. This seems to require what we have called a liminal space for playing with possibilities (of whatever is relevant in the particular context or to the problem).
3   Developing mastery of disciplinary concepts and skills and methods of inquiry which mediate how we interact with, and make meaningful connections in order to understand and act on and in, our world. This involves working with symbolic modalities (language, mathematics, diagrams, etc.) that Vygotsky and Wartofsky call tools or artefacts and Dennett calls 'mindtools'.
4   Repositioning learners as knowledge producers, within a set of social practices.
5   What we might call the 'educational style': This involves repositioning the student and teacher relationship so that it accentuates the educator and the learner simultaneously facing the knowledge question/problem (shoulder to shoulder), thereby modelling a way of working – of being a professional practitioner or a member of a disciplinary community. It may, or may not, also involve arrangements in the learning environment or learning space.

Conclusion 211

The implications of what was learned from the cases, however, have the effect of shifting the explanatory processes of the cognition involved. One of these shifts involves *unlearning* the assumption that learning is located solely in the mind in the area bounded by the skull. That model of cognition conceptualises the mind using the metaphor of filing cabinet with learning constituted by memorisation. The historical socio-cultural approaches to cognition and learning centred on Vygotsky's notion of mediation and extended mind theory were brought into the analytic process to explain how the imagination forges links and relations that cross the usual boundary of the mind container[1] by incorporating mind-tools/artefacts, disciplinary methodologies/processes and the ways that (relevant) communities work with knowledge.

One further objective of the original research on which this book was based was to analyse the value of Ricoeur's theory as a heuristic device with which to interpret teaching that fosters imagination, which will be considered later in the chapter. In the last part of the chapter I consider the implications for educators and areas for future research.

1 Questioning assumptions, asking 'What if?' questions and openness to knowledge being reconstructed

Questioning assumptions and asking 'What if?' questions are skills involving imagination that were raised in all the ethnographic cases. This capacity underpins openness to the idea that knowledge can be reconstructed in the future.

In quantum physics this involved learning to place the assumptions of the known world in parenthesis, to posit that the physics principles that work for our human-sized world make the quantum world or the galactic world seem 'weird' – that assumptions or perspectives about weirdness are context specific. The students were also encouraged to question assumptions by learning about scientists in history whose work broke assumptions or whose work was later found by others to contain a flawed assumption. These examples furnished students with incontrovertible evidence that progress in physics knowledge proceeded through questioning assumptions. This begs the question: What other assumptions may yield a different perspective, shifts in the kinds of questions and a different theory?

In history, questioning assumptions took the form of not assuming that the present was like the past. Learning to think like an historian meant encountering difference. One educator observed, for example, that students had difficulty making sense of religious nuns in medieval Europe (particularly, but not only, the visions they claimed to have). A twentieth- or twenty-first-century perspective may assume that the convent was an instrument of the church's control of women, without giving sufficient weight to the context of choices available to certain women in medieval Europe, when avoidance or delay of marriage offered some power of choice to women, including relative independence, at a time when marriage and children was a predestined path, including childbirth

212   *Conclusion*

with all its attendant dangers. The different logic of actors in the past may not be our own, although the actors share our humanity.

I discovered a related example when reading for the history ethnography that nicely illustrates this point. It is from Geoffrey Blainey's *The Story of Australia's People*:

> We usually condemn nomads as careless and improvident, perhaps because in our society the nomads traditionally are poor — the swagman, gypsies, hawkers, seasonal workers, surfies, dropouts and indeed, in recent times, uprooted Aborigines. But the traditional Aboriginal groups mostly moved because they believed they were in charge of their future. We view personal possessions partly as a result of our material success but to Aborigines they were a burden. Somebody had to carry them. That their groups moved to new sites was an indication of their knowledge and skill. In moving camp and winning a living from a variety of botanical environments they faced reality rather than evaded it. In moving around they were not creatures of whim but of purpose; their wanderings were systematic . . . it was characterised by a keen ability to exploit the different seasons of the year. These people were nomadic because season after season they could utilise the intimate relationship between weather, the maturing of plant-foods, and the breeding of migrating habits of birds and reptiles, insects and marsupials.
>
> (2015, pp. 4–5)

The extract illustrates the point that history involves making a rhetorical argument whose purpose is to persuade readers to a new understanding. This passage questions assumptions and performs a work of translation. From a sedentary, agrarian social viewpoint, such as we may have, the Australian Aboriginal nomadic way of life may appear idle. As this passage demonstrates, and as observations of the medieval European class showed, 'doing history' involves the historian in a process of combining historical evidence into an argument by straddling differences in values and way of life of the past and translating them into meaningful modern terms so that they prevail over common values that can create misunderstanding. Thus, historians use their experience and imagination to question and challenge assumptions, as well as to reconsider normative perceptions. From that point they generate 'possibility thinking' in order to infer explanations for how the sources answer their questions.

While some questioning of assumptions appears to emphasise self-scrutiny and critical thinking, one can also see in it the drive to explore — sometimes referred to as curiosity, or play. Arguably, it stems from the same reason why young children in particular ask so many questions and many great scientists insist their discoveries derive simply from the drive to understand.

The finance class's moment of surprise was the pedagogy which most aligned to teaching that encouraged students to question assumptions and reflect. The illegal trading incident was the case in point in which many students were seduced into trading illegally with a blacklisted bank by the high profits to be made. Here the pedagogy used surprise to disrupt students' prevailing assumptions about the goal of profit-making when unhitched from consideration of values and trust between institutions or the wider role of banking professionals in society.

In pharmaceutical science, the students were challenged to review their understanding of the process of scientific inquiry by exposure to many examples, historical and contemporary.

Questioning assumptions underpins the notion of imagining alternative possibilities because the one can lead to the other. 'Possibility thinking' in education, Craft, Jeffrey and Leibling (2001) say, is about learners posing the question 'What if?' or moving from 'What is' to 'What might be', which has obvious implications for the practice of problem solving. Ricoeur goes further and argues for the role of imagination in relation to the power and motivation to act on 'what might be'. In doing so he relates imagination to agency, practical problem solving and action in the world – and points to the expansion of this ability by language (thence the link to extended mind theory).

> And it is indeed through the anticipatory imagination of acting that I 'try out' different possible course of action and that I 'play', in the precise sense of the word, with possible practices. . . . Next imagination is involved in the very process of motivation. It is imagination that provides the milieu, the luminous cleaning, in which we can compare and evaluate motives as diverse as desires and ethical obligations, themselves as disparate as professional rules, social customs, or intensely personal values. Imagination offers the common space for the comparison and mediation of terms as heterogeneous as the force that pushes as if from behind, the attraction that seduces as if from in front, and the reasons that legitimate and form a ground as from beneath. . . . Extending Austin's brilliant analysis of the famous article 'ifs and cans', one can say that in expressions of the form 'I could, I could have . . .', the conditional provides the grammatical projection of imaginative variations on the theme 'I can'. . . . This conditional form belongs to the tense logic of the practical imagination. What is essential from the phenomenological point of view is that I take possession of the immediate certainty of my power only through the imaginative variations that mediate this certainty.
>
> There is thus a progression starting from the simple schematization of my projects, leading through the figurability of my desires, and ending in the imaginative variations of 'I can'. This progression points towards the idea of imagination as the general function of developing practical possibilities.
>
> (Ricoeur, 1991, pp. 177–178)

As we have discussed earlier, a commonality observed in the case studies related to questioning assumptions was encouraging openness to new perspectives. Working mathematically in physics often meant there was no one right way to proceed. This meant students had to experiment with what they could

214 *Conclusion*

try next. The physics common room, which was a space for unsupervised learning, was a space where honours students could practise physics embedded within a community. In history, the teachers taught that the conjectural skill of interpretation through questioning of historical sources – what, why, who, etc. – were more likely to emerge from a slow, close reading of the historical sources. This entailed re-learning how to read. This skill gave students a strategy for remaining open to finding meaning and significance in the sources. Openness to change and shifting perspectives also emerged when, in the lecture, the educator validated the experience of being confused by re-framing it as a signal of a learning moment. She stressed that if students were reading historical sources and were confused, their confusion was not failure to comprehend. On the contrary, the confusion was a pregnant moment for an historian: it signalled the need to become alert to something that had to be painstakingly unpicked and meaningfully put back together. She proposed taking a risk by confronting confusion, rather than avoiding it, giving up or thinking you are stupid and turning away. In finance, we saw this openness in the teacher's encouragement of risk-taking and trying new strategies. Removing inhibitors to risk-taking behaviour was also worked into the allocation of marks in the assessment regime. Bankers have to learn strategies to mitigate risk. Finding out the consequences of various strategies in a simulation environment was the basis of the pedagogy used by the finance educator. In pharmaceutical science, the variety of examples of scientific inquiry demonstrated the need to question any assumption that it involves a linear process.

In these ways, taking risks was modelled by many of the teachers as a way professionals worked when they questioned assumptions and went about their disciplinary/professional practice. Each of these instances draws attention to the importance placed on the authentic context of the learning situation – whether that expert is an historian, physicist, banking professional or pharmaceutical scientist – or a novice swimming teacher or parent. Risk is an ever-present aspect of tackling complexity. Tolerating uncertainty and integrating it into a way of working was modelled as a skill inherent in learning something new.

Emotions

A theme of emotions involved in questioning assumptions and openness to new perspectives emerged from various pedagogies. It is because we have emotions that inquiry often has a purpose – whether it be wonder or curiosity, to relieve anxiety or to fulfil a desire (Bleazby, 2013, p. 100). As we have seen, confusion, and the unsettling feeling that can attend risk-taking, can involve a feeling of disequilibrium, or dissatisfaction, that is mentioned by theorists such as Nussbaum (2001), Csikszentmihalyi and Getzels (1988), and Dewey (in Bleazby, 2013, p. 99) as auguring creative insight. These theorists also argue that learning something new is not easy or automatic and so entails some discomfort. The pharmaceutical science educator went to some lengths to allay the anxiety or discomfort of beginning university. These findings are significant because they manifest that inquiry is certainly attended by, sometimes guided by and often impeded by, emotions. Ignoring that fact ignores the deliberate modulation of emotion to enhance learning. The findings demonstrate the need to acknowledge that our emotions colour learning moments, as they do creative moments, and can be promoted, or stifled, by teaching approaches.

While forming new and meaningful connections is a defining characteristic of the imagination, if those connections become calcified, or there is an unquestioning over-identification with the new rule or concept that blinds a further act of re-seeing, there results a rigidity which heralds the shrinking of imaginative capacity. Kuhn's *The structure of scientific revolutions* (1962) provides several examples of highly imaginative ideas that were regarded as so contrary to dominant paradigms that they were resisted (e.g., the Copernican revolution). Similarly, the ability to continue to approach situations with a fresh, flexible and questioning attitude is important to the capacity to find new problems that others have not yet identified, as well as to being able to solve well-recognised problems. The physics educator called this ability the ability to 'read against the grain of [his] own text' (transcript, post-class interview). That self-scrutiny emphasises the process of imaginative thinking and demonstrates the desirability of a supple dialectic between critical and imaginative thinking if imagination is to remain vital.

2 Making new meaningful connections, discerning patterns

In each case study, the pedagogy emphasises personally forming meaningful connections. For example, in each of the case studies, making new connections between concepts was encouraged and practised as a way to give insight or understanding into the situation they were trying to understand, make a case for or, in the case of finance, manipulate.

In physics, for example, the educator played a game asking for ways to link the quantum coherence function, quantum correlation and quantum degree of coherence. It was also evident in the pedagogical process of trying to join up what physical interpretation of quantum concepts was suggested by pictorial, mathematical and linguistic descriptions of them. Interpreting them in relation to the other appeared to be a process capable of reorganising and shaping their conceptions of the quantum concept that was not given in experience, but it had to be composed via these tools that functioned as 'proximate terms'. Forming connections, too, was demonstrated in the way that analogies with known systems or things, or the movement of their physical bodies, were employed – reproductive imagination – not simply to recall them, but in order to postulate relationships or functions and provide a felt image for an emerging meaning.

Similarly, in finance, making connections appeared to entail the students representing financial data in graphs and interpreting those graphs in the light of theory so they could predict the strategies most likely to be successful. In history, students learned how to combine findings from historical sources and

216   *Conclusion*

structure evidence in arguments or webs of meaning in essays – an essay being a kind of apprenticeship in writing a chapter of a book, which is the primary form used by historians.

In pharmaceutical science, student-made diagrams of the process of scientific inquiry were used to model a grasp of the logic at work in the key stages of the process, but the pedagogy allowed an appreciation of the gap between it and actual investigations which entail an openness to the possibilities that there are other steps and loops that may be needed because inquiry doesn't evolve in a closed environment.

In each ethnographic case, it appeared that pedagogy that cultivated imagination through fostering the making of new connections emphasised the active production of knowledge, strategy or personally meaningful understanding, rather than passively memorising, or consuming, pre-existent history, physics or finance. Therefore, it emphasised the students' agency. It was also important that educators tried to trigger sources of internal motivation in students such as by providing quasi-real contexts. We saw this in the simulated banking scenarios, in the physics students' common room and in the pharmaceutical science task of making a hypothesis and designing and implementing an experiment to test it.

Ricoeur's central point in the prior passage quoted at length is that the imagination as a general mental function co-opts and internalises possibilities of thought – new meaningful connections – that are enabled by forms of language – in this case grammar of the conditional tense – in order to extend its reach. Thus we are led back again to the way in which imagination weaves its way through the tools/ artefacts of culture significance and turbocharges the effects of imaginative ability.

Another notion that threaded its way through the ethnographic cases is that making new meaningful connections appears to happen in a kind of hiatus, a liminal space prior to the arrival of an idea – what Ricoeur refers to as 'the milieu, the luminous clearing', in which juxtaposing, comparing and playing with hypothetical possibilities are opened up before criticality kicks in. This is a very important point. Because while agency seems to be about action and making choices, for actions to be original and significant, a certain hiatus, an uncommitted space of possibility, precedes them, whether lightning quick or years long in gestation.

3   Mastery of skills and knowledge, methodologies, processes: developing expertise

The importance of forging personally meaningful connections as a way of cultivating imagination meant these teachers valued the *process* of learning and not just the outcome or product. However, valuing the process reinforced, rather than reduced, the need to gain fluency in disciplinary skills and to practise when and how to use received theoretical knowledge, which, after Vygotsky (1978), Dennett (1995) and Clark (1997) I have referred to as 'tools'. Mastery of these skills is important because of the value of the tools: it is impossible to think as far with our brains alone, without the power of the augmentation from hard-won mastery over vocabulary, disciplinary practices and concepts that can be built on (whether these are mathematical operations, linguistic terminology, pictorial representation, theories or disciplinary methodologies). This is also why creation is always creation from something, and the idea of unalloyed originality appears, at least to me, as untenable. Imagination works with cultural tools or artefacts (this includes language and mathematics, not just material artefacts such as houses, computers and sextants). Ideas that are accepted as creative always build on something else (even if it is unexpected). Arguably, mastery of disciplinary thinking tools is accentuated in higher education rather than school education. Using imagination by making connections between concepts in their disciplines, therefore, often involved students making inferences from what was given to what was possible, where what was 'given' was not direct perception of reality but a situation mediated by the tools and artefacts. Using embodied analogies or graphs, which abbreviate the relationships between variables in real situations, connects these possibilities back to everyday experience so that students can see the applicability and meaning of knowledge to the world in which they live and move. Fluency in using disciplinary tools underpinned the expansion of the horizons of current understanding made possible by the creation of yet more new, meaningful connections.

The findings suggested a close relationship between imagination and critical thinking required by disciplines in higher education, at least in the classes I observed. Wielding the tools and techniques of disciplines involved students in a constant interplay of imaginative conjecture and critical analysis, allowing new syntheses of ideas to arise that were grounded in evidence or found to be corroborated by other data. In history, this grounding involved the connections that were to be 'found' in the documents or sources, which had to be actively linked and woven into a rhetorical, structured argument about the research question. In quantum physics their conceptions of the physical situation needed to accord with what was suggested by the maths or measured in experiments. In pharmaceutical science, the gap between the artefact and actual inquiry was a source of critical thinking and expansive learning. These findings accord with the 'extended mind' view that the interactive coupling between the objects and the mind, using tools, *is* the cognitive processing (Menary, 2010).

Vygotsky emphasised the importance of making connections but also the structure or organisation into which they are shaped; it is not random connections that we are talking about. He maintained that the ability to combine elements of knowledge to produce a structure – to combine the old in new ways – was the basis of creativity (2004, p. 12). Similarly, Ricoeur's theory of imagination, emphasising as it does the act of configuration (in metaphor, narrative plot and scientific models) focuses on insights arising from the semantic shift in perspective.

4   Repositioning learners as knowledge producers

The ethnographic cases demonstrated, from first to fourth year and postgraduate levels, the emphasis these educators gave to working with authentic disciplinary or professional tasks. Students were learning to think and work

218   *Conclusion*

like historians/physicists/financiers/pharmaceutical scientists, and so on, and it positioned them as knowledge producers.

In history, for example, the students wrote essays which involved developing the skills of making an historical argument from historical source material, in history books (text) and film.

In pharmaceutical science, in the period following the period of observation, the students made up a hypothesis and designed and implanted an experiment to test it.

In physics there were extended periods in class when all the students were involved in trying to answer questions about what physical pictures/causes were suggested by the maths and pictorial representations: for example, what a harmonic oscillator was and their evolving conceptualization of what a photon is.

In finance, the simulation pedagogy required students to form multiple strategies – one would not work – to accord with a changing financial situation.

5   Repositioning the student and teacher relationship: educational style

The findings from the ethnographic cases suggested that teaching for imaginative learning occurred in a range of educational environments or spaces. Traditional didactic lectures, small 'master-classes', high tech simulation environment, the honours student common room – they were all used to effect. There was no single pre-eminent teaching/learning environment for fostering imagination.

In each of these different educational environments, however, these higher educators *modelled* disciplinary methodologies/processes of inquiry and tool use, attitudes to knowledge and acknowledged emotions. They told stories that embodied personal attitudes to confusion; they modelled agile self-questioning, not knowing what to do and risk, as well as questioning assumptions. This entails persisting to engage purposively including, or especially, when you don't know what to do or when the outcome is uncertain. When they did so, teachers frequently positioned themselves shoulder-to-shoulder (figuratively speaking) with their student learners, as fellow physicists, historians, financiers or scientists, face-to-face with a situation or problem, and working through it together – reminiscent of what Lave and Wenger (1991) call 'legitimate peripheral participation'. It is in this way that 'problem finding' may also be modelled by educators, although this was not observed in my research. It was not a 'do as I do' model of working, however. But it also implicated learners in how they saw their identity – as historian, scientist, financier, lifelong learner and so on. Arguably, this is because imagining yourself as an historian or scientist, for instance, happens by imagining a relationship between self, practices (or methodologies) and possibly certain locations – like a library, laboratory and so forth. Learning becomes meshed with learning to be. It is about imagining yourself as – possibly – an expanded version of yourself, as someone other than you are now. In this way, these pedagogies appeared to involve empathy, in the sense that the educator empathised with the range of feelings students may have about their learning and their identity as learners. The educators modelled the management of those feelings, which may help or impede students' growth as learners and towards becoming knowledge producers and people able to respond constructively to complexity in their world.

Reflection on the usefulness of Ricoeur's theory

One objective of this study was to consider the value of Ricoeur's theory as a heuristic with which to interpret imaginative teaching and learning. Some emergent themes from the case studies were:

- There is a relationship between reproductive and productive imagination and the presence or absence of critical consciousness in high order learning (see Figure 2.1).
- The displacement of concepts reorients perspectives when we conceive or hear fresh metaphors or novel models/analogies for things.
- The imaginary making of connections is aided by historical, cultural and disciplinary tools such as language, discourse, mathematics, graphs, diagrams and body movements.
- Semantic innovation can involve learner identity.
- The liminal space in which imaginary possibilities are momentarily entertained and in which possibilities can be entertained and characteristics compared before evaluation closes them off.

Reproductive imagination was used to recall an object that is perceptible by the senses (like the vibrating violin string in physics, the use of graphs in finance and the diagram/model of a process in pharmaceutical science). But the purpose of recalling it was to be able to help learners think about a concept's parameters, shape and behavioural possibilities in hypothetical terms or to postulate relationships or functions. These are much more abstract functions than having a visual image *of* something. This meant the relationship between reproductive and productive imagination in the teaching was not in the end about distinguishing one from the other, because the former could be used to achieve the later. Reproductive imagination was used in the educators' pedagogical approaches to prompt students to actively generate ideas and postulate relationships – to enable students to use, but go beyond, experience. They formed strategies, and they used multiple symbolic modalities to expand their learning and conceive new things. In pharmaceutical science, the diagram/model of the scientific inquiry process, which appeared to be a form of reproductive imagination, was used in the pedagogy to anchor reflection on the complexity and variability that were evident in accounts of historical experiments and in the words of living scientists. This difference between the diagram and actual examples made available to learners the idea that mental agility is needed at various stages to remain alive to ways of solving emerging problems.

220 *Conclusion*

What this suggests is that there is a movement from reproductive to productive imagination, an intentional slippage from one to the other, which was activated by pedagogies that scaffold reflection on their tools/artefact whether that was a diagram, body movement or a graph. The pedagogies pulled learners' thinking to go *beyond* conceptions of tool-enabled knowledge, internalising new relations to it. Once again, we are reminded of the y axis in Figure 2.1 representing Ricoeur's notion of productive imagination's critical consciousness of the constructedness of the imaginary product with, at the other end of the axis, belief in the imaginary image or product.

Ricoeur's characterisation of productive imagination as including the human subject's critical consciousness that distinguishes the real from the imaginary is particularly useful to higher education. Three of the ethnographic cases in particular displayed the active role of imagination in the provisional nature of knowledge and inquiry. Through teacher attitudes to error and confusion, through the admonition to question assumptions and approach problems in ways that were meaningful to the individual students, to the creation of new understandings, concepts and theories were treated as working ideas that guided and enabled inquiry but could be reconstructed or falsified in the future. Productive imagination entails an awareness of the fictiveness, or constructedness, of what is created. For learners, this implies an openness to reconsider how knowledge may arise in the future. This suggests that imagination's importance for opening up possibilities is essential in the renewal of knowledge and for learning to be never-ending.

However – and this has implications for future research – Ricoeur's theory was inadequate by itself to explain epistemological imagination (Taylor, 2006) and required a connection to theories of cognition and learning. By integrating Ricoeur's theory of imagination with Vygotsky's and Wartofsky's social-cultural notion of tool mediated learning, and Clark's notion of tools in the extended mind theory, the findings from the ethnographies show how concept formation and cognitive capacity are mediated and transformed by tool use. Tool use in higher education was embedded in social-cultural, disciplinary practices involving methods for using the tools, building fluency in the use of those skills and ways of collaborating in disciplinary communities. This is why Vygotsky refers to tools as artefacts; it points to their cultural origins. The students learned procedures – the five 'W' questions in history, for example – as well as traditions for interaction with, and interpretation of, the tool that characterised practice in those disciplinary communities. The tools were deployed to redescribe or represent a situation, which could then be acted on. These complex disciplinary methodologies and practices are unique to each discipline and are represented by 'Rules' in Engeström's activity theory diagram (see Figure 5.1).

In addition, the pedagogies went beyond the instrumental: *motives* to use the tool were present and were accompanied by development of 'Why' use it, 'How' and 'When'. I argued too that imagination is involved when learners are positioned in relation to knowledge in terms of their identity as historians, scientists, financiers and so forth – that is, people who see the possibilities for acting using those tools. (Although, as we discussed in Chapter 2 in relation to tired metaphors, these identities that we imagine ourselves to be can, like metaphors, desiccate and become limiting self-imposed roles as well.) An amalgamation of Ricoeur's theory of imagination with historical social-cultural notions of tool mediated learning was needed to help us understand how it is that students in higher education learn the working processes and thinking 'tools' of disciplines and practices of the professions that enable the creation of new knowledge and practices. Engeström has identified contradictions as prime sources of new knowledge and changes in practices (1990a, 2009). What we have seen is that pedagogies (always involving the use of tools in various ways) can involve imagination and, when they do, can lead students towards learning in the sense of changing one's mind. When students experience being taken from a familiar model of the world (the reproductive) to an unfamiliar model (the productive), that shifting is just as important as the content of the new model – and often involves metacognition. If they can treat concepts and theories as working ideas that guide and enable inquiry but are always open to future revision and reconsideration, then learning will involve imagination and the seeking of other possibilities. Learning is not simply a matter of the continuous acquiring of new knowledge, concepts or skills; it is what you do with them. Actions that make new connections or are based on novel kinds of understanding can build openness to complexity and reconsideration. It makes the imagination of fundamental importance to higher education.

Implications for practice

The ethnographic chapters (5, 6, 7 and 8) contain narratives of educational approaches that, I argue, foster the imagination of students. One aim of this book was also to clarify what imagination is so that educators and their students have clearer understanding of how to develop it. In Chapter 1, I also said that my aim in this book was to create narratives which allow readers to, in a sense, 'go visiting' these classes to 'exchange experiences' with them in all their complexity. Because good teaching involves judgement and is responsive to particular needs of students and the unique characteristics of the student cohort, this is not a direct process of simply applying lessons or doing certain activities. What the ethnographies afford is the opportunity for educators to reconsider their teaching practices in the light of the theoretical interpretations in these narratives and to gain a new perspective on how disciplines draw on the imagination of their practitioners – in ways in which educators may not always be consciously aware.

However, as I have learned in the process of this research, drawing diagrams can also be used to generate learning of something new, and Figure 9.1 summarises key features that I have discussed in this book. In effect, it is my attempt to offer an explicit stimulus, or mediation tool, that helps readers move their understanding from what Vygotsky calls the intermental plane to the

222 *Conclusion*

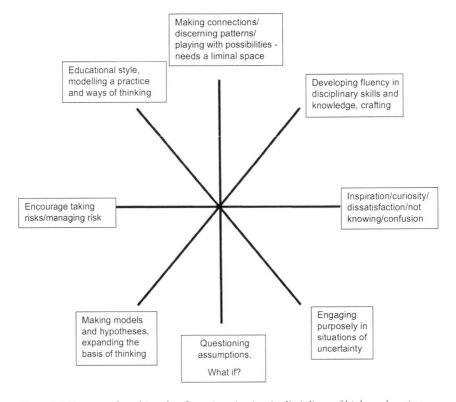

Figure 9.1 Features of teaching that foster imagination in disciplines of higher education

intramental plane. I have visually represented the features discussed prior as a constellation, in tangents in which what is at one end forms a relationship to what is at the other.

Questions and ideas for teaching approaches that foster imagination

The following are questions directed at teaching practices, and ideas for activities, that are suggested by the evidence in my research findings. They are related to the five features at the start of this chapter. They are supported by the emphasis on combinatorial activity emphasised in Ricoeur's theory of imagination. These are not discipline specific. Readers will need to align their use with desired learning attributes and outcomes.

- What opportunities are given for students to challenge and question knowledge?
- How do I, as an educator, model that?

Conclusion 223

- When, and how, are students required to organise, reorganise, analyse, synthesise or evaluate knowledge and information?
- What did I ask the students to do or produce to forge and demonstrate links between concepts (etc.)?
- What opportunities were given to the students to inspire them?
- Why did the learning matter?
- Who did it matter to?
- What opportunities were learners given to elaborate their conceptions by sharing and discussing learning artefacts with each other?
- Are there opportunities to play a game that asks students on what basis concepts could be linked with each other?
- What ways do I as an educator offer to demonstrate that not-knowing and uncertainty about the outcome involve risk? What models for how to do that are offered? Historical, personal?
- Can I provide more opportunities for students to use multiple mindtools/ artefacts/modes (language, diagrams, mathematical symbols, body movements, role play, maps, etc.) to represent their understanding and articulate and reflect on it? How do I, as an educator, model that?
- Try asking students to think up a metaphor that represents a concept and then discuss the relationship between attributes they share. The idea is to generate ideas and to bound the process with constraints.
- Consider asking students to recount a narrative from the perspective of a cell, a molecule, an animal, a toxin, the immune system, a historical figure, etc. (this demands forming new connections from a different perspective).
- Design something in a context with surprising conditions: for example, ask the question, 'How would you need to support human fertility on a mission to MARS?' for a course in reproductive technology.
- Ask yourself what kind of disciplinary tools or professional activities in your field involve combining knowledge and skills? Many involve mimicking authentic forms, such as writing a report, running a court case, designing a museum exhibit or conducting a patient interview, a symposium or similar. The relevance of essays has been challenged recently, but the essay form has in-built requirements to link evidence together in an argument and so can be fit for encouraging the making of new connections in ways that are open ended. Making a museum video exhibit and running an exhibition will do a similar thing. Asking students to perform their knowledge in some way can engage emotions and harness social motivations.
- Find a problem. The ability to find significant problems that are worth solving and define or decompose that problem is open ended and involves imagination and other attributes in the 'hand' of creativity, especially deep knowledge of an area or field – and possibly the application of values. Students need to be given the opportunity to generate ideas that make a difference.
- Focus on problem-solving processes: In order to solve a problem successfully, you may need to discover, or select, a set of appropriate methods

224   *Conclusion*

that are likely to help solve the problem. Writing a research paper, for example, will involve selecting appropriate methods of locating information, choosing research strategies, discarding irrelevant sources, identifying relevant evidence, evaluating credibility of sources and possibly collaboration. Designing a medicine to combat a disease, or organising a symposium on democratic models, will similarly demand a combination of skills and include the development of personal attributes.

- What opportunities are there for students to witness experts modelling a disciplinary or professional process? Pedagogies that include modelling can position the students and educator as together facing the problem. In this way educators can model asking questions, such as: What else could we try? What other possible explanations could explain the data? What other sources of data might corroborate or falsify this hypothesis or illuminate more of the process? What resources could we draw on to help us think through this (problem/task)? What other problem is this like? Or how is it unlike that (precedent)?
- Have I used strange or intriguing problems? Have students had opportunities to be exposed to extremes or limits to known knowledge? Problem finding may also emerge from this.
- How did the students know what a quality product or performance should look like?
- Is creativity developed over each level of the degree?

Future directions of research

These ethnographic cases indicate some general properties of teaching which encourages imagination, but more ethnography on other non arts-based areas and ones that use different teaching contexts may produce greater appreciation of discipline-specific practices and how they interplay with imagination.

Given that Ricoeur's theory of imagination emphasises novel combinatorial activity, research in interdisciplinary teaching contexts would yield the opportunity to observe cross-disciplinary teaching and how students put into play selected (new and traditional) tools and methods of working with them, as well as other resources, to grasp situations in order to act on goals. As well, how imagination is involved in the very construction of motives for action, and what that may mean for emerging identities, would also be of interest given the kind of engagement in real-world problems that is needed.

Another interesting area that did not emerge strongly in my research in Chapters 5, 6, 7 and 8, but which was discussed by Csikszentmihalyi and Getzels (1988) is problem finding. Problem finding research distinguishes between 'presented' (given) and 'discovered' problems, and theorists contend that problem *finding* is characteristic of creative thought processes. Perhaps because my research design focused on imaginative teaching, and its impact on learning, rather than focusing on imaginative learning per se, its methods, while capturing *educators'* encouragement of personally meaningful learning approaches, did not uncover the learner processes equally well. Coursework classes focus on the curriculum and seldom veer off course, so diverging class attention to noticing some new problem tends not to happen. Analysing student assignment work when it is completed does not show an observer how the student has found sub-questions or resolved them. My focus groups with students also did not include questions on whether and how they identified and pursued new questions or problems that arose during their assignments. Future research methodologies that include asking participants to demonstrate their practices and skills with speaking-aloud commentaries about their thinking and methods of problem solving – what have sometimes been called 'knowledge harvesting' (Trowler, 2013) – may offer opportunities to explore this area further, as it is not well understood but is a priority in higher education.

The implied provisional nature of knowledge underpins the openness to the possibility of revising and constructing new propositions, models or possibilities for new projects. This needs to include the notion of choices and values – and how they arise in social communities. I have argued that Ricoeur's theory of imagination in combination with socio-cultural theory interpretations of practice, and extended mind and predictive processing theories of cognition, together provide rich theoretical perspectives which can contribute to an understanding of how imagination interacts with tool use, and disciplinary and professional practices, and/or how individuals and communities influence each other in order to frame, approach and solve problems.

Note

1 I have used the eloquent language of Hutchins (2014) in making this point.

References

Blainey, G. (2015). *The story of Australia's people: The rise and fall of ancient Australia*. Melbourne: Viking.

Bleazby, J. (2013). *Social reconstruction learning: Dualism, Dewey and philosophy in schools*. New York: Routledge.

Clark, A. (1997). *Being there: Putting brain, body and world together*. Cambridge, MA: The MIT Press.

Clark, A. (2015, March 4). *The extended mind: HDC, a history of distributed cognition* [seminar on web]. Retrieved from http://www.hdc.ed.ac.uk/seminars/extended-mind

Craft, A., Jeffrey, B., & Leibling, M. (2001). *Creativity in education*. London: Continuum.

Csikszentmihalyi, M., & Getzels, J. W. (1988). Creativity and problem finding in art. In F. G. Farley & R. W. Neperud (Eds.), *The foundations of aesthetics, art, and art education* (pp. 91–106). New York: Praeger.

Dennett, D. C. (1995). *Darwin's dangerous idea: Evolution and the meanings of life*. New York: Simon & Schuster.

Engeström, Y. (1990a). *Learning, working and imagining: Twelve studies in activity theory*. Helsinki: Orienta-Konsultit Oy.

Engeström, Y. (1990b). When is a tool? Multiple meanings of artifacts in human activity? In *Learning, working and imagining: Twelve studies in activity theory* (pp. 171–195). Helsinki: Orienta-Konsultit Oy.

226   *Conclusion*

Engeström, Y. (2009). Expansive learning: Toward an activity-theoretical reconceptualization. In K. Illeris (Ed.), *Contemporary theories of learning: Learning theorists . . . in their own words* (pp. 53–73). Abingdon, Oxon: Routledge.

Hutchins, E. (2014). The cultural system of human cognition. *Philosophical Psychology, 27*(1), 34–49. doi:10.1080/09515089.2013.830548

Kuhn, T. (1962). *The structure of scientific revolutions.* Chicago; London: University of Chicago Press.

Lave, J., & Wenger, E. (1991). *Situated learning: Legitimate peripheral participation.* Cambridge, UK; New York: Cambridge University Press.

Menary, R. (2010). Cognitive integration and the extended mind. In R. Menary (Ed.), *The extended mind* (pp. 227–244). Cambridge, MA: A Bradford Book, The MIT Press.

Nussbaum, M. (2001). *Upheavals of thought: The intelligence of emotions.* New York: Cambridge University Press.

Ricoeur, P. (1991). Imagination in discourse and in action (K. Blamey & J. B. Thompson, Trans.). In J. M. Eadie (Ed.), *From text to action: Essays in hermeneutics* (Vol. 2, pp. 168–187). Evanston, IL: Northwestern University Press.

Taylor, G. H. (2006, Spring-Fall). Ricoeur's philosophy of imagination. *Journal of French Philosophy, 16*(1 & 2), 93–104.

Trowler, P. (2013). Can approaches to research in art and design be beneficially adapted for research into higher education? *Higher Education Research & Development, 32*(1), 56–69. doi :10.1080/07294360.2012.750276

Vygotsky, L. S. (1978). *Mind in society: The development of higher psychological processes.* Cambridge, MA: Harvard University Press.

Vygotsky, L. S. (2004). Imagination and creativity in childhood. *Journal of Russian and East European Psychology, 42*(1), 7–97.

Wertsch, J. V. (2007). Mediation. In H. Daniels, M. Cole, & J. V. Wertsch (Eds.), *The Cambridge companion to Vygotsky* (pp. 178–192). Cambridge: Cambridge University Press.

Index

abstract thinking 42
action 37–38
agency 21, 24, 33–35, 40, 153, 155–156, 183; *see also* metacognition; resourcefulness
Amabile 206
analogy 22, 24, 34, 49, 90, 91, 102, 106, 111, 122, 206, 217, 219
Anderson, N. and Krathwohl, D. 5–7, 9, 154
artefacts 202–204, 210, 207; *see also* models; tool mediation

Biggs, J. and Tang, C. 2, 5–7, 9, 154
Black, M. 28–29, 52
Bloom's taxonomy 5–7

Clark, A. 4, 12, 46, 53–66, 105, 172, 181, 201, 203–205
collaboration 3, 72, 75, 88, 106–108, 143, 152, 154, 181, 184, 188–189, 206; *see also* learning communities
combinatory *see* imagination, forming connections; imagination, synthesis
confidence 4, 81, 84, 104, 135–136, 206
configuring meaning 26, 30, 32–33, 43, 60, 66, 93, 121, 139, 142–143, 147, 191–197, 202, 204, 217; *see also* imagination, synthesis
connections *see* imagination, synthesis
creativity: absence in assessment 2; chapter 4; definition 3–4; educators' view about 85–87; environments conducive to 57, 79, 172, 185–187, 210; as a graduate attribute 2; intention to development of 81–83; originality 70–71; overlapping terms 4–5, 69, 72–73; personal traits 70–71; as process 73–79, 183; as product 70–73; relationship with critical thinking

27, 55, 77–79, 135, 147, 156, 164; systems model 79–80, 107 (*see also* Csikzentmihalyi, M.)
critical thinking 2, 25, 31, 39, 77–78, 129, 143–144, 190, 217; critical consciousness 20–21, 31, 129
Csikszentmihalyi, M. 1, 71, 76, 79–80, 83, 87, 107, 137, 214
curiosity 3, 6, 76, 77, 81, 83, 90, 136–137, 188–189, 190, 195, 197, 212, 214, 222

Dawkins, R. 27–28, 33, 37, 52, 55, 77–78, 117, 135, 156, 163–164
Dennett, D. 55–57, 66, 105, 162, 210
Dewey, J. 7, 35–36, 41, 76, 113, 115, 117, 123, 156, 158, 165, 170, 170, 185, 214

embodied cognition 4, 8, 38, 54, 58, 60, 120–121
emotions 35–36, 109, 115–116, 136, 145–147, 157–159, 214–215
Engeström, Y. 107, 110, 123, 158, 172, 184, 202–203, 220–221
ethics 35–36, 38–39, 129, 147, 157–160, 174, 177, 188, 195, 213; *see also* emotions
expertise 78–79, 83, 216
extended mind theory 54–56, 61, 203–204, 211

higher order thinking 5, 9, 46, 76, 131, 137
historical discoveries 112, 188–189, 191

identity 136–138, 154, 218–219
imagination: deployed in learning 9; forming connections 3–5, 8, 9, 23–24, 31, 32, 35, 74, 85, 91, 118–120, 134–135, 170, 215–217, 222 (*see also* imagination, synthesis); Imaginative Curriculum Project 88–89; importance 1; instruction

228 *Index*

processes 89, 90–91, 92; lack in higher education 2; liminal space 38–39, 216; memory 13, 20, 24, 26, 38, 42, 50, 62, 102, 122; and mindtools 5, 102–106; moral imagination 42; possibility thinking 101; probable imaginary constructions – what if? 39–40; productive imagination 5, 20, 21, 27–34, 102, 160, 163–164, 205–206; relationship to reality 20–21, 37, 41–43, 165, 170; reproductive imagination 20, 21, 102, 160, 162, 164, 205–206; role in creativity 4; storytelling and identity 93–94; synthesis 3, 5, 6, 26, 32, 61, 63, 117–120, 138–143, 151, 207
inference 7, 41, 58–59, 117, 159, 165, 170, 195, 197, 217
innovation 1–2, 4, 39, 52, 57, 72–73, 80

Johnson, M. 35–36, 38, 42, 78, 115, 147, 158

Kant, E. 20, 22, 24, 34, 53, 63

Lakoff, G. and Johnson, M. 29–30, 112
learning: making meaning 8, 43; unsupervised learning 62, 64–66, 197, 214
learning communities 88, 106–108, 153, 195, 206, 210, 214, 217

memory 13, 20, 24, 26, 38, 42, 50, 55, 56, 57, 61, 62, 102, 166
metacognition 153, 198, 200
metaphor 22–6, 29–32; making assumptions 29–31
modelling 57, 83, 102, 113–115, 135–137, 184–185, 218–219
models 27–29, 33–35, 46, 50, 52–53, 60, 108, 163–164; daydreaming 62, 64; generative models 58, 62–64, 65; probabilistic models 59, 61, 64; scientific models 27–29, 31–32, 64, 78, 108
motivation 39, 49, 75–76, 79, 81, 84, 85, 89, 92, 114–115, 159, 177–178, 189, 193, 213, 220; *see also* curiosity

narrative 12, 14, 32–35, 36–38, 53, 55, 62, 64, 93–94, 105, 111, 118, 120, 130, 134, 139, 143, 153, 170, 189, 198, 207, 217, 223
Nussbaum, M. 35–36, 94, 115, 147, 158, 214

perception 21–22, 24, 26, 42, 46, 49, 50–53, 58–66, 144, 204–205; learning 58–59, 211; and representations 12 (*see also* artefacts)
Polanyi, M. 8, 12, 46, 53–54, 57, 105, 123, 201
predictive processing 58–65, 205–206; and imagination 61–62; and learning 58–59
problem finding/ problem formulation 76–77, 83, 137

questioning assumptions 6, 112–113, 129–130, 174–175, 210, 211–215

reflection *see* metacognition
resourcefulness 30, 55–56, 66, 72, 106–108
Ricoeur theory 9–20, 219–220
risk 4, 70, 73–74, 81, 82, 84, 87, 92, 114, 116, 135152, 155–156, 157, 161–162, 167–168, 171–173, 174, 175–177, 185, 214, 218, 222, 223

simulation 150
SOLO taxonomy 5–7, 9, 154
speech/language 49; tools 55, 56
surprise 157–159, 170–172

tacit knowledge 53–54
tool mediation 47–48, 102–105, 184, 191–205; dialectical unity of it and practical activity 49, 50; and epistemic action 50; by language 47–49, 53; as a social process 49; and tacit knowledge 54; *see also* extended mind theory; imagination, and mindtools; Wartofsky

uncertainty 6, 58, 84, 116–117, 144, 158–159, 214, 222, 223

visualisation 104
Vygotsky, L. 5, 11, 41–42, 46–50, 53–54, 57, 60, 64, 74, 78, 107, 127, 143–144, 181, 186, 197, 202, 218, 210, 211, 217, 220

Wartofsky 51–53

ZPD 49